The Mensa Quiz Book

THIS IS A CARLTON BOOK

This edition published in 2017 by
Carlton Books Ltd
20 Mortimer Street
London W1T 3JW

ISBN: 978-1-78739-021-8

Printed in Denmark

The Mensa Quiz Book

Test your knowledge against the highest IQs in the world

CARLTON BOOKS

Contents

Preface

The questions in this book have been used for the Brain of Mensa quiz. As such, the word trivia is hopefully not applicable to describe them, but at the same time, they are written in the hope that at least one contestant (or member of the audience, if applicable) could answer them. Some might require lateral thinking, i.e. you might think that you don't know the answer but could arrive at the answer with a bit of thought. And if you are unable to arrive at a correct answer, then I hope that a fair number will at least be educational.

Brian Daugherty

Introduction

The first and biggest organisation for people with a high IQ, Mensa has been bringing intelligent people together from all over the world for decades. Our mission is three-fold:

- to identify and to foster human intelligence for the benefit of humanity;
- to encourage research into the nature, characteristics, and uses of intelligence; and
- to provide a stimulating intellectual and social environment for our members.

The only requirement for membership that Mensa has ever had is to score at or above 98% in an approved standardised IQ test. Even our name was chosen to highlight our egalitarian spirit – the Latin word mensa means "table", and represents the theoretical round table at which we all sit as equals, regardless of age, gender, race, or status. We are non-political, non-religious, and non-discriminatory in every sense – except for IQ, of course!

There are now well over 130,000 Mensans in countries around the globe. More than 50 nations have their own national Mensa organisations, and for the rest, Mensa International serves as an umbrella covering the entire planet. Antarctica is the only continent without any members, but then so far, the continent has no permanent residents. The youngest person to join British Mensa was the UK's Elise Tan-Roberts, who became a Mensan at the age of just two years and four months, while our oldest member to date was 103, and didn't join until she was in her 90s.

Similarly, our membership ranges from people who didn't achieve highly at school to professors with multiple doctorates, and includes programmers, truck drivers, artists, farmers, soldiers, musicians, fire-fighters, models, scientists, builders, writers, fishermen, accountants, boxers, and police officers. Some are world-famous names, whilst others are totally outside the public's awareness. It doesn't matter in Mensa – all are equal.

As a high IQ society, Mensa has a core interest in intelligence – what it is, how to nurture it, and how to make the most of it. We are a strictly non-profit organisation, and are involved with numerous programs for gifted children, improving literacy, and making education accessible. The Mensa Foundation regularly publishes a scientific journal of research into relevant scientific areas. But we are also a social group, and bringing intelligent people together is very important to us.

Mensa holds a lot of events for its members at all levels from the local to the international. There are regular local and regional gatherings in towns and cities all over the world, ranging from semi-formal meet-ups to lectures, tour groups, dinner and lunch sessions, and nights of cinema, theatre, or gaming. In some larger cities, there are events available most days. Lots of national Mensa organisations also arrange frequent country-wide meetings, including spectacular annual gatherings with workshops, speakers, dance evenings, games, children's events, and much more. They also issue national membership magazines, such as British Mensa's Mensa Magazine, and American Mensa's Mensa Bulletin, both monthly.

But members also come together frequently to share common ground. These special interest groups (SIGs) cover all manner of subject that you can imagine, from the everyday to the extremely obscure. SIGs issue regular bulletins and zines, and many also organise meet-ups, provide email discussion lists, and more. If you can't find a particular interest group that you're looking for, starting one yourself is extremely simple.

Simply put, Mensa can be as large or small a part of your life as you like. For some members, the organisation is a family, full of friends; Mensa marriages have taken place. For others, it is a casual interest, a little something to help get the grey matter ticking over. Wherever you might fall on that spectrum, it's fine. We're all equal, remember.

We do encourage all our members to use their brains, of course. Mental exercise is not just a lot of fun, it can definitely be of help in keeping the mind fit and healthy. Research over the last decade has clearly demonstrated that regular puzzle solving and social interaction can help to actively stave off Alzheimer's disease. The brain remains responsive to the ways we use it all through our lives – a principle called neuroplasticity – so the more we challenge it, the stronger our abilities to meet those challenges will become.

Besides, solving puzzles and answering tricky questions are amongst the most basic of human behaviours. You find recreational puzzles, games and riddles in every culture around the world, and in every time period we have half-decent archaeological remains from. It's a core need, and something we work hard to encourage.

At the end of the day though, Mensa is about you – take what you want from us, and ignore the rest. We're here for you, not the other way around.

Mensa is the international society for people with a high IQ. We have more than 100,000 members in over 40 countries worldwide.

The society's aims are:

to identify and foster human intelligence for the benefit of humanity

to encourage research in the nature, characteristics, and uses of intelligence to provide a stimulating intellectual and social environment for its members.

Anyone with an IQ score in the top two per cent of population is eligible to become a member of Mensa – are you the 'one in 50' we've been looking for?

Mensa membership offers an excellent range of benefits:

Networking and social activities nationally and around the world

Special Interest Groups – hundreds of chances to pursue your hobbies and interests – from art to zoology!

Monthly members' magazine and regional newsletters

Local meetings – from games challenges to food and drink

National and international weekend gatherings and conferences

Intellectually stimulating lectures and seminars

Access to the worldwide SIGHT network for travellers and hosts

For more information about Mensa: www.mensa.org, or

British Mensa Ltd.,
St John's House,
St John's Square,
Wolverhampton
WV2 4AH
Telephone: +44 (0) 1902 772771
E-mail: enquiries@mensa.org.uk
www.mensa.org.uk

The Quizzes

1. The Roman Empire reached its greatest extent under which emperor?

2. Who was the sculptor from Cyprus who made a statue of a woman which he then fell in love with?

3. Which now-ruined city in Africa was the birthplace of the Roman emperor Septimus Severus?

4. The words 'merchant' and 'mercantile' stem from which source in Roman mythology?

5. Which German city was founded by the first Roman emperor and was named in his honour?

6. Which tree with a distinctive spirally-grooved bark was brought to Britain by the Romans?

7. Which Greek city was destroyed by the Romans in 146 BC?

8. Spartacus's rebellion was put down by which Roman general?

9. The largest lead mines under Roman control were situated in the region of which river in present-day Spain?

10. Name the building opposite, and state who commissioned it.

11. Who was the first Roman emperor to be chosen by the Army?

12. Which Roman poet was exiled in AD 8 to an area in present-day Romania?

13. Why does February have only 28 days whereas it had 29 days in the past?

14. What was the effect of the Roman law known as the 'Lex canulia'?

15. Why was Naples spared during the great Vesuvius eruption of AD 79 that destroyed Pompeii?

16. The Colosseum in Rome was named after a large statue of whom, which used to stand in the vicinity?

17. According to legend, during the attack on Rome by the Gauls in 390 BC, what type of animal gave the Gauls away after they had ascended the Capitoline Hill undetected?

18. Which American city is named after a society which itself was named after a Roman dictator of the early republic?

19. Which socialist group is named after a Roman general who opposed Hannibal?

20. The general Germanicus Caesar was the father of which Roman emperor?

Answers see page 278

1. Who is credited with the discovery that Jupiter has moons, the planet's four largest moons now being collectively named after him?

2. What forms clouds on both Uranus and Neptune?

3. The Trojans are a group of asteroids that orbit in a gravitationally neutral area between Jupiter and the Sun. What is the inappropriate name borne by the first Trojan to be discovered in 1906?

4. Which comedian discovered a white spot on the planet Saturn?

5. Fragments from which comet hit Jupiter in 1994?

6. Most Solar System objects have names from Roman or Greek mythology. However, four of the five main satellites of Uranus have names derived from which other source?

7. What is studied by aerographers?

8. Who first noticed the gap between the A and B rings of Saturn?

9. What name links a figure in Greek Mythology and a small moon in the Solar System – in mythology she was a priestess of Hera who was changed into a heifer by Zeus?

10. Which feature on Jupiter was first observed by Robert Hooke in 1664 and is still there?

11. On which body of the Solar System would you find craters called Beethoven, Shakespeare and Tolstoy?

12. Who found that planets follow an elliptical orbit about the Sun?

13. Which is the largest volcano in the Solar System, pictured opposite?

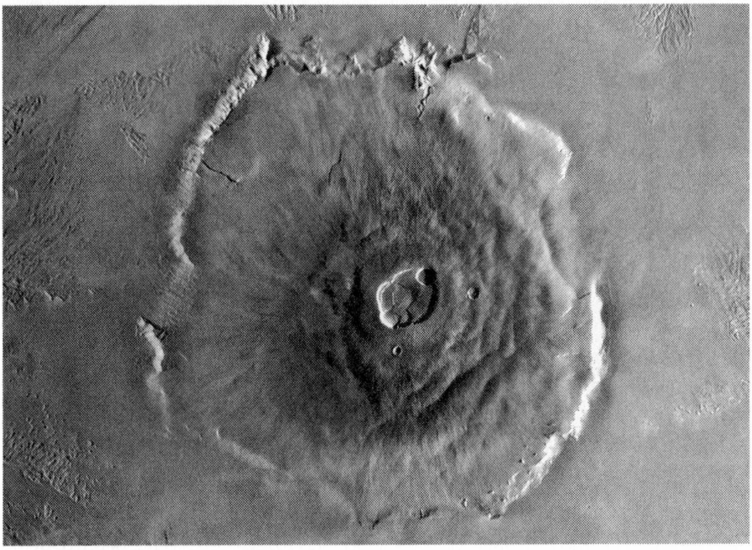

Answers see page 278

Stick Men

Can you work out why C is the odd one out from this group?

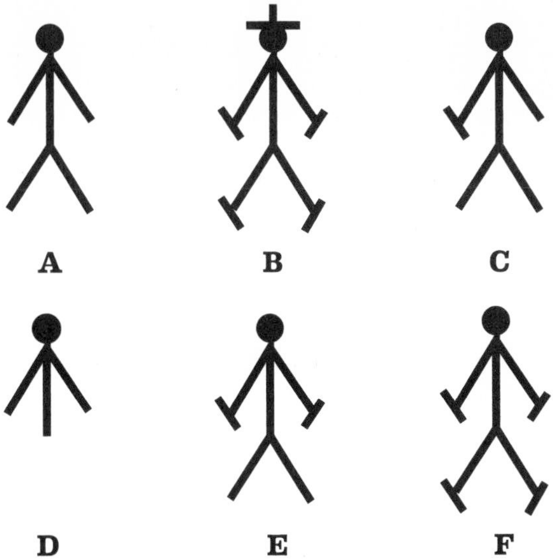

Answer see page 278

1. Tracy Emin stems from which seaside town?

2. Name one of the two artists associated with The Yellow House in Arles?

3. Who painted *Impression, Sunrise*?

4. The story of which artist is told in the film *The Agony and the Ecstasy*?

5. Which artist won the Turner Prize in 1995, prompting Norman Tebbit to declare: 'Have they gone stark raving mad'?

6. What special feature of many works of the artist Georg Baselitz was first displayed at an exhibition in Köln in 1970?

7. Who painted the pictured 17th century painting *Las Meninas,* in which the artist portrays himself working on a painting?

8. Who succeeded Bellini as official artist of the Venetian Republic?

9. Which group of artists were reputed to refer to Joshua Reynolds as 'Sir Sploshua'?

10. Who painted the two pictures of Nell Gwyn to be found in Chirk Castle?

11. Which impressionist painter is particularly associated with horse-racing and ballet dancers?

12. Gallery 1853, in Bradford, specialises in the work of which artist?

13. Who painted *Primavera* in 1478?

14. What was the surname of two 18th century painters, uncle and nephew, one being associated with Venice, the other working in Germany and Poland?

15. With what type of painting do you associate Andrei Rublyov?

16. Elizabeth Siddal posed as Ophelia for a picture by which painter?

17. Which painter safeguarded Paris's art collections during the time of the Commune but was later imprisoned for allegedly allowing the destruction of Napoleon's triumphal column on the Place Vendôme?

18. From which Spanish town did Picasso originate?

19. Who painted *Storm on the Sea of Galilee*, which was stolen from the Gardner Gallery in Boston?

20. Which family of painters from Augsburg travelled widely outside that city, one being buried in Alsace, another being based in Basel for a certain period?

Answers see page 278

1. In which prison was Nelson Mandela incarcerated for 18 years?

2. The capital of British Columbia is situated on which island?

3. What was the name of the ship featured in *Treasure Island*?

4. On which island is the main part of Copenhagen (a smaller part lies on the island of Amager)?

5. The descendants of the Bounty mutineers moved from Pitcairn to which other island?

6. Which fictional character was imprisoned on an island just south of Marseilles?

7. On which island would you find the Emerald Coast?

8. Which island was the site of a brief struggle between Spain and Morocco in the Summer of 2002?

9. Where is the island of Bimini?

10. In which group of islands is Bikini Island?

11. Robinson Crusoe Island belongs to which country?

12. Cape Breton Island is a part of which Canadian province?

13. Which is the most southern of the Balearic Islands?

14. Who commanded a Portuguese trading expedition to India in 1506 which, on the outward journey, discovered a group of previously unknown islands in the Atlantic?

15. The island of If lies off which city?

16. Which island in present-day North Carolina was the site of attempts to form an English colony in 1585 and 1587 – although the original colonists vanished?

17. The town of Marsala lies on which island?

18. Which journalist campaigned against Devil's Island in his 1923 publication *Au bagne*?

19. Thira is the main town on which Mediterranean island (or group of islands) formed from the rim of an ancient volcano?

20. In AD 26, Emperor Tiberius, pictured below, retreated to live on which island?

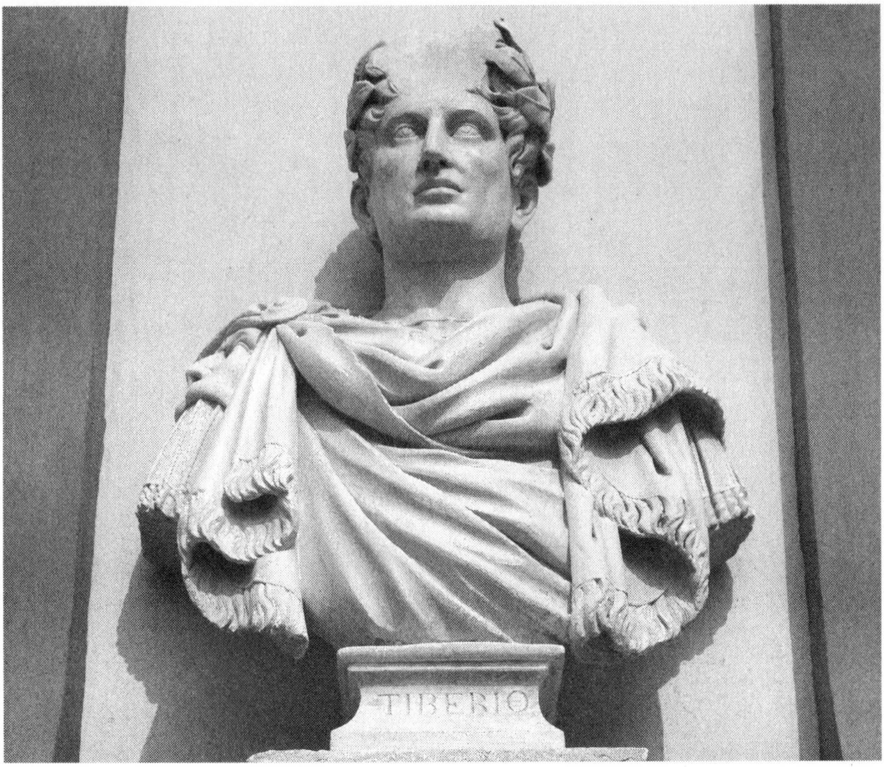

Answers see page 279

1. Which Japanese city was devastated by an earthquake in January 1995?

2. Which play was staged in East Berlin in January 1949, with Helene Weigel in the title role, a production which effectively marked the foundation of the Berliner Ensemble?

3. The peace conference for the First World War was initiated on 18th January 1919, in which town or city?

4. Which newspaper was founded on 1st January 1930 and claims to be the world's only daily, socialist newspaper in the English language?

5. Which former President of Zimbabwe was sentenced to 10 years imprisonment in January 1999?

6. What was the nature of the trademark dispute brought by Hormel Foods before the British High Court in January 2005?

7. Which computer became operational in Urbana, Illinois on 12th January 1997?

8. Where was the allied summit meeting held in January 1943, although Stalin was unable to attend because of the Battle of Stalingrad?

9. Lloyd George sent 10,000 troops and tanks to which British city in January 1919 as a result of industrial unrest?

10. Which European capital city was flooded in January 1910, the water forcing its way through the sewers and underground railway tunnels, rather than by the river breaking its banks?

11. Which socialist leader was shot dead in January 1919, near the Lichtenstein Bridge in the Zoo area of Berlin, and then thrown into the canal?

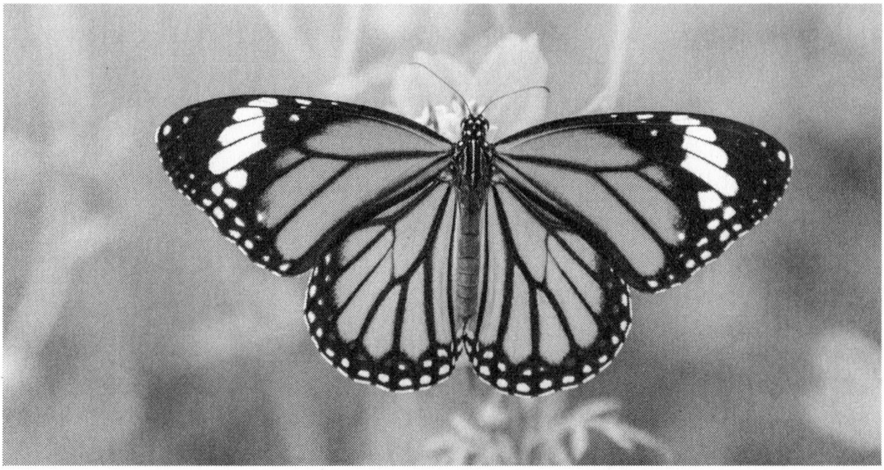

12. In January 2002, a freak cold front in Mexico is estimated to have killed 250 million of which type of butterfly, pictured above?

13. On 1st January 1962, which became the first Polynesian state when it achieved independence from New Zealand?

Answers see page 289

Odd One Out

Which of the following is the odd one out?

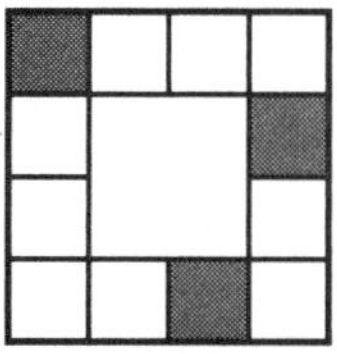

A

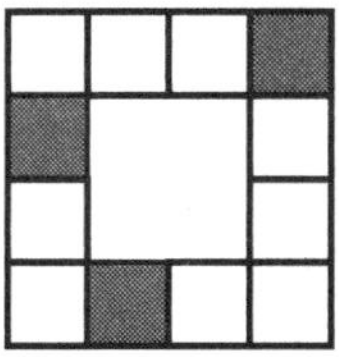

B

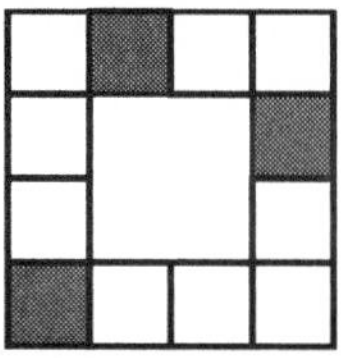

C

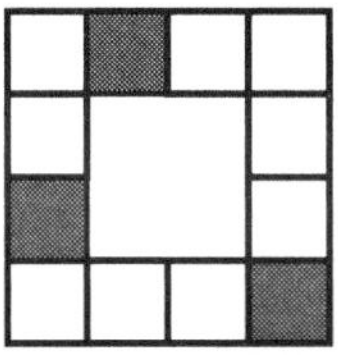

D

Answer see page 279

Puzzle Around

What number should replace the question mark?

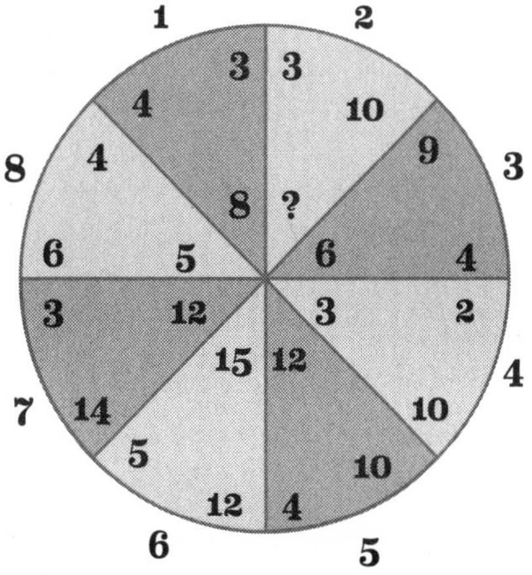

Answer see page 279

1. Which character did Humphrey Bogart play in *The African Queen*?

2. Who played Mrs. Robinson in the film *The Graduate*?

3. In the film, *The Great Escape,* how many people successfully escaped?

4. Who had a hairy stunt in the film *Steamboat Bill, Jr.* where a wall falls on him, but he is saved by standing where the window is?

5. In *Moby Dick,* starring Gregory Peck, who played the part of the preacher who gave a fiery sermon in the early part of the film?

6. Which Brazilian footballer had a role in *Escape to Victory*?

7. Which role did Marilyn Monroe play in the film *Some Like it Hot*?

8. In *Anchors Aweigh,* Gene Kelly danced with which cartoon character?

9. In the Errol Flynn film *Robin Hood,* what role was played by Basil Rathbone?

10. Who played Szell, a Nazi who has evaded justice, in the film *Marathon Man*?

11. Who was 'coated in gold' for the film *Goldfinger*?

12. In the film *Chaplin* starring Robert Downey Jr., who played the role of Chaplin's mother?

13. Who was, in 1960, one of the original *Magnificent Seven* and a year earlier had played opposite Hayley Mills in the film *Tiger Bay*?

14. What character did Peter Sellers play in the film *I'm Alright Jack*?

15. Hattie McDaniel was a distinguished actress who won an Oscar for her role in *Gone with the Wind*. Why did she not attend the premiere of the film?

16. Who went from being *Gregory's Girl* to being a singer with *Altered Images*?

17. Who made the transition from silent films to talkies with the film *Unaccustomed As We Are*?

18. In the 1935 film of *Midsummer Night's Dream* directed by Max Reinhardt, which had Mickey Rooney playing Puck, who played Bottom?

19. Which role did Ingrid Bergman play in the film *Casablanca*?

20. Who played *Shaft* in the first film of that name?

Answers see page 279

1. What was invented by John Pemberton?

2. Which inventor disappeared, presumably overboard, from the ship Dresden?

3. Who won a prize of £20,000 for inventing a clock that enabled sailors to accurately calculate longitude at sea?

4. Which European research institute is often credited with the invention of the World Wide Web?

5. What did Newcomen invent in 1712?

6. Who invented the Spinning Jenny?

7. The Royal Society was moved to set up a committee to decide whether Isaac Newton or Gottfried Leibniz first invented the calculus. This committee decided in favor of Newton - which scientist chaired the committee?

8. In its struggle against the influence of English, the *Academie Francaise* has had enormous success with its invention of the word *baladeur*, a word which carries allusions to the words *ballade* (*with two l's*) meaning 'ballad' and *balade* (*with one l*), meaning 'a walk' or 'a stroll'. What is the meaning of the word 'baladeur'?

9. Which company invented Astroturf?

10. Which invention of the 1930s has a name derived from the Spanish for 'diving board'?

11. Which totally-bogus foreign-sounding name was invented by Polish-American Reuben Mattus to promote his ice-cream?

12. In 1839, what name did the astronomers Maedler and John Herschel give to a new invention of LJM Daguerre?

13. Harry Ferguson, who appeared on the twenty pound note issued by the Northern Bank of Northern Ireland, is known for making or inventing what?

14. Marie Harel is usually attributed with the invention of which cheese?

15. Which inventor of a machine-gun also produced an experimental steam-powered flying machine which did at least lift off the ground briefly?

16. What was the name of the hypothetical being that Clerk Maxwell invented to theoretically counteract the Second Law of Thermodynamics?

17. Which device was alleged to have been invented by Santos-Dumont when he desired to use his hands just for steering his aircraft?

18. Who invented a modern open-hearth method of steel production in the mid-19th century which now bears his name?

19. Which library is often credited with inventing parchment to get round a ban on the export of papyrus by the Egyptians?

20. Who invented the VHS and are now called Panasonic?

Answers see page 280

1. The Mumbles lies south of which city?

2. What is the second largest city in Austria?

3. Which city has an area called Le Panier which was deliberately destroyed by the Germans during World War II?

4. Anderlecht is a suburb of which city?

5. Which protestant city in the Low Countries was converted into one of the most Catholic cities in Northern Europe by virtue of the so-called 'Spanish Fury' of 1576, led by the Duke of Alba?

6. Euroairport is a tri-national airport, situated in France but serving three cities - one Swiss, one French and one German. Name one of these cities.

7. Which two European capital cities are only 60 kilometres apart?

8. Rusholme's Curry Mile is to be found in which city?

9. In which town or city are the inhabitants sometimes referred to as 'Mackems'?

10. Puccini came from which Italian city?

11. El Greco lived in which Spanish town or city from 1577?

12. Haydn's 104th Symphony is named after where?

13. In which city did Gutenberg, depicted opposite, operate his printing press?

Answers see page 280

Square Solution

Can you work out the reasoning behind these squares and replace the question mark with a number?

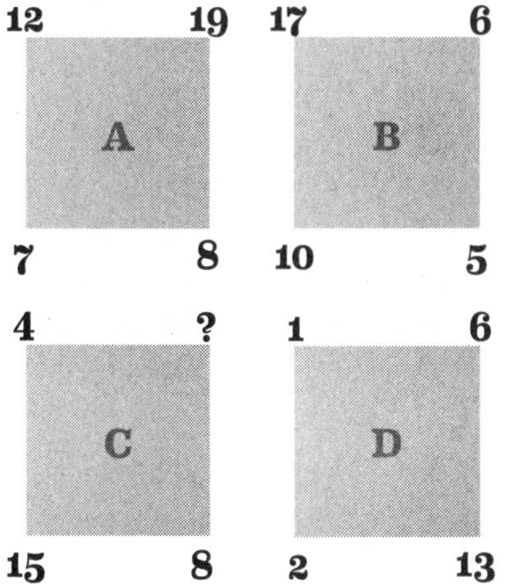

Answer see page 280

Odd One Out

The weight of each suitcase is shown. Which is the odd one out?

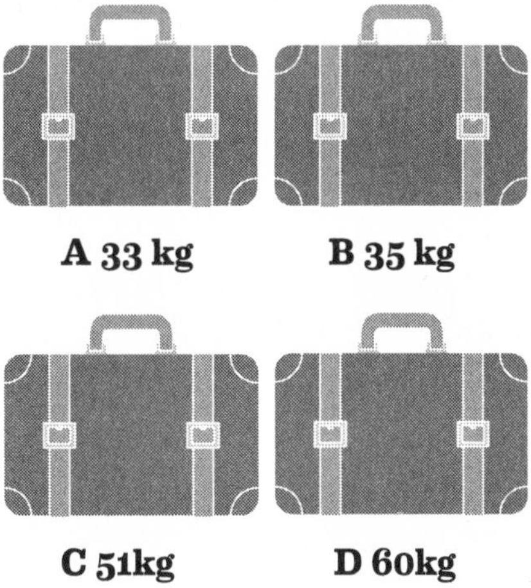

Answer see page 280

1. Who was the leader of the third expedition to reach the South Pole?

2. To whom did Beethoven originally want to dedicate his third symphony?

3. What other name is used for the Third Battle of Ypres?

4. The Third International was established in 1919. By what single word was it probably better known?

5. Dr. J. Allen Hynek introduced a classification of what?

6. What is the third-longest river in Europe, after the Volga and the Danube. Like the Volga, it enters the Caspian?

7. Brussels and Antwerp are the two largest cities in Belgium. What is the third largest?

8. What is the first line of the play *Richard III*?

9. The title music for the film *The Third Man* is played on the pictured instrument. What is it?

10. What was the aim of Captain Cook's third and final voyage?

11. Which millionaire was Max Ernst's third wife?

12. Which work of fiction is described here : a man manages to upset three separate people within a short period of time and sets up three duels. When he arrives at the first duel, he finds his opponents' seconds are the two men he is supposed to be meeting in the second and third duels?

13. Which is the third largest town in Turkey – under the name of Smyrna it can claim to be among the oldest settlements known?

Answers see page 280

Dartboard Dilemma

You have three darts to throw at this strange dartboard. Each dart must score and more than one dart can land in the same segment, but separate scoring rounds may not contain the same three values in a different order. How many different ways are there to score 32?

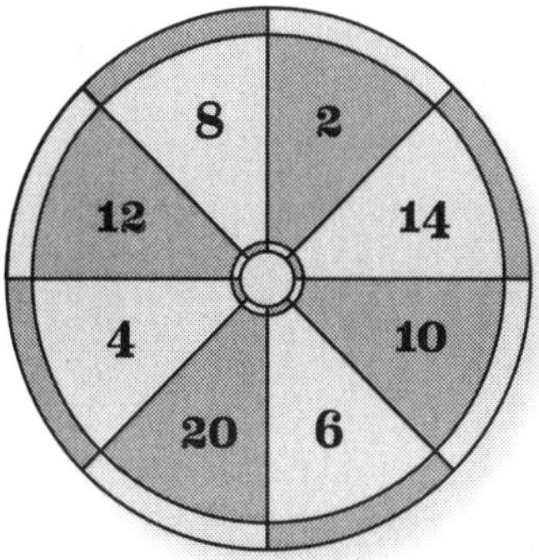

Answer see page 281

Squared Up

Remove eight of these lines to leave only two squares, at least one of which must be a small square with one line on each edge. How can this be done?

Answer see page 281

1. The headless statue of Nike in the Louvre came from where?

2. Which sculptures were removed from the Parthenon in 1799?

3. The statue of Christ the Redeemer which overlooks Rio de Janeiro was commissioned to celebrate what event?

4. On the 50th anniversary of the Easter Uprising the IRA blew up a statue in O'Connell Street off its pillar. Whose statue was destroyed?

5. The statue of which poet can be viewed adjacent to platform 5 of London's St Pancras Station?

6. Much publicity has been given to the fourth plinth in Trafalgar Square. Name one of the people represented by the statues on any of the other three plinths.

7. Which sculpture by Antony Gormley is on show in Gateshead?

8. A statue of which king was unveiled in Winchester in 1901 among great ceremony?

9. The statue in Dublin which is apparently known locally as *The Tart with the Cart* is actually a representation of which person?

10. Which statue by Rodin stands in front of Calais Town Hall?

11. Who produced sculptures for the then-new British Medical Association building in the Strand, sculptures which proved to be controversial and have now been destroyed?

12. *The Colossus of Rhodes* was a statue of whom?

13. What was the family name of the sculptors Pietro, the father and Gianlorenzo, the son? A famous work of the son is the pictured opposite, *Ecstasy of St Teresa* in Rome.

Answers see page 281

1. In the North of England, what is a tarn?

2. The word 'Jackpot' comes originally from which activity?

3. Which items of manufacture are described by a name derived from the Italian for 'cowrie shells', a word which itself is derived from the word for 'little pigs'?

4. What three-letter acronym, forming an English word, was the name of an early Commodore computer?

5. Which word originally referred to Jewish exiles but now is used increasingly to refer to any group of ethnic exiles?

6. The word 'Sioux' is not a name actually used by that tribe to describe themselves. From which language did the word enter into English?

7. What is the origin of the word 'scarper', as in telling someone to go away?

8. The word 'maglev' is short for what?

9. What single word can be used to describe an area of 100 square metres?

10. Which English word derives from non-English words and from an astrological belief that a bad situation can be caused by bad stars?

11. Which three-letter word was the designation for a fore-runner of the Euro?

12. In York, England, the word 'gate' indicates a street – what word actually indicates a gate on the city walls?

13. The word 'alkali' comes from which language?

14. What word originally denoted a groom or horse-servant but came to indicate a high military rank?

15. The word 'Formosa', sometime used for Taiwan, stems from which language?

16. Which word derived from Greek and Aramaic is an alternative name for Calvary, where the Crucifixion took place?

17. The full name of Stanford is 'Leland Stanford Junior University'. Explain the word 'Junior'.

18. The word 'transistor' is short for what?

19. What three letter word describes the center of a tornado?

20. What other name was brought in to describe the Snap-dragon (above), leading George Orwell to complain that a simple English word had been replaced by a word that required reference to a dictionary in order to spell it correctly?

Answers see page 281

1. With which sixties group, sometime backing group for Bob Dylan, was Robbie Robertson a member?

2. Which music group has supported the British space probe *Beagle 2* , and in 1999 released a record which contained a song called *Beagle 2*?

3. Who was a co-founder and singer with the Spencer Davis Group before leaving to form Traffic?

4. Paul Jones and Mike D'Abo were lead singers with which group?

5. Which band had a song with the line: 'Take a look at my girlfriend, she's the only one I've got'?

6. The events related by Deep Purple in their song *Smoke on the Water* took place in which town?

7. Which city, pictured here, was the name of a song released by the Beautiful South in 1996?

8. Which band was fronted by Peter Noone?

9. *Top of the Pops* was for many years introduced by Led Zeppelin's *Whole Lotta Love* but it was actually performed by another band – which one?

10. What is the first name of the band whose second and third names are Black Mambazo?

11. Which of TS Eliot's cats (as in the musical Cats) was also the name of a pop group?

12. According to the song by Toto, what 'rises over the Serengeti'?

13. What group fronted by Vivian Stanshall first came to prominence on the TV program *Do Not Adjust Your Set*?

Answers see page 281

Box Clever

Which of these is not a view of the same box?

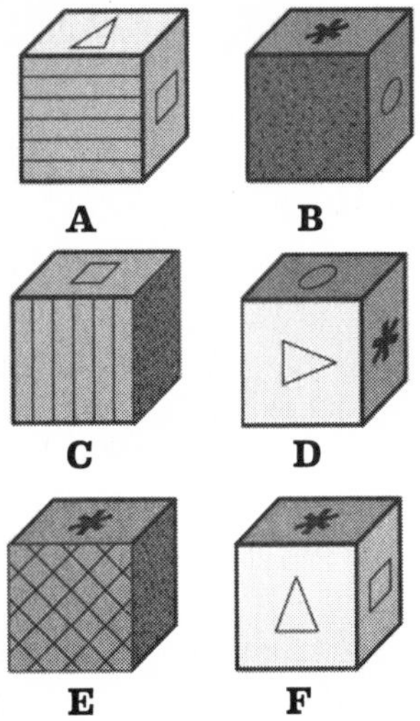

Answer see page 281

Time Travel

This clock was correct at midnight (A), but lost one minute per hour from that moment on. It stopped one hour ago (B), having run for less than 24 hours. What is the time now?

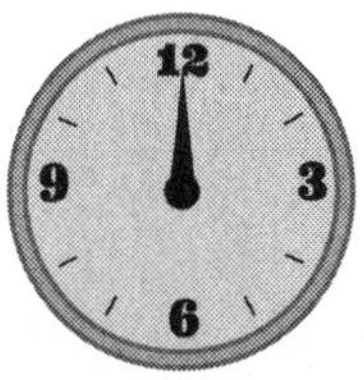

A – midnight

B – a.m.

Answer see page 281

1. Which oil tanker caused a spill off Pembrokeshire in February 1996?

2. Which European country was nominally unified in the same year that the American Civil War started, holding its first parliament on 18th February?

3. In February 2004, Dynamo Moscow lost to Rochdale in which sport?

4. Name one of the coastal towns targeted by RAF as the result of a strategic change in February 1942?

5. The weather area of Finisterre was renamed what, in February 2002?

6. The month of February has a name derived from the Latin word meaning what?

7. Which country suffered disastrous flooding in February 1953, leaving 2,000 dead and 72,000 evacuated?

8. Although George Washington was born on 11th February, why do celebrations take place on 22nd February?

9. Which ship left Kuwait on 19th February 1967, eventually bound for Milford Haven, but never reached there?

10. After the American landings in Morocco and Algeria in November 1942, where did they suffer a major defeat at the hands of the Germans in February 1943?

11. Which painting was stolen from the National Gallery in Oslo in February 1994, but was recovered in May of the same year with the help of Scotland Yard?

12. Who was the British Prime Minister when the Tolpuddle Martyrs were arrested in February 1834?

13. Which island is still a popular diving venue, thanks to an attack by US forces on Japanese naval forces in mid-February 1944, during Operation Hailstorm?

Answers see page 281

Pattern Poser

Can you work out which shape should replace the question mark in this square?

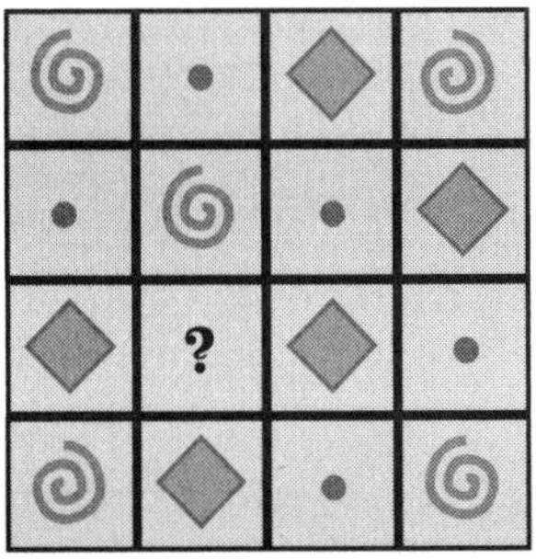

Answer see page 282

Odd One Out

Can you work out which is the odd number out in this circle – and explain why?

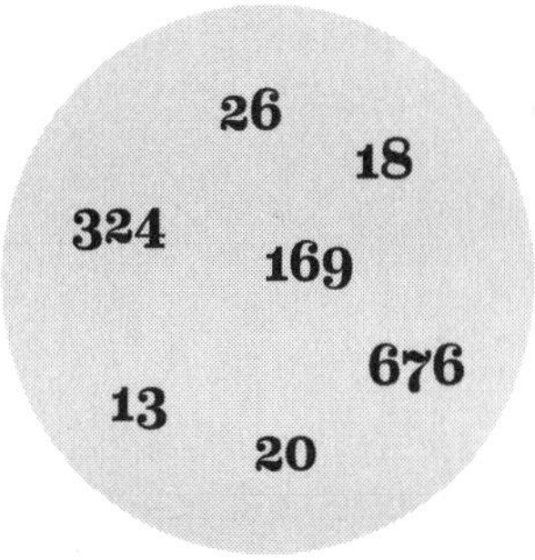

Answer see page 282

1. In the 1890s what became Brazil's first planned city, and the capital of Minas Gerais state?

2. Who was born in Rosario, Argentina in 1928 and is often seen in images derived from a photograph taken of him by Alberto Korda?

3. What did Henry Wickham steal, or smuggle, from Manaus in Brazil – an act which did great damage to the local economy?

4. Which early president of Chile had obvious Irish ancestry?

5. Pele played for which Brazilian club for 19 years?

6. Which language was the official language of the Inca Empire?

7. Who was president of Argentina in 1981/2?

8. Penthesilea was the queen of which group of people?

9. Which present-day capital city was founded by Pedro de Mendoza?

10. A French colony on the Falklands was settled by so many people from one particular town that a new name for the Falklands came into being, based on the name of this town. What was it?

11. The Venezuelan Ilich Ramírez Sánchez who took part in events such as the attack on El Al aircraft at Orly Airport and the attack on OPEC offices in Vienna during 1975, was commonly referred to in the press as 'The Jackal'. What name or 'nom de guerre' did he himself use?

12. Which stadium hosted the 1970 and 1986 World Cup Finals?

13. A Carioca is a person from where?

14. What is the bear pictured called and what's unique about it?

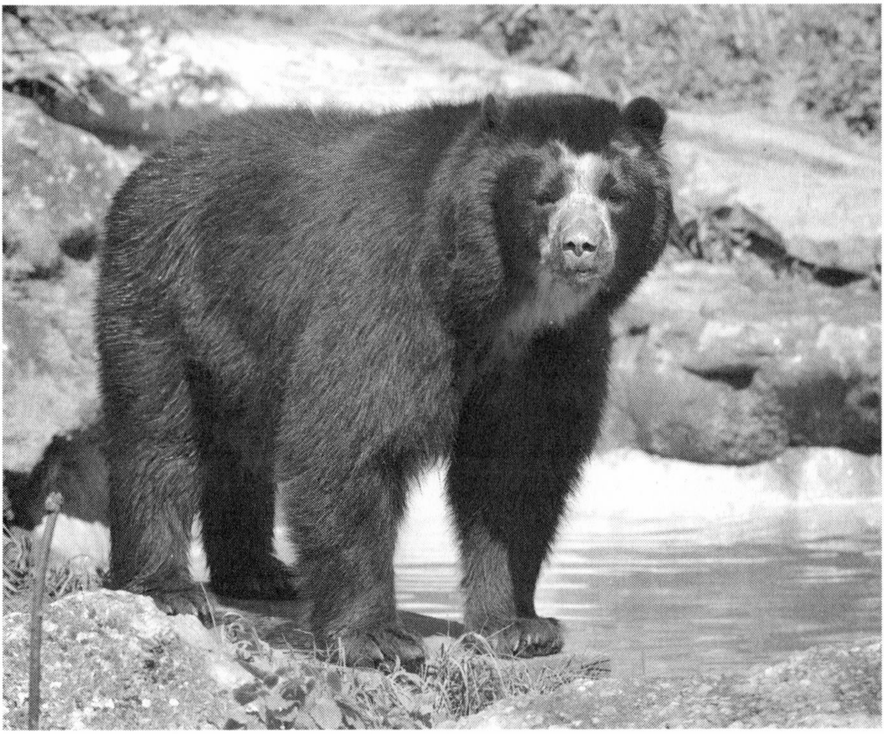

Answers see page 282

Round the Dial

The hands on these clocks move in a strange but logical way. What is the time on the fourth clock?

Answer see page 282

Missing Number

What number should replace the question mark?

6	7	4	8
2	3	0	0
4	5	2	4
5	6	3	?

Answer see page 282

1. Which actor played the main villain in *On Her Majesty's Secret Service* opposite George Lazenby?

2. In which Bond film did Ursula Andress appear?

3. Which genuine Soviet spy organization, apart from the KGB itself, features in early James Bond books?

4. *Never Say Never Again* was a remake of which film?

5. Which French actor played Drax in a Bond film and the investigating officer in *The Day of the Jackal*?

6. In which film does James Bond travel with a companion on the Orient Express?

7. Who appeared in the first staging of *The Threepenny Opera* in Berlin, as well as an early Bond film?

8. Jill Masterton features in which Bond adventure?

9. In *You Only Live Twice,* what is the name of the head of the Japanese Secret service, whom James Bond first meets in a not-yet-in-use underground railway station?

10. In a Bond film, who or what was Little Nellie?

11. The title of which James Bond novel stems from James Bond's first attempt at writing a haiku?

12. Which book finishes with James Bond lying on the floor, poisoned, and facing an unknown fate?

13. Which actress, pictured here, played Miss Moneypenny in many of the original Bond films?

Answers see page 282

Time Travel

This clock was correct at midnight (A), but began to lose 10 minutes per hour from that moment. It stopped 2 ½ hours ago (B), having run for less than 24 hours. What is the correct time now?

midnight p.m.

Answer see page 282

Box Clever

Which of these is not a view of the same three sides of a box?

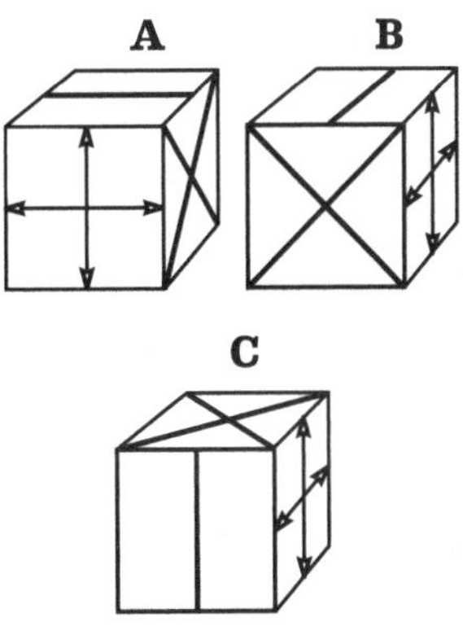

Answer see page 282

1. What name is given to the delta region of the River Rhone?

2. Which major river of Ethiopia shares its name with a soap product?

3. The Saar River is a tributary of which river?

4. Which river, with a name indicating another country, is formed in New Mexico, flowing through the Texas Panhandle into Oklahoma?

5. Which river surrounds Brasilia on three sides?

6. The Ponte Vecchio crosses which river?

7. Which two countries are separated by the Yalu river?

8. On what river does Albany, the capital of New York State, lie?

9. The (Russian) River Don flows into which sea?

10. What name is given sometimes to a single gorge or sometimes to an entire gorge system on the River Danube in Transylvania, where it divides the Carpathians and the Balkans?

11. The River Meander lies in which country?

12. Which two countries of the same name are separated by a river also of the same name?

13. On which river close to St. Malo was a tidal generating station built in 1967?

14. Which river flows from the Baikal Sea and was the source of a name adopted by a political figure?

15. To try and gain tourism advantages, a section of the Mae Klong river in Thailand has officially been renamed as what?

16. The River Amur forms, for about 1,800 kilometres, the boundary between which two countries?

17. Which river joins the Murray River at Wentworth, and is a contender with the Murray for the title of longest river in Australia?

18. The Lachine Falls lie on the St. Lawrence River. How did they get their name?

19. Which city was founded in AD 762 on the banks of the River Tigris at its point of closest approach to the Euphrates?

20. The Grand Coulee Dam shown below lies on which river?

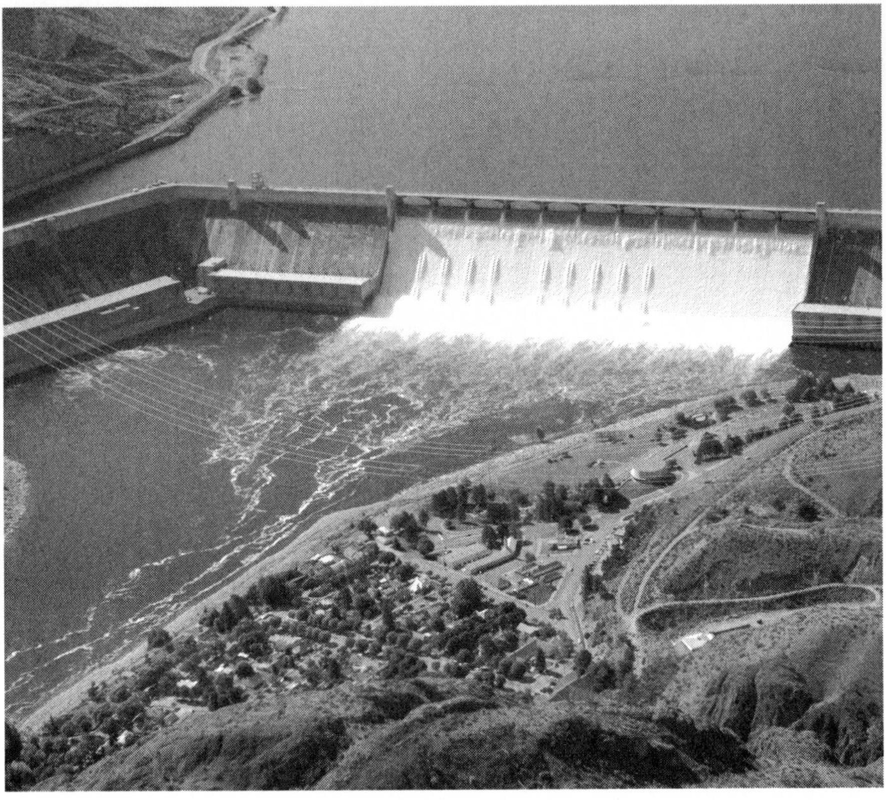

Answers see page 283

1. Which Anna Sewell book was once banned in South Africa?

2. The book *Anne of Green Gables* is set in which part of the world?

3. Which book by Johann Wyss appeared in 1827 and was part of the contemporary fascination for Robinson Crusoe style books?

4. The long-running legal case of *Jarndyce versus Jarndyce* features in what book?

5. Which Joseph Conrad book is based in Costaguana and tells a story of silver mining?

6. *The Piper at the Gates of Dawn* is the name of a chapter in which book?

7. In the book *Moby Dick*, Captain Ahab and Ishmael set sail from the island pictured here. What is it called?

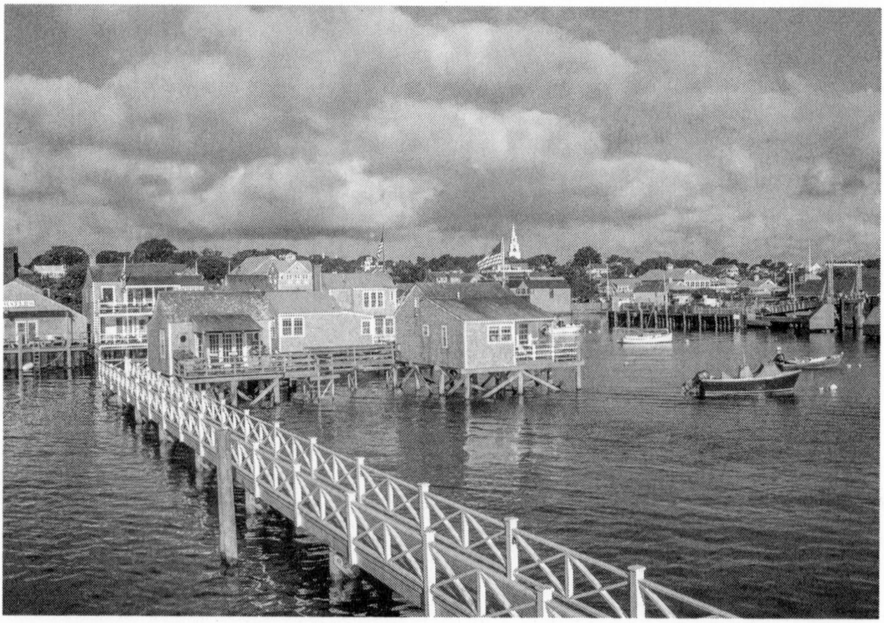

8 John Cleland was the author of which controversial book?

9. Which book by H.G. Wells tells of a disaffected draper who eventually ends up working in a pub?

10. *On the Banks of Plum Creek,* one of the books upon which the TV program *Little House on the Prairie* was based, was written by whom?

11. Which book starts off with Buck Mulligan in the vicinity of a Martello Tower called Sandy Tower?

12. Some of the leading characters from which book lived at Thrushcroft Grange?

13. Which book by Kafka tells of a man, referred to as K., who travels to take up an appointment as a Land Surveyor only to find, when he gets there, that no job is waiting for him?

Answers see page 283

Make Up

Which of these cubes cannot be made from this layout?

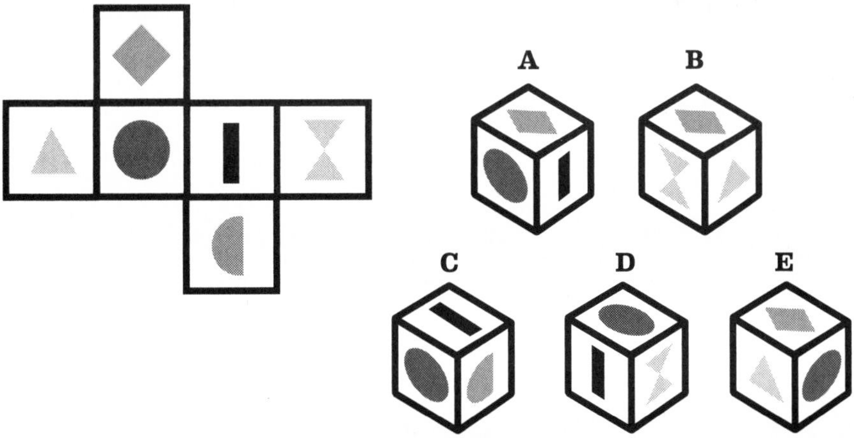

Answer see page 283

1. What type of food stuff is *Quark*?

2. A dish of poached eggs and wilted spinach could be referred to by what name (sometimes Parmesan cheese sauce is added)?

3. From the point of view of British supermarkets, what greengrocery item is their most profitable food item?

4. Which unit of energy is used in science in preference to calories and is usually also displayed alongside calories on food packaging?

5. What is a 'Jersey Royal'?

6. A pantry was originally a store area for what type of food?

7. Gulliver's Travels features a military dispute between the 'Big-Enders' and the 'Little-Enders'. Explain the origin of these names.

8. Which oil can be used in oil paints, putty, wood finish, floor covering and food?

9. Which foodstuff item, which first appeared in 1922, was named after a village just South of Burton on Trent?

10. Which vegetarian sausages typically contain cheese, breadcrumbs, leeks and herbs? Caerphilly Cheese is often used nowadays, instead of the original cheese which gave them their name, which is no longer made.

11. Who was the father of Agamemnon, a figure who is associated with a story about serving up a meal made from human remains?

12. What is both the German word for meal and the name of a city, producing a humorous anecdote about God creating the city and finishing with a phrase which could also mean 'dinner is ready'?

13. What are the three main ingredients of custard (of the type that could also be described as crème anglais?)

Answers see page 283

Puzzle Around

Can you work out the sequence, and what the square with the question mark should look like?

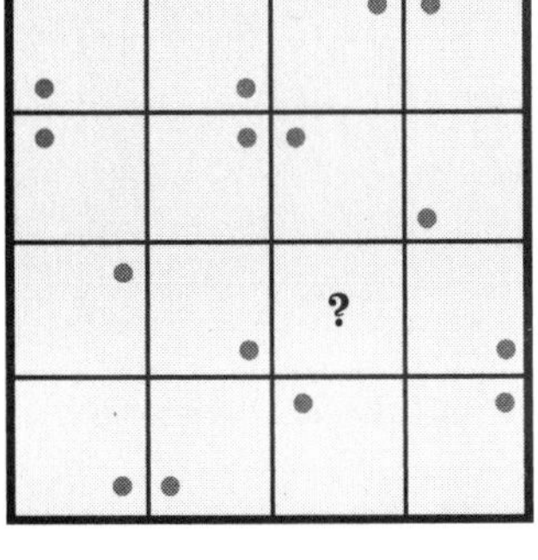

Answer see page 283

Piece It Together

These pieces make up a circle when put together correctly However, one piece is missing. Which is it?

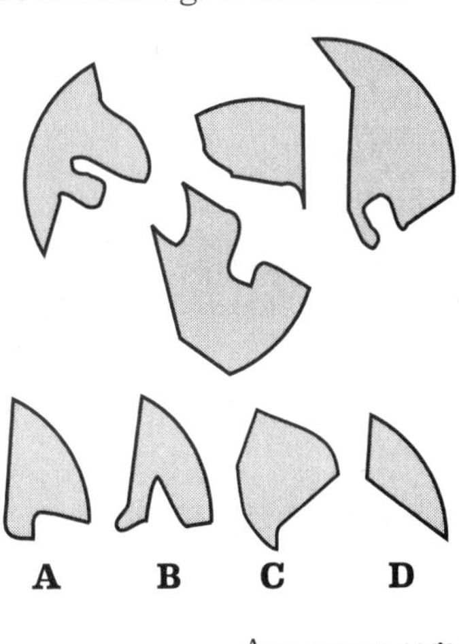

Answer see page 283

1. What are the dimensions of an A4 sheet of paper?

2. What was the name of Prince Llewelyn's dog, which he killed by mistake?

3. Which instruments represent the Wolf in Prokofiev's 'Peter and the Wolf'?

4. Yossarian features in which book?

5. Who was the mother of the last three Valois kings of France?

6. Which was the largest cut diamond in the world until 1985, being cut from the Cullinan Diamond (pictured here in its rough form)?

7. The European Southern Observatory operates telescopes in which country?

8. Leon Gambetta was a Prime Minister of which country?

9. Which company was set up by Allen Lane in 1935/6 to sell a particular product at an attractive price?

10. In San Francisco, what is BART?

11. Which poet was the editor of the 'Shell Guides' to British counties?

12. Peter Longhurst was at one time destined to become a well-known name in Britain, but it turned out not to be. In which activity was he engaged at the time?

13. Who wrote the approx. 6 hours long opera *The Trojans*?

14. Which naturalist was head of BBC2 TV from 1965-68?

15. Base Jumping gets its name from the four locations from which the jumping takes place – name them.

16. How did Thomas Bouch achieve infamy for a certain event in 1879?

17. Who played Eliza Doolittle in the New York production of *My Fair Lady* in 1956 but was denied the film role? She had to wait until 1964 for a part in a Hollywood film.

18. Which disaster-ridden oil rig had the same name as a Norwegian writer?

19. What type of animal is a Gadwall?

20. After the death of Moses, who led the Israelites into the Promised Land?

Answers see page 283

1. Who was the youngest US president?

2. Who was the first US vice-president to resign because of criminal charges?

3. Who was actually president of the United States in 1861 when the Confederate States of America was proclaimed?

4. Which capital city is named after the fifth president of the United States?

5. What was the name of Franklin D. Roosevelt's wife?

6. Who was Kennedy's Republican rival in the 1960 Presidential election?

7. Who was the railway magnate sent by the US President to purchase parts of Mexico?

8. Orlando Bosch has caused great controversy in some circles for being released by President Bush Sr., despite being a prime suspect in the 1976 bombing of an aircraft from which country?

9. The Watergate Scandal involved a raid on the offices of which presidential hopeful?

10. Which American president was in office when prohibition was introduced, although he personally tried to block it?

11. Who is the only ex-US president to be subsequently elected to the Senate?

12. What was the surname of the only grandfather and grandson to have become US presidents?

13. Who was president when the USA annexed California and various other former Mexican possessions?

14. Which American socialist leader was in prison during World War I but campaigned as a candidate for President in 1920 while still behind bars?

15. Who was four times governor of Alabama and four times presidential candidate?

16. In 1932, who was the American general who ignored the orders of the president and destroyed a Hooverville (i.e. shanty town) in Washington DC?

17. Which radio station was named after the daughter of an American president?

18. Which party did Theodore Roosevelt form when he failed to gain the nomination for presidential candidate?

19. Which president was forced to flee the White House (as it was later called) by the British invasion of Washington in 1814?

20. In 1800 what man, pictured here, tied with Thomas Jefferson in the presidential election?

Answers see page 284

1. The book *Catcher in the Rye* gets its name from a misquotation of verse by which poet?

2. Which poet wrote about 'First looking into Chapman's Homer'?

3. Which Spanish poet and dramatist, who wrote *The House of Bernard Alba*, was executed by the fascists in 1936?

4. Which poet was arrested for treason in 1945 but was judged unfit to stand trial. He was detained in hospital for 13 years

5. Which Scottish writer was offered the post of Poet Laureate in 1813 but declined?

6. Which poet wrote verse about Laura who he first met in 1327?

7. Under what name did the poet Christopher Grieve write?

8. Give the next line of poetry : 'Rough winds do shake'

9. What was invented by Gilbert Romme, its nomenclature being added by the poet Fabre d'Eglantine?

10. Which poet had a friendship with fellow poet Paul Verlaine from 1871–1873, a friendship which ended when Verlaine shot him in the wrist, and received an 18-month prison sentence?

11. Which poet released a record album called *Banana Blush*?

12. Which poet represented the Communist Party for a few years in the Chilean parliament and was their candidate for president in 1970?

13. The poem Bronze Horseman by Pushkin tells of a statue of which person?

14. Which silversmith became famous for an alleged exploit during the beginning of the fight for American Independence, as described in a poem by Longfellow?

15. Which poem contains the line: 'As idle as a painted ship upon a painted ocean'?

16. Which poem/song by Banjo Paterson starts off by telling of someone making a cup of tea?

17. Which poem first appeared as a piece of unnamed verse in the preface to the epic *Milton: A Poem in Two Books* but was set to music by Hubert Parry in 1916, initially as a boost to the war effort, but it was soon adopted by the suffragette movement?

18. What adjective did McGonagall use to describe the River Tay in the first line of his poem on the Tay Bridge Disaster?

19. Wordsworth wrote a poem 'above' which abbey?

20. Ramesses II became known by what name to the Greeks – a name used by Shelley in a famous poem inspired by the pictured statue?

Answers see page 284

1. Which scientific effect causes sound to increase in pitch when the source is traveling towards you, and decrease when traveling away (the same idea as used by police radar traps)?

2. What is Cherenkov radiation?

3. The CERN research institute (part of which is pictured, right) is physically located in which two countries?

4. Name one of the two places where anyone can demonstrate the existence of cartilage in the human body straight away?

5. What is the Magnus Effect?

6. Who would be interested in a Hertzsprung-Russell diagram?

7. What name is given to the effect, observable under a microscope, whereby smoke particles or pollen can be seen to exhibit an irregular movement due to being bombarded by molecules?

8. Which mathematical curve assumed naturally by hanging cables has come to be better known in the context of wires carrying overhead electricity?

9. What special name is given to a length of 10 to the power of minus ten metres, or one ten-millionth of a metre. It received this name as a result of an astronomical work of 1869.

10. Which scientific effect, named after a Swiss mathematician, describes the 'sucking' effect that allows a carburetor to work?

11. What name is given to the quantum phenomenon whereby a sub-atomic particle can pass through a barrier which classically would be impenetrable?

12. In Quantum Mechanics, which constant is represented by the letter 'h'?

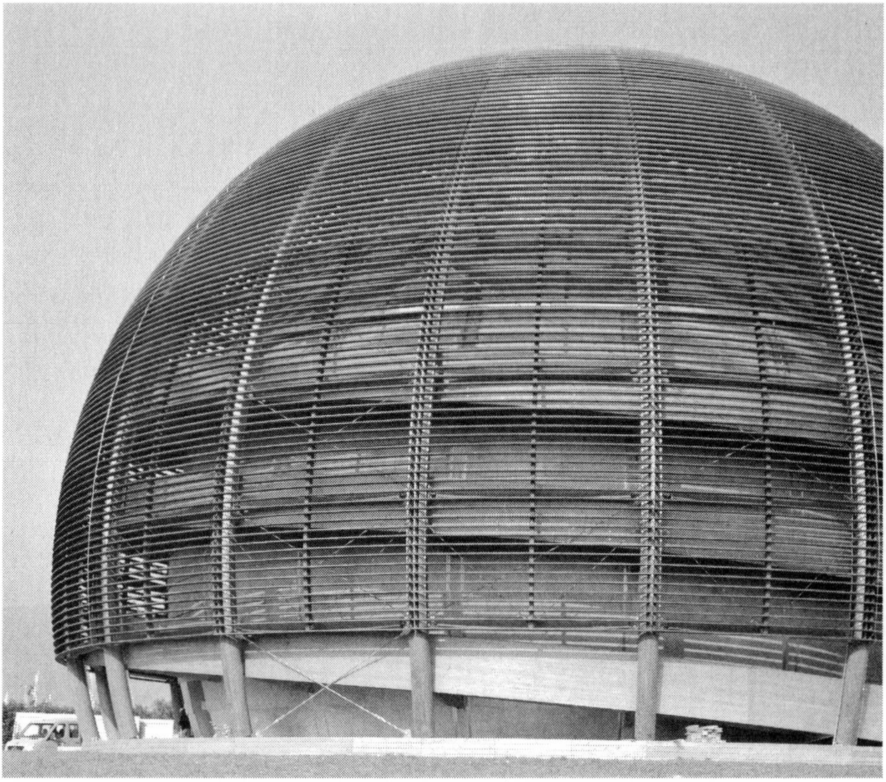

13. Which metal is derived from the ore bauxite?

Answers see page 284

In The Balance

Each large ball weighs one and a third times each small ball. There are 9 small balls on the left scale. What is the minimum number of small and large balls we need to add to the 2 balls on the right scale to make them balance?

Answer see page 284

1. Which play by George Bernard Shaw takes place during a war between Serbia and Bulgaria?

2. Lady Teazle is a character in which 18th century play?

3. Which opera by Richard Strauss is based on a play by Oscar Wilde?

4. In the play *Forty Years After* by Alan Bennett, a teacher complains that when he was younger the works of Lawrence were banned but are now a part of the exam syllabus. Someone points out he is in error – which error has he made?

5. *Pyramus and Thisbe* provides a play within which other play?

6. Who was the salesman in Arthur Miller's *Death of a Salesman*?

7. Which playwright has one of his characters, Thomas Stockmann, declare: 'The majority are always wrong'?

8. Big Daddy is a character in which play?

9. The musical Cabaret was preceded by a stage play called *I am a Camera* , based on the same Christopher Isherwood stories. What was Walter Kerr's famous but scathing three-word critical comment on the play?

10. Which folk group formed by Pete Seeger get their name from a play by Gerhard Hauptmann?

11. The Rod Taylor film *Young Cassidy* was based on the life of which Irish playwright?

12. Verdi's opera *Falstaff* is based on which play?

13. What was the name of Schiller's play telling the story of the pictured queen?

Answers see page 285

1. Which house on the banks of Loch Awe is the home of the head of the Campbell clan?

2. What are the two main conditions to be satisfied before a whiskey can be described as Scotch whisky?

3. In the Scottish legal system, who is the official who prepares the case for prosecution?

4. The Caledonian Canal exits into which Firth at its eastern end?

5. Which Scotsman is considered to be the founder of the American Navy?

6. What is Lallans?

7. Prior to her escape in 1568 (soon after which she fled to England), Mary Queen of Scots was imprisoned on which loch?

8. Which Scottish town was formerly known as St. John's Town?

9. The father of Robert Louis Stevenson and other relatives were responsible for constructing about half the total of a particular type of building in Scotland. What type of building?

10. Where can you view Mons Meg?

11. Which Scottish town is dominated by an incomplete replica of Rome's Colosseum, called McCraig's Folly?

12. What was the first National Park in Scotland?

13. Who was King of Scotland at the time of the Norman Conquest in 1066?

14. Which is the second highest mountain in Britain?

15. Who raised his standard by the banks of Loch Shiel?

16. Where did several thousand Scottish emigrants attempt to settle in 1698 and 1699, a disastrous venture that almost brought Scotland to its knees?

17. Which book finishes with the hero about to enter the bank of the British Linen Company in Edinburgh – a sequel starts with the same person emerging from the same bank?

18. Loch Ness lies in which rift or valley, which runs between Fort William and Inverness?

19. Which Scottish game is similar to hurling, so similar that Ireland-Scotland internationals have been held between the two codes?

20. In which town between Glasgow and Edinburgh will you see the pictured rotating boat lift, that transfers boats between the Forth and Clyde Canal and the Grand Union Canal?

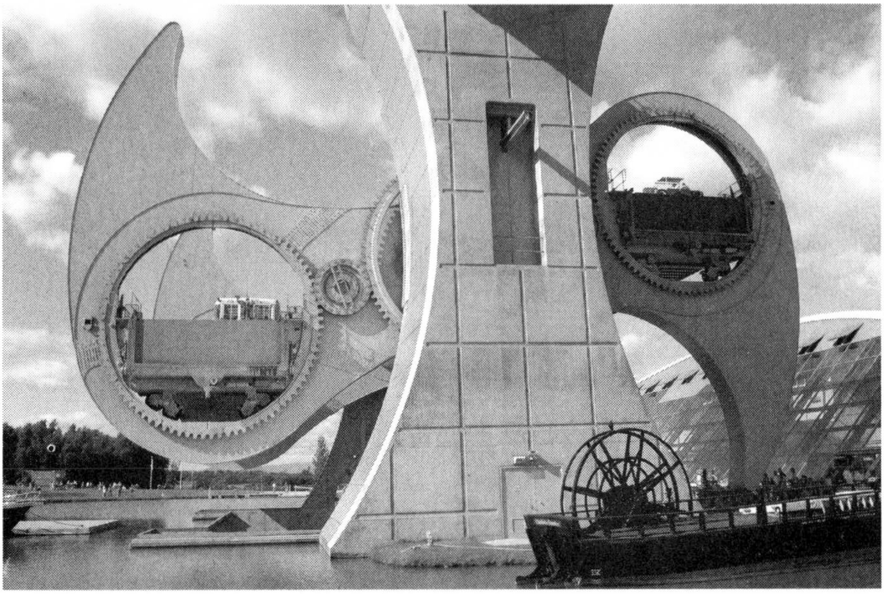

Answers see page 285

1. What was the name of the peace treaty signed on 3rd March 1918 between Soviet Russia and Germany?

2. Where was the bridge used by the Allies to cross the German Rhein from 7th March to 17th March 1945?

3. In which village were 507 people shot dead on 16th March 1968, by troops under the command of Lieutenant Calley?

4. On what date is the vernal equinox?

5. Which city was bombed on 9th March 1945, leaving at least 80,000 dead?

6. Which college was the subject of controversy in March 2002 for allegedly accepting students in return for financial favors?

7. What was the last mainline steam engine to be built in Britain, coming into service in March 1960 with an expected service life of 20 years, only to be withdrawn in 1965?

8. What event of March 3rd 1943 resulted in many deaths in Bethnal Green, London, despite the fact that no German bombers appeared on that date?

9. In March 2003, which European state voted to expand the powers of the monarchy?

10. Which new car was introduced by Jaguar in March 1961 at a ceremony in Geneva?

11. In which French town did a gunman attack council members in March 2002, killing 8 and wounding 19?

12. Which Triumph works was turned into a co-operative in March 1975?

13. Who was seen on video being beaten up by members of the Los Angeles police in March 1991?

Answers see page 285

Squared Up

Can you work out the number needed to complete the square?

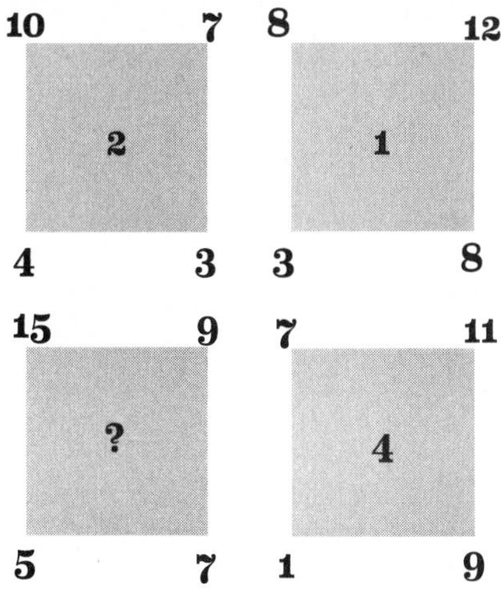

Answer see page 285

Odd One Out

Can you find the odd one out of these symbols?

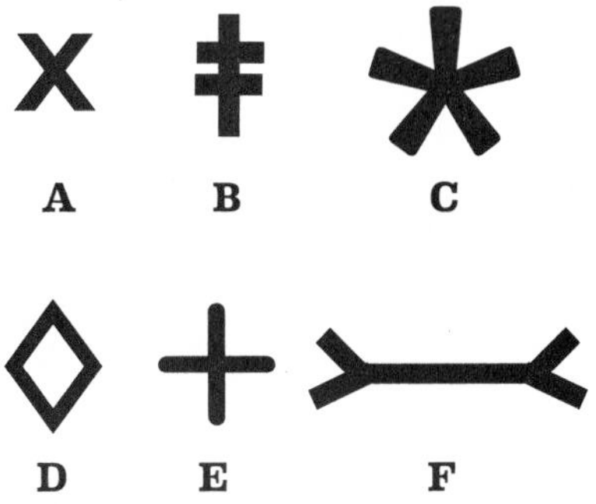

Answer see page 286

1. Which month of the revolutionary French calendar provided the title of a book about mineworkers by Emile Zola?

2. Which name is given to the female figure who represents the embodiment of the French Revolution?

3. Which town was two-thirds surrounded by the River Rhone in its early days, and has been a part of France since the time of the Revolution?

4. Touissant L'Ouverture led a rebellion in what part of the world, in the wake of the French Revolution?

5. Who wrote a *History of the French Revolution* and then had to re-write it because the manuscript was burnt whilst in the possession of John Stuart Mill?

6. Who said, with reference to the French Revolution: 'Bliss was it in that dawn to be alive'?

7. Who painted *Marat Assassiné* during the period of the French Revolution?

8. During the French Revolution the Church of St Genevieve, patron saint of Paris, which was built under Louis XV, was changed into what?

9. In which month of the revolutionary calendar was Robespierre executed?

10. What surname is shared by a Geneva-born philosopher who was one of the inspirations for the French Revolution, a French dramatist/poet, and a French painter?

11. The French revolutionary month of Ventôse is named after what?

12. What is the French word for 'sling' or 'catapult' that was used for a series of revolts against Louis XIV?

13. Delacroix (pictured above) famously painted *Liberty Leading the People*. It commemorates the revolution of which year?

Answers see page 286

Sum Body

Can you unravel the reasoning behind this diagram and find the missing number?

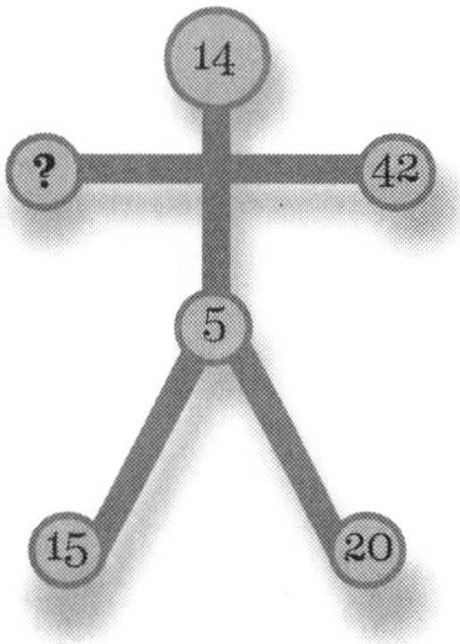

Answer see page 286

Squared Up

This square follows a pattern. Can you unravel it and replace the question mark with a number?

9	3	3	3
5	8	2	1
4	3	8	1
8	2	1	**?**

Answer see page 286

1. With respect to the Great Train Robbery, name either of the towns between which the train was traveling?

2. What does TGV stand for?

3. Which form of iron replaced cast iron as a material enabling construction of proper railways in their early years?

4. Why were there no (legal) high-pressure steam engines in production before 1800?

5. Which is the only surviving A3 Pacific locomotive to have been built by Nigel Gresley, being also the first locomotive to have officially travelled at 100 m.p.h.?

6. At 1,065 metres, which is the highest railway station in Britain?

7. Which city has a light railway called the DART, as seen here?

Rank these moons in order of size.

A

B

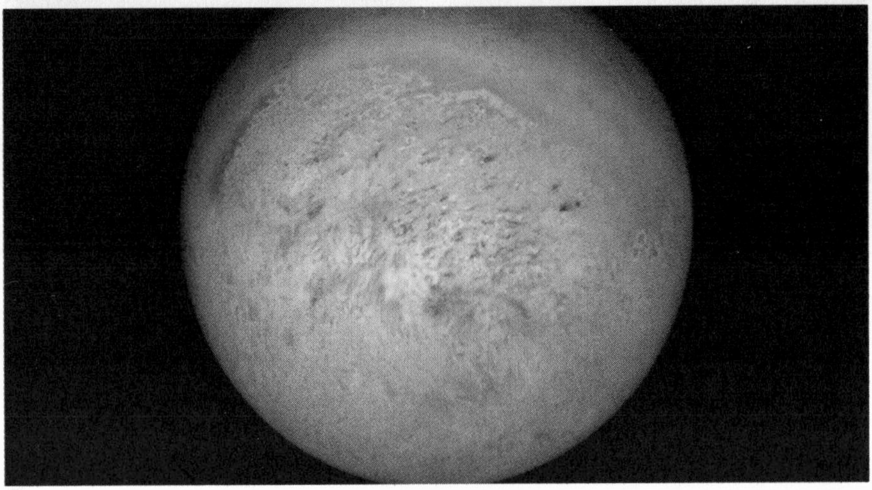

C

D

E

Answer at the back of this section

Which animal is the odd one out?

A

B

C

D

E

Answer at the back of this section

These pictures and others were exhibited by Edvard Munch under what general title?

Answer at the back of this section

Following traditional rather than modern customs, on which anniversaries would the pictured items be appropriate gifts to give to a spouse?

A

B

C

D

E

Answer at the back of this section

Which country does each of these desserts come from?

A

B

C

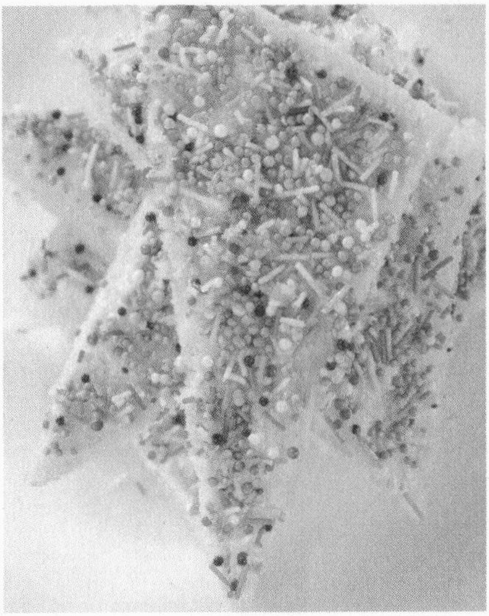

D

E

Answer at the back of this section

Rank these sports by when they were invented.

A

B

C

D

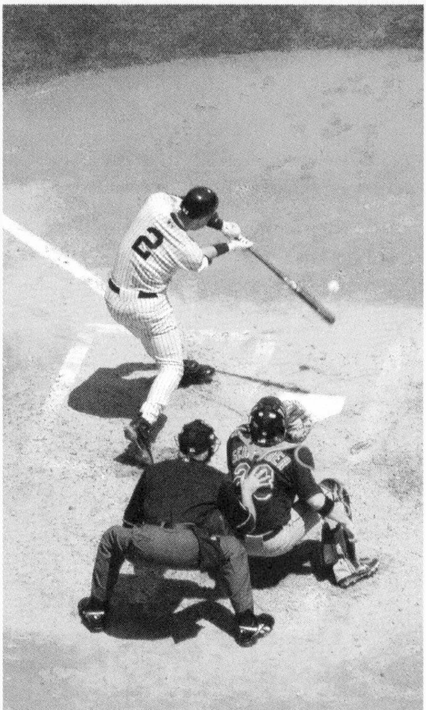

E

Answer at the back of this section

If someone lives in Australia, which of these flags would be the correct one to fly at home?

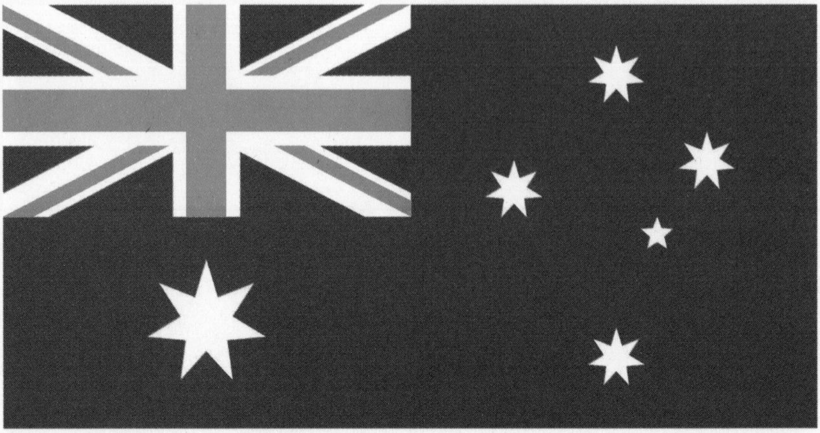

A

B

C

D

E

Answer at the back of this section

What cultural milestone do the people pictured here all have in common?

Carl Jung

Marilyn Monroe

Edgar Allen Poe

Robert Peel

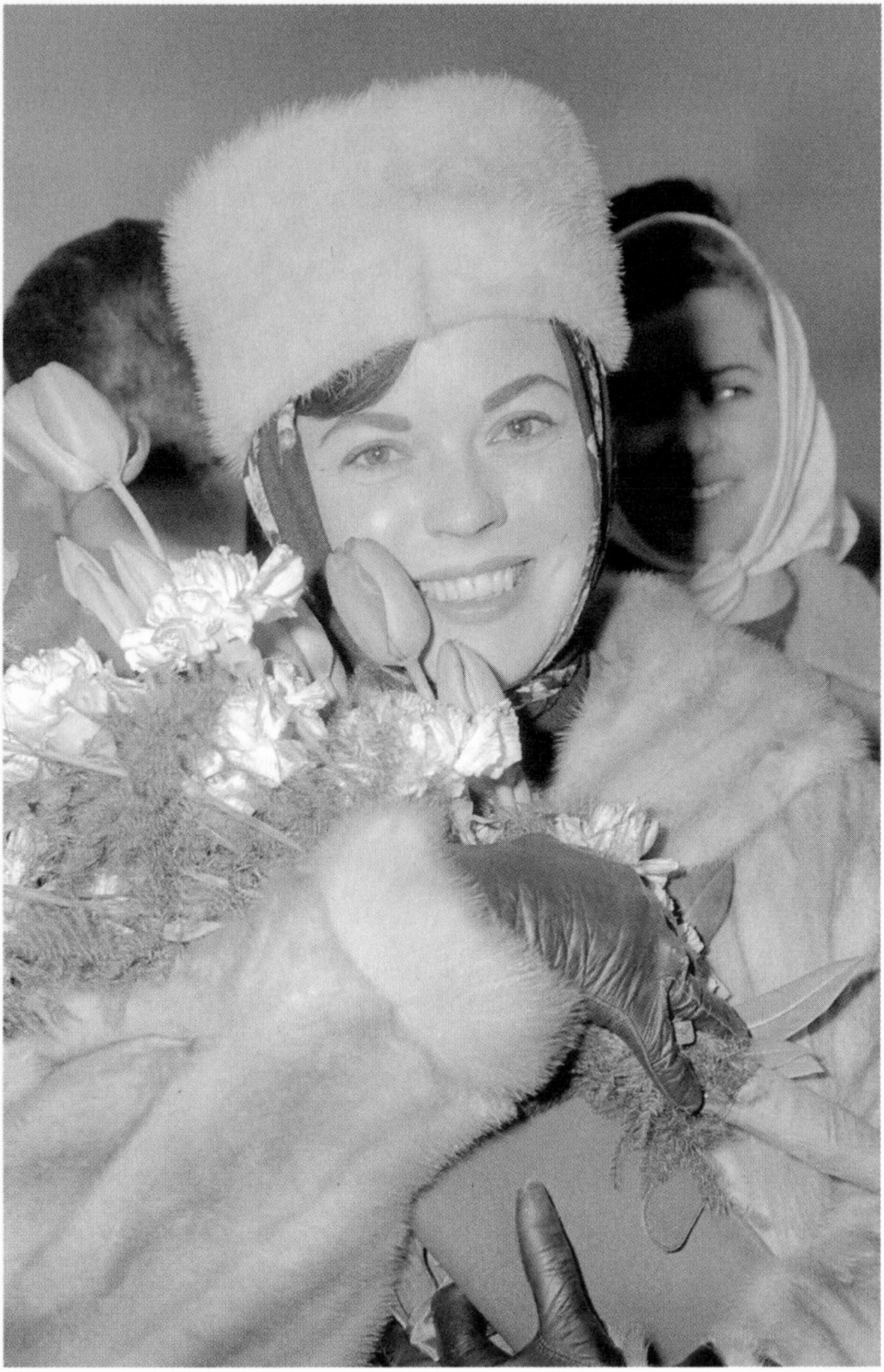

Shirley Temple

Answer at the back of this section

Answers

Moons of the Solar System

b (Ganymede), a (Callisto), d (Io), c (Triton), e (Phobos)

Black-and-White Animals

The Valais Blackneck goat (c), which the only animal that isn't common to Africa.

Edvard Munch

The Frieze of Life

Anniversaries

a: 3rd (Leather), b: 22nd (Copper), c: 5th (Wood), d: 17th (Furniture), e: 65th (Blue sapphire)

Dessert

a: Egypt (Basbousa), b: Malaysia (Ais kacang, can also be found in Singapore and Brunei), c: India (Rasmalai), d: Australia/New Zealand (Fairy bread), e: Lithuania/Poland (Šakotis)

Sport

d: Tennis (12th century), c: Rugby (1823), e: Baseball (1845), a: Basketball (1891), b: Volleyball (1895)

The Cross and the Ensign

They should fly a., which is Australia's current flag.

The other two with a Blue Ensign are from 1903–1908 (e) and 1901–1903 (c), while the red Civil Ensign (seen in its 1903–1909 version in d and its current one in b) is now for use only at sea.

Famous Faces

They all appeared on the cover of ***Sgt. Pepper's Lonely Hearts Club Band*** by The Beatles.

8. Which railway was built in the late 1890s as part of a plan to connect Manchester with Paris?

9. The song *Homeward Bound* by Simon and Garfunkel was allegedly inspired by time spent at which railway station?

10. Which event in 1927 caused the railway to offer early morning trips from Manchester to Southport, returning in time for the start of work in the morning?

11. The Blue Train runs on a journey of about 1,600 kilometres in which country?

12. Which country has the largest railway network, in terms of length?

13. Who was killed on the opening day of the Liverpool to Manchester Railway?

Answers see page 286

Arrow Hunt

The arrows in this grid go in a clockwise spiral starting from the top left corner. In which direction should the missing arrow point?

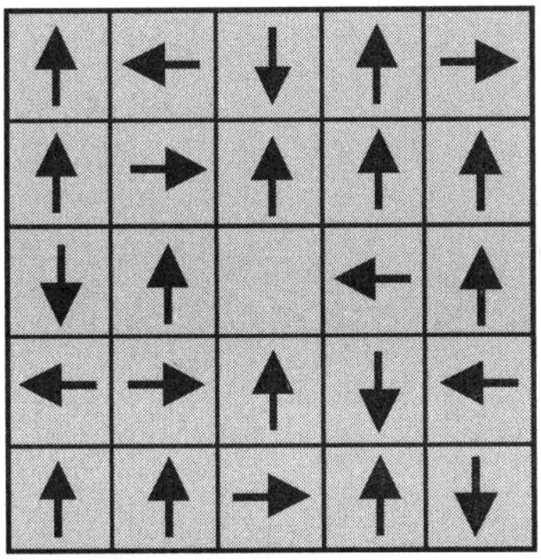

Answer see page 286

Word Slice

By taking a segment and finding its pair the names of three scientists can be found. Who are they?

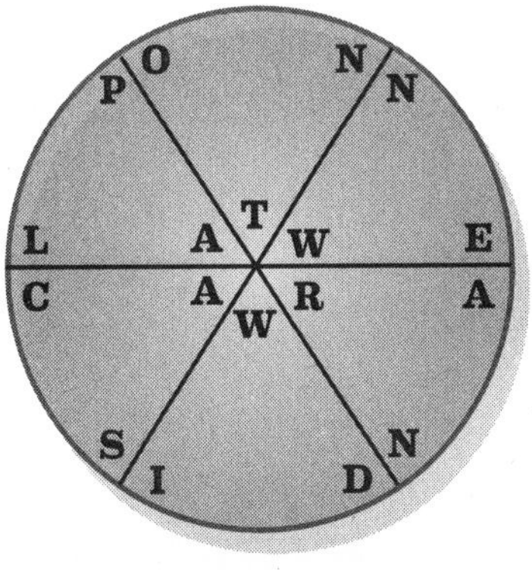

Answer see page 286

1. Who wrote *Chitty Chitty Bang Bang*?

2. In which film was a Starling used to catch a Buffalo?

3. The book *Gone to Texas* was filmed under what title?

4. Which film was based on a Graham Greene book and starred Richard Attenborough as Pinkie Brown?

5. Who wrote *Witness for the Prosecution* which was turned into a film starring Charles Laughton and Marlene Dietrich?

6. What was the name of the motel featured in the film *Psycho*?

7. Who played the title role in the film *The Exorcist*?

8. Which novel (later made into a film) relates, in its opening paragraphs, how Joe Buck exits from a shop in Houston, after just buying a new pair of boots?

9. Name one of the two films that features the character of Dave Bowman?

10. Which book by Martin Cruz Smith was filmed with William Hurt in the main role of Inspector Renko?

11. Which film is based on *Jack's Return Home* by Ted Lewis?

12. *Murder She Said* has Margaret Rutherford in the role of Miss Marple. Which future Miss Marple had a minor role in this film?

13. In 1954, the BBC screened a version of *1984* with Peter Cushing as Winston Smith, and two years later an American film had Edmond O'Brien in the Winston Smith role. Which actor appeared in both versions?

14. The 1940 film of *Rebecca* by Daphne du Maurier (pictured), starring Laurence Olivier and Joan Fontaine, was directed by whom?

15. The controversial Disney film *Song of the South* is based on which set of stories?

16. Which book by Charles Portis, featuring an ex-member of Quantrill's Guerillas and a Texas Ranger, was made into a film starring John Wayne?

17. Who had his *Motorcycle Diaries* published in 1993, a film subsequently being made?

18. The film *The Colditz Story* is based on a book by which of its former prisoners?

19. The book called *Q & A* was filmed under what name?

20. Which novel by Paul Theroux is named after an area of Honduras, and has been made into a film?

Answers see page 286

1. What three types of animal were *Rag, Tag and Bobtail*

2. Until recently, the Wapiti (also known as an 'elk' in America) was automatically assumed to be the same species as what type of European animal (some doubt now exists in some quarters)?

3. Which animal has a variety called Grevy's?

4. *Canis lupus* is what type of animal?

5. The common Central European animal known as a Waschbär in German is actually an escapee from fur farms and gets its German name from its habit of washing its food. What is its English name?

6. Which mammal can come in a white variety which is not white, and a black variety which is not black but which could have been named purely to distinguish it from the so-called white variety?

7. Sadly, including the one pictured here, three types of modern tiger have become extinct. Name one.

8. Which animal is 'lutra lutra'?

9. What type of animal was Beatrix Potter's 'Timmy Tiptoes'??

10. Which pig in *Animal Farm* was responsible for spreading Napoleon's propaganda amongst the other animals?

11. A colony of which type of animal has established itself around Turin – and is causing concern for conservationists in general, in case they spread elsewhere?

12. What type of animal is a pinniped?

13. Which animal belongs to the genus Ornithorhynchus and has a common name meaning 'broad-footed'?

Answers see page 286

Symbolic Value

Each similar symbol in the diagram has the same value – one of which is a negative number. Can you work out the logic and discover which number should replace the question mark and the values of the symbols? Bodmas does not apply.

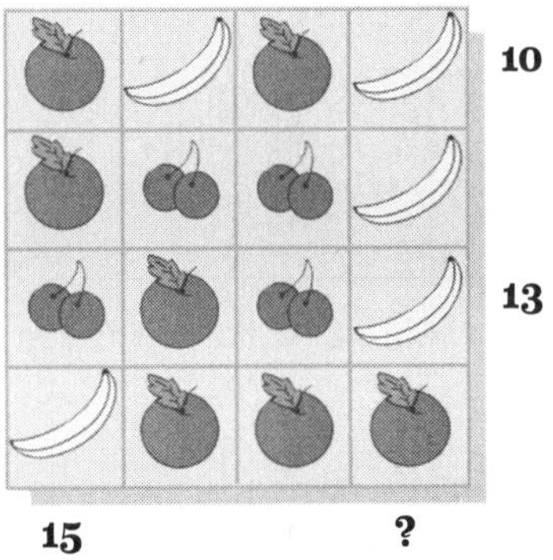

Answer see page 287

Box Clever

There is a different symbol on each side of the box. Which of these is not a view of the same box?

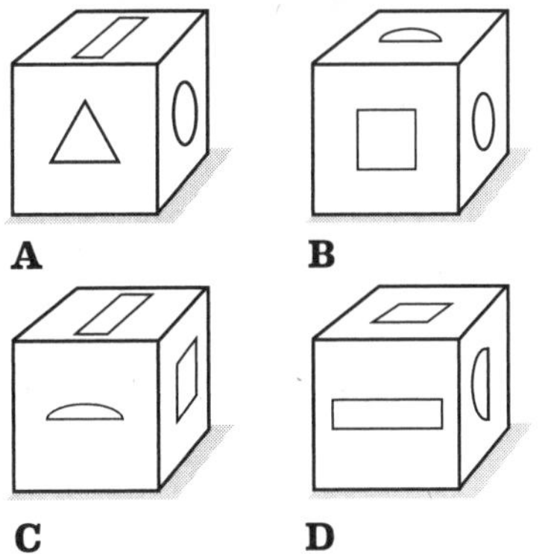

Answer see page 287

1. Which is the largest of the Society Islands?

2. Which former Portuguese colony forms an island republic west of Angola?

3. Island Records was actually founded on which island?

4. In 1942, which island under the control of Vichy France was attacked and taken over by the British?

5. Which islands are also called the Sandwich Islands?

6. Apart from Britain, which other major island was invaded successfully by the Normans?

7. Robert Graves spent his last years on which island?

8. In the 1930s who disappeared while travelling to the island of Howland?

9. What is the official borough name of Staten Island?

10. On which island can you find Aberdeen, Stanley, Victoria and Causeway Bay?

11. Bastia is a port on which island?

12. Which islands separate the Bering Sea and the Pacific?

13. Josephine (of Napoleon fame) was born on which island?

14. What is the name of the flying island visited by Gulliver on his travels?

15. Which name beginning with 'M' is an alternative name for the Spice Islands?

16. Orangutans in the wild are nowadays restricted to two islands. Name one.

17. Which islands north of Novaya Zemlaya are named after an Austrian Emperor?

18. Pearl Harbor is on which Hawaiian island?

19. The so-called ABC Islands consist of Aruba, Bonaire and which other island?

20. On which island did Daedulus enter the Labyrinth to fight the Minotaur?

Answers see page 287

1. Which country was the first to beat Germany at football after their World Cup win in 1990?

2. Which Asian country reached the quarter-finals of the World Cup in 1966?

3. Which country won the first football World Cup?

4. Who was captain of the Italian team that won the World Cup in 1982, and went on to make a record number of appearances for Italy?

5. In the opening match of the 1974 World Cup, who beat the host nation West Germany by 1-0?

6. Where was the Women's Football World Cup of 2003 held?

7. Which South American country made its World Cup debut in 2002?

8. In the 1994 World Cup, which Colombian player triggered off a craze for wearing blonde wigs?

9. In which city did the opening game of the 2006 World Cup take place?

10. Which African player was the top scorer in the 1966 Football World Cup?

11. Who did Zinedine Zidane head-butt in the World Cup Final 2006?

12. Which country did Australia beat 31-0 at football in a World Cup qualifying match?

13. In the World Cup of 2010, which squad had the most French-born players, apart from France itself?

14. In which three years did Brazil win the World Cup, allowing them to keep the trophy outright?

15. What man, pictured here, was President of FIFA at the time of the first World Cup competition in 1930?

Answers see page 287

Pattern Poser

Find the missing number.

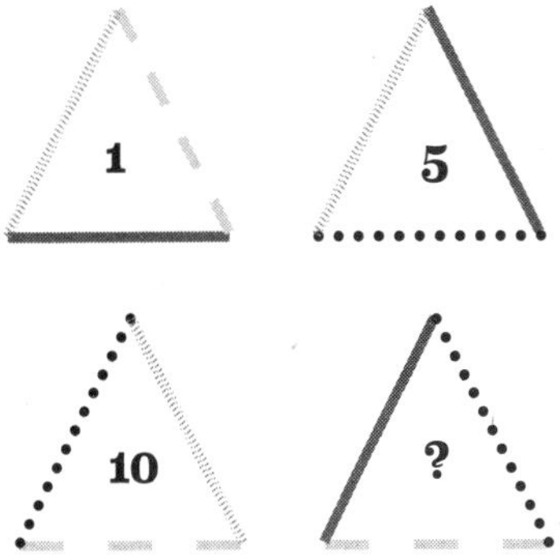

Answer see page 287

Shape Shift

Can you find the odd shape out?

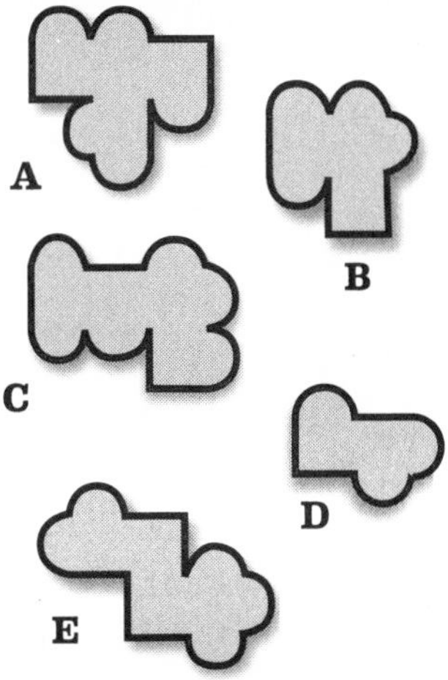

Answer see page 287

1. Who sang the words on Hawkwind's well-known record 'Silver Machine'?

2. The song 'In the Ghetto' by Elvis Presley is 'set' in which American city?

3. Which Mexican folk song became known in an 'upbeat' form due to a record released by Richie Valens in 1958?

4. In a Donovan song, who came singing songs of love?

5. Which song provided Johnny Cash with his first million seller, and became the song with which he started many of his concerts?

6. The Simon and Garfunkel song Mrs Robinson mentions which baseball player?

7. Who sang the song Mama, I'm coming home, which appears on the album *No More Tears*?

8. In what style of music is the song 'The Girl from Ipanema'?

9. Who wrote the song 'Mighty Quinn'?

10. Which song did HAL, the computer in 2001, sing while he was being disabled?

11. The song 'O Danny Boy' is sung to which tune?

12. Who sang the British Eurovision Song Contest entry 'Boom-bang-a-bang'?

13. Which record released by Ike and Tina Turner in 1971 was a song originally written by John Fogerty for the group of which he was a member?

Answers see page 287

Arty Anagram

Can you work out what letter needs to be inserted in the middle to form four famous artists by combining opposite segments in anagrams?

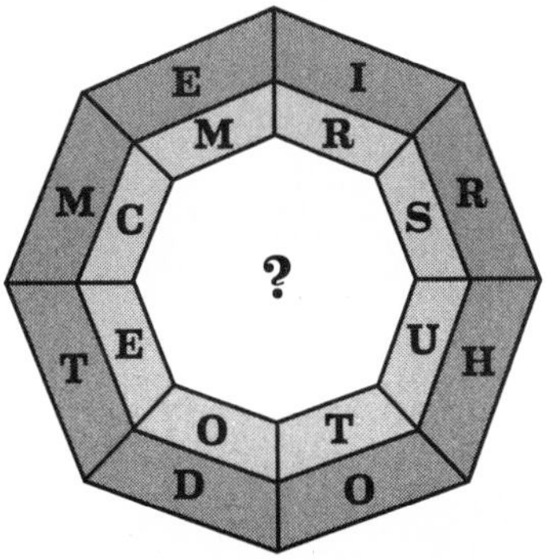

Answer see page 288

Squared Up

Can you work out what number each symbol represents and find the value of the question mark?

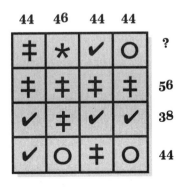

44	46	44	44	
‡	*	✔	O	?
‡	‡	‡	‡	56
✔	‡	✔	✔	38
✔	O	‡	O	44

Answer see page 288

1. What is the English name of the lake known locally as *Lac Leman*?

2. On which lake in America was London Bridge re-built?

3. Which ship that sank in Lake Superior was immortalised in a 1976 song by Gordon Lightfoot?

4. Friedrichshafen on Lake Constance featured in the early days of air transport due to which firm?

5. Where would you find the Great Bitter Lake?

6. On which lake was Malcolm Campbell killed?

7. Which is the largest lake in the African Rift Valley?

8. Lake Volta lies in which country?

9. The Niagara Falls are situated between which two lakes?

10. Name one of the lakes on the Caledonian Canal.

11. Which lake has been formed by the Aswan High Dam?

12. What is the oldest existing freshwater lake and contains 20% of the world's fresh water?

13. Which Swiss lake is known locally as *Lac des Quatre-Cantons or Vierwaldst¨attersee*?

14. The freshwater lake, the IJsselmeer, occupies, roughly speaking, the area formerly occupied by which stretch of water?

15. Which Brazilian racing circuit has a name meaning 'between the lakes'?

16. What is the largest lake in Italy?

17. The lake known as the Serpentine in Hyde Park is known by what name in Kensington Gardens?

18. Lake Ladoga lies adjacent to which major city?

19. Which is the largest lake in Wales?

20. Bowness and Ambleside lie on the lake pictured here. What is its name?

Answers see page 288

Circular Logic
From the information given, can you work out the missing total and the values of the different images?

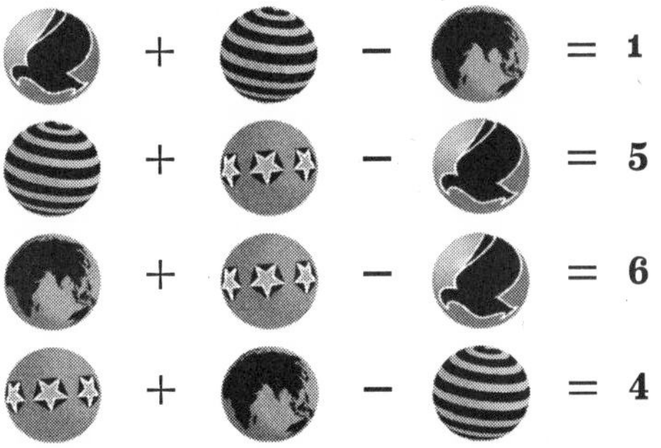

Answer see page 288

1. Tverskaya Street, the main street in Moscow, was formerly named in honour of which writer?

2. Who wrote *Sebastopol Sketches,* based on personal experiences in the Crimean War?

3. Which science-fiction story contains the characters Rick, Rheya and Dr Sartorius?

4. Which play by Chekov provided the symbol used by the Moscow Art Theatre?

5. Who was preparing to write the libretto for Glinka's opera *Russlan and Ludmilla* but was shot dead before he could carry this out?

6. Which book by Nikolai Gogol tells a story of Cossacks in the Ukraine?

7. Which book begins with the following scenario: Two men are sitting in a park in Moscow, discussing the existence of God. One of them is told by a foreign-sounding gentleman that he will die by decapitation, which he laughs off, but only minutes later he slips in the street and has his head sliced off by a tram?

8. Which story by Nikolai Leskov with a Shakespearian allusion provided the basis for a controversial opera by Shostakovich?

9. Who first achieved fame with his book *Red Cavalry* relating his experiences serving with Russian forces in Poland in the wake of the revolution. He also wrote about his native town of Odessa?

10. Olga was one of Chekhov's *Three Sisters*. Name one of the other two.

11. Who or what is Baba Yaga?

12. Which man of literature lived at Yasnaya Polyana?

13. How does Anna Karenina die?

Answers see page 288

1. In one of his works first performed in Leipzig in 1913, Delius heard the first what of spring?

2. Which expressionist playwright became leader of the Soviet Republic of Bavaria in April 1919, but was overthrown shortly after by a vicious unit of the Freikorps?

3. Who played a major role in the overthrow of the French monarchy in August 1792, then became a founder member of the Committee of Public Safety but was executed in April 1794?

4. What is the name of the new Airbus, first flown on 29th April 2005?

5. The Duke of Wellington was brought out of retirement to 'deal' with a demonstration by which group of people in April 1848, in South London?

6. Which country underwent an revolution initiated on 25th April, 1974?

7. Which Act of Parliament was passed in June 1832, although an earlier version had failed in April 1831?

8. Which military aircraft project was cancelled in April 1965, the government announcing they were to purchase the F-111 instead?

9. Who was the man who on 28th April 2001 flew into space, after paying for the experience?

10. Which city experienced an earthquake on 22nd April 1906?

11. April Dancer was known as what, in the TV program of the same name?

12. Which refugee camp in Northern Palestine was the scene of a controversial and widely-reported Israeli action in April 2002?

13. Which horse races make up the Spring Double?

Answers see page 288

Safe Path

Here is an unusual safe. To reach the OPEN button, all the other buttons must be pressed in the correct order. Each button has a compass direction together with the number of steps needed. Which is the first button you must press?

4SE	1E	4S	1SE	4SW
2S	1E	1NE	1SE	1SW
1E	1NW	open	2NW	2W
3E	3NE	1SW	3NW	1SW
2N	1N	1N	3N	1N

Answer see page 289

Missing Number

What number should replace the question mark?

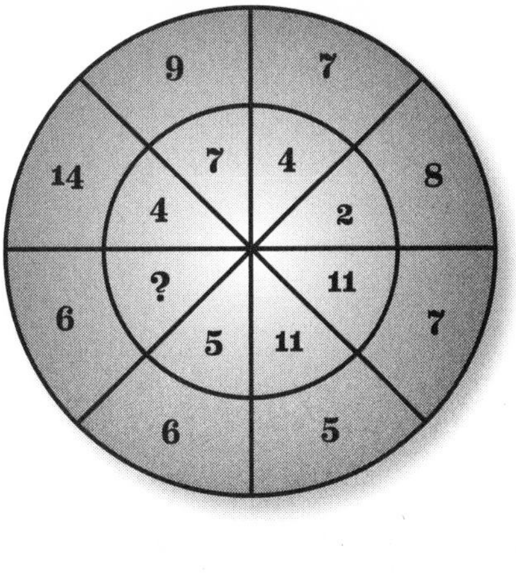

Answer see page 289

1. Italy intervened in the Austro–Prussian War of 1866 in order to win which territory?

2. Which pass between Poland and Slovakia was the scene of much fighting in both World Wars? A football team was named after the nearby village of the same name in recognition of its wartime role.

3. What was the name of the present-day Russian town of Sovetsk when it was a town in Germany, a name famous for one of the peace treaties signed during the Napoleonic Wars?

4. Which war could be have said to have started due to a dispute over the Holy Sepulchre Church in Jerusalem because the Armenian Church had the key to the front door while the Catholic Church only had the key to the side door?

5. Which English-speaking duchy in the Southern Alps, with a population of 6,000, decided to declare war against the United States in 1956?

6. Which French playwright financed the supply of a large amount of armaments to the Americans during the War of Independence, but was never actually paid for them - finally the Americans paid his family in 1835?

7. Bonnie Prince Charlie's uprising of 1745 can be conceived of as a part of which wider-ranging European conflict?

8. The five treaties known collectively as the 'Paris Suburb Treaties' were concerned with what topic?

9. At the time of the Plague and the Great Fire of London, England was at war with which country?

10. Which writer was the brother-in-law of Baron von Richthofen, the First World War ace?

11. Thucydides wrote a history of which war, a war in which he himself had participated?

12. Many black people who had fought with the British during the American War of Independence were originally settled in Nova Scotia, but many of them were then re-settled where?

13. Who became a brigadier general during the American Civil War at the age of 23, one year after he graduated from the United States Military Academy ranked last in his class?

14. The Eighty Years War is a name given to the independence struggles of which country?

15. Which author said: 'Probably the battle of Waterloo was won on the playing-fields of Eton, but the opening battles of all subsequent wars have been lost there'?

Answers see page 289

1. In which range of mountains in New York state did Rip Van Winkle fall asleep for several years?

2. Zermatt lies at the foot of which mountain?

3. Which was the first 8,000 metre-plus mountain to be scaled?

4. Which mountain violently erupted in North-West America in the 1980s?

5. What is the highest mountain in the world when measured from its base (as opposed to measuring height above sea level)?

6. Within 100 metres either way, the summit of Mount Everest lies at how many metres above sea level?

7. Where are the Sperrins mountain range?

8. Which railway celebrated its opening day in 1896 in an unfortunate way when one of its locomotives went over a cliff?

9. A corrie is a mountain feature where glaciers once formed. What is the Welsh word for a corrie?

10. Which range of mountains is about 1,100 km long and forms the eastern border of Lesotho?

11. Which important mountain pass lies near the meeting point of Kentucky, Tennessee and Virginia?

12. Which range of mountains is horseshoe-shaped, enclosing the great Hungarian plain?

13. Which city lies adjacent to and on the slopes of Mount Carmel?

14. Which city traces its name to a visit to the area by Magellan and his shouting a statement that he could see a mountain?

15. Mount McKinley, above, is in which American state?

16. Where are the mountains known as the Cuillins, specifically?

17. In the classification of geological ages that starts with the Cambrian, which age is named after a range of mountains in Switzerland and France?

18. In which country would you find the Southern Alps, containing 17 peaks over 3,000 metres?

19. Which dormant volcano in Russia close to the border with Georgia could lay claim to be the highest mountain in Europe (if it was agreed that it lies in Europe)?

20. The highest point that can be reached in Europe by railway is on which mountain?

Answers see page 289

1. Glenn Miller played which instrument?

2. The USA chose between two countries as the location of a canal linking the Pacific and Atlantic. They chose Panama but which was the other country?

3. What is a gricer interested in?

4. What connects Elena Kondakova and Svetlana Savit-skaya?

5. In transport, what is the meaning of the acronym SPAD?

6. Which duck escaped from Slimbridge in the 1950s and in 2003 became the subject of an eradication order from the British Government, supported by the RSPCA?

7. Which London Underground line was built in the 1960s, the first new line since the early 1900s?

8. The Czech town of Zlin is particularly connected with the shoe company Bata. Which playwright was born there in 1937 and first came to prominence with a play of 1967?

9. What profession did Yasser Arafat practise before entering politics?

10. *Thomas the Tank Engine* is set in Sodor which, if based on any real-life location at all, is based on where?

11. Bridge is derived from which other card game?

12. Who was the author of *The Godfather* novels on which the films were based?

13. Grange-over-Sands overlooks the sands of which bay?

14. Which singer fronted The Partridge Family?

15. Who was the oldest actor to receive the Oscar for Best Actor?

16. In a book by Dickens, who married Peggotty?

17. What are 'cuisses de nymphes aurore' if seen on a menu?

18. Who persuaded Isaac Newton to publish his *Principia*?

19. The first scheduled jet passenger flight flew from London to where?

20. As an MP which constituency did Gordon Brown represent when he became Prime Minister of the United Kingdom?

Answers see page 289

1. Who wrote a book called *My Universities* despite never having been to University?

2. Having attended the Versailles Conference, who then expressed his misgivings about the proceedings in a 1919 book called *The Economic Consequences of the Peace*?

3. Who wrote a book in 1492 called *The Prince* which systemized various devious political strategies?

4. *The Affluent Society* was published by which Canadian economist?

5. Who delivered his views on evolution in a book called *The Malay Archipelago*?

6. Which book by Dale Carnegie and published in 1936, gives hints as to how to deal with social and business situations?

7. Who wrote about his experiences with a donkey called Modestine?

8. Sue Prideaux's book subtitled *Behind the Scream* is a biography of whom?

9. Whose first major book was called *The Development of Capitalism in Russia*?

10. *The Selfish Gene* was the first book by whom?

11. Which Archbishop of Canterbury was responsible for compiling the Domesday Book?

12. Who wrote *How Mumbo-Jumbo Took Over the World: A Short History of Modern Delusions*?

13. Which biographer of Charlotte Brontë (pictured) also wrote the novels *Mary Barton* and *North and South*?

Answers see page 290

Cycle Logical

These bikes took part in an overnight race, and their start and finish times became mathematically linked. Can you discover the link and work out when bike D finished?

C start: 5:28

Finish: 2:11

A start: 3:15

Finish: 2:06

B start: 3:20

Finish: 1:09

D start: 7:39

Finish: 3:17

E start: 6:28

Finish: ?

Answer see page 290

1. What name is shared by an actor born in 1930 and the winner of the Turner Prize in 1999?

2. Who was shortlisted that same year for an exhibit called *My Bed*?

3. Which art movement is indicated by the initials PRB?

4. What name is given to a type of colloid used famously for paints involving the suspension of tiny particles of one liquid in another liquid?

5. Who painted the picture of the Duke of Wellington, dating from 1814, on show in the National Gallery?

6. This 1590 painting by Lucas van Valkenborch shows which city with the frozen river Schelde?

7. A song by Nat King Cole shares its name with which painting?

8. In 1888, Van Gogh joined which other painter in Arles?

9. What was Raphael's surname?

10. The film *Lust for Life* tells the story of whom?

11. Which art school is a department of University College, London and is to be found in Gower Street?

12. In which town or city can you view Da Vinci's *Last Supper*?

13. Picasso's painting *Guernica* commemorates the attack on the town of Guernica by which organization?

Answers see page 290

Number Pattern

What number should replace the question mark?

2	1	4	7
5	4	5	9
3	1	8	6
8	3	?	4

Answer see page 290

A Question of Balance

Each shape has a value. Scales 1 and 2 are in perfect balance. How many squares are needed to balance scale 3?

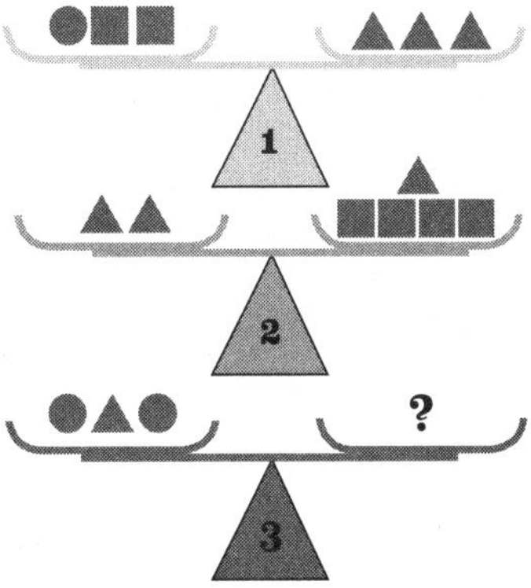

Answer see page 290

1. What is the main island of Japan?

2. At which circuit is the Japanese Grand Prix staged?

3. Who was president of the Philippines when the Japanese invaded?

4. What was the Japanese word for the 'Divine Wind' that stopped a Mongol invasion of the country?

5. With its length of 2,479 metres, the Steel Dragon in Japan is the longest what in the world?

6. The 1936 Olympic Marathon winner staged a bit of a protest. Why?

7. Which city was known as Edo until 1868?

8. Who was the Admiral in command of the Japanese attack on Pearl Harbor?

9. The Kuril Islands have been a bone of contention between which two countries?

10. The peace treaty for the Russo-Japanese war of 1904/5 was signed in Portsmouth, in which American state?

11. What is the largest of the Ryukyu Islands?

12. What type of aircraft dropped the A-Bombs on Japan?

13. Who designed the pictured Imperial Hotel in Tokyo in 1916, incorporating anti-earthquake devices – something it very soon had need to take advantage of?

Answers see page 290

Perfect Fit

Which of the surrounding pieces fits perfectly on top of the block A to make a rectangular block?

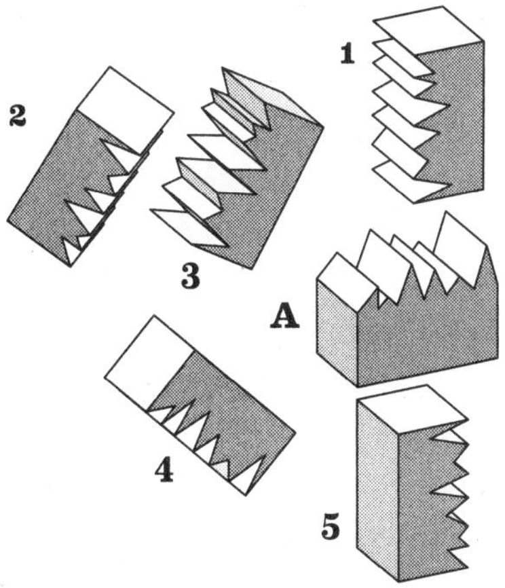

Answer see page 290

Figure It Out

Can you work out what number would replace the question mark?

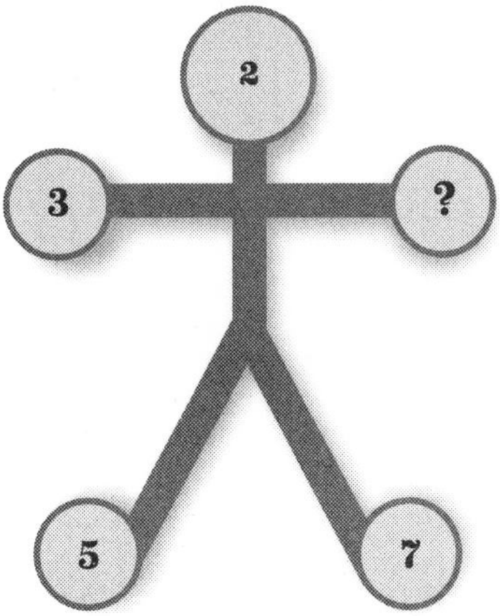

Answer see page 290

1. Which musical opened in London in 1968, the day after theatre censorship was abolished?

2. Mrs Johnson is a leading character in which musical?

3. What was the first Rodgers and Hammerstein musical?

4. 'Money makes the world go around' comes from which musical?

5. The musical *Half a Sixpence* was based on which novel?

6. The musical *Jersey Boys* is concerned with which pop group?

7. Which character does Dick Van Dyke play in Mary Poppins?

8. *The Sound of Music* is based in the vicinity of which city, seen here?

9. According to its own publicity, what was a 'new musical ripped-off from the motion picture' and is 'funnier than the Black Death'?

10. Who composed the music for a musical based on *Cry the Beloved Country* called *Lost in the Stars*?

11. *Hey! Big Spender* is a song from which musical?

12. *There's no Business like Show Business* is a song from which musical?

13. What is the name of the young boy in *Les Misérables* who is shot dead at the barricades while collecting ammunition?

Answers see page 290

Missing Link

Can you work out which of the squares A to E would complete the diagram?

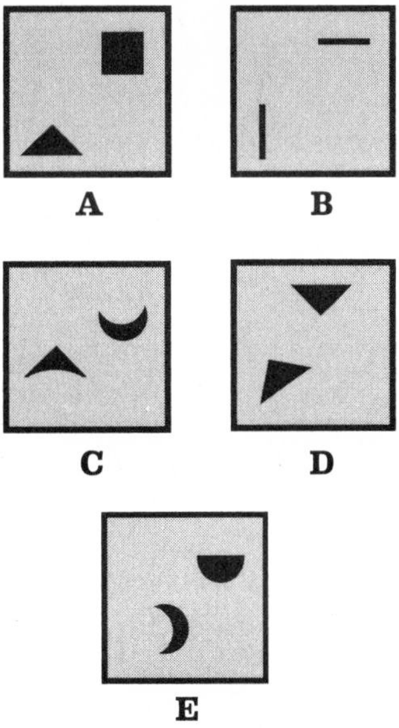

Answer see page 291

1. In *Psycho*, which actress was stabbed to death in the shower?

2. Which writer was sentenced to death in 1849 and had to undergo what turned out to be a sham execution procedure before he had his sentence commuted to a less severe punishment?

3. In which country did Lord Byron die?

4. Which city was besieged for 15 months by Cardinal Richlieu, who built a large seawall to stop the British Navy supplying the town, the siege resulting in the death of three-quarters of the population?

5. Which animal appears to have become extinct with the death of a specimen in Hobart Zoo in 1936?

6. Who was sentenced to death in 1916, but was reprieved and later elected as an MP to the British Parliament?

7. Where was Archimedes living at the time of his death?

8. Whose death is being related in the song which contains the lyrics: 'That dirty little coward that shot Mr. Howard'?

9. Elizabeth Siddal was the model for which Millais painting of 1852 based on a theme from Hamlet?

10. How did Pliny the Elder die?

11. Who became mayor of Palm Springs and was later elected to the House of Representatives in 1994, his term being cut short by his death in a skiing accident in 1998?

12. Walter Raleigh was sentenced to death in 1603, but this was commuted to life imprisonment. Later he was released an allowed to go on an expedition to Guiana, but events there led to the death sentence finally being enacted by King James. Which events actually offended the King?

Identify all of the images pictured.
Can you spot anything that isn't a seed?

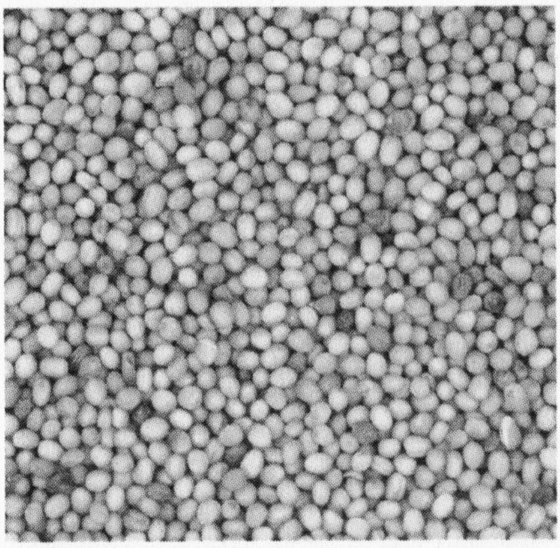

A

B

C

D

E

Answer at the back of this section

What do all of these cocktails have in common?

A

B

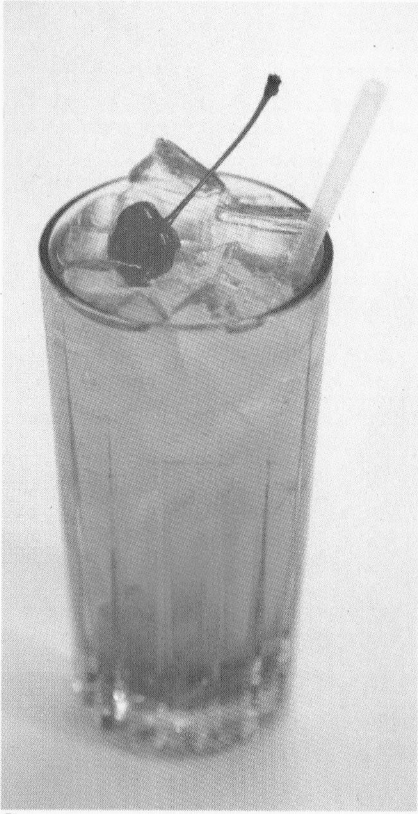

C

D

E

Answer at the back of this section

These are all examples of northern Renaissance paintings. Can you identify which artist created each painting, and also which one was widely believed to have invented oil paint?

A

B

C

D

E

Answer at the back of this section

Identify all of these early bicycles.

A

B

C

D

E

Answer at the back of this section

These burial sites are among the ten oldest free-standing buildings in the world. Where can you find each one?

A

B

C

D

E

Answer at the back of this section

Which US presidents did each of these pets belong to?

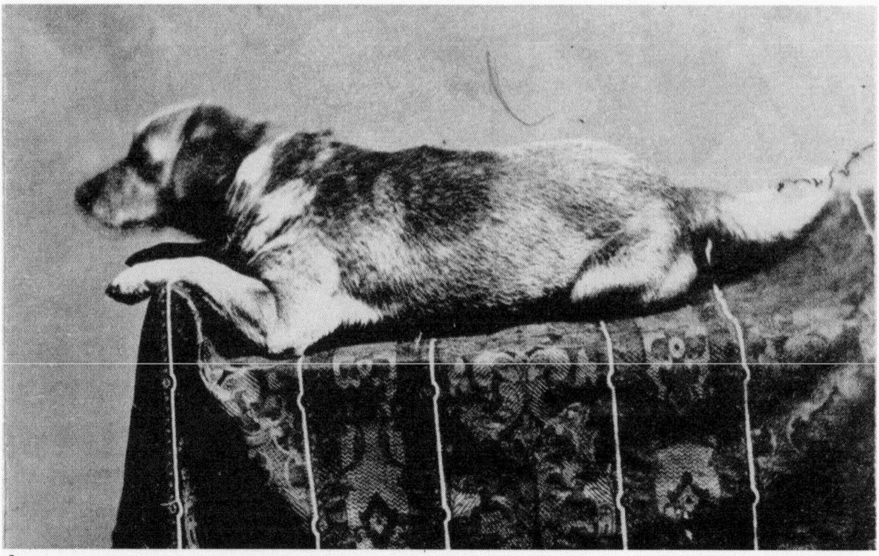

A

B

C

D

E

Answer at the back of this section

Starting with the earliest, arrange these items by the date of their invention.

A

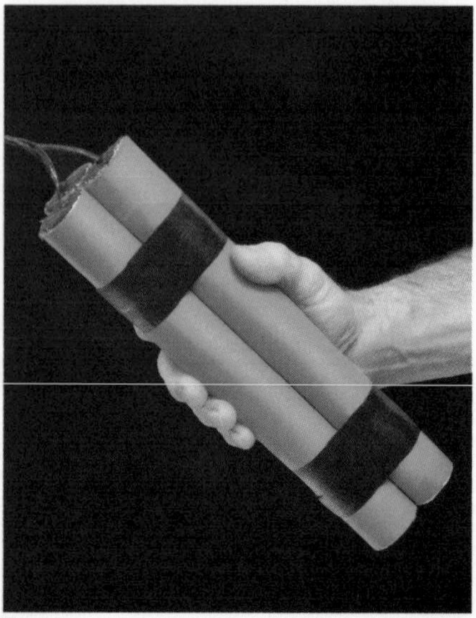

B

C

D

E

Answer at the back of this section

Identify all of these animals. Can you find the link between them and identify which is the odd one out?

A

B

C

D

E

Answer at the back of this section

Answers

Seeds

a: Mustard, b: Coriander, c: Caraway, d: Fennel, e: Cumin. Only mustard is a seed. Coriander, cumin, caraway and fennel are all referred to as seeds but are actually fruits.

Cocktails

They all share their names with real people (a: Jack Rose, b: Ralf Roletschek, c: Shirley Temple, d: Rossini, e: Rob Roy)

The Northern Renaissance

a: Hans Holbein the Elder, b: Jan van Eyck (or someone from his workshop), b: Albrecht Dürer, c: Hieronymus Bosch, e: Hans Holbein the Younger

Jan van Eyck was believed to have invented the technique of oil painting.

Velocipede

a: Vélo Torpille (Torpedo Bike), b: 'Boneshaker'/Michaux velocipede, c: 'Cyclomer' amphibious bicycle, d: Coventry Rotary Quadracycle, e: Hemming's Unicycle/'Flying Yankee Velocipede',

Neolithic Burial Sites

a: Sardinia, Italy (Monte d'Accoddi), b: Gozo, Malta (Ġgantija), c: Avebury, England (West Kennet Long Barrow), d: Orkney, Scotland (Knap of Howar), e: Bougon, France (Tumulus of Bougon)

Presidential Pets

a: Abraham Lincoln (Fido), b: Richard Nixon (King Timahoe, Vicki and Pasha), c: Calvin Coolidge (Rebecca), d: Warren G. Harding (Laddy Boy), e: Bill Clinton (Buddy)

Inventions

a: Chocolate (1819), b: Dynamite (1867), d:Christmas lights (1882), e:Escalators (1891), c:Toaster (1927)

Unusual Animals

a: Bramble Cay melomys, b: Bermuda petrel/Cahow, c: Golden toad, d: Paradise parrot, e: Pinta Island tortoise

The connection between the animals is that they are all extinct, except for the Bermuda petrel/Cahow, which was thought to be extinct for 300 years before 18 pairs were found nesting on an uninhabited rock.

13. According to folklore, who said prior to execution : 'I fear that the town of Rouen will suffer for my death'?

14. It was intended that Beethoven should go to Vienna as a pupil of Mozart. This was annulled by Mozart's death but Beethoven went to Vienna anyway as a pupil of which other composer?

15. An assassination attempt on Franklin Roosevelt in 1933 resulted in the death of the mayor of which city?

16. According to Oscar Wilde you would have to have a heart of stone to be able to listen to the account of whose death without laughing?

17. Which Billy Wilder film begins after the death of the main male character?

18. Who was the only one of Jesus's disciples to die a natural death?

19. Stuart Sutcliffe,who died early from a brain haemorrhage, was a member of which pop group?

20. The Astor Place Riots, depicted here, were a major riot in New York in 1849 resulting in many deaths. It was sparked off by a production of which Shakespeare play?

Answers see page 291

1. Which mountain was about 3,000 metres high on 18th May 1980 but only about 2,500 metres high the next day?

2. Which fort on Lake Champlain was captured from the French in 1759, and was captured by the Americans in May 1775? Its name is possibly better known to some people by virtue of it being used as the name of a US Navy ship.

3. Which reservoir was the main target of the Dambusters in May 1941, its destruction causing flooding of the Ruhr Valley?

4. Which successful football team was wiped out in a plane crash in May 1949, the club never having been able to achieve its former status since then?

5. Which Billy Wilder film is set in May 1927?

6. Manet's painting *The Execution of Emperor Maximilian* was influenced by the painting Executions of May 3 1808 by which artist?

7. Which new National Trail walking route was opened in May 2003, becoming, in the process, the most expensive path in Britain per unit length?

8. Which neutral city was bombed by the Luftwaffe in May 1941, an event which they claimed was a mistake?

9. Which chemist introduced the word 'oxygen' but was executed in May 1794?

10. In May 1671 who, disguised as a clergyman and accompanied by a few confederates, attempted to steal the English crown from the Tower of London?

11. In 2005, several students injured themselves when they engaged in a May Day tradition and jumped off a bridge into which river?

12. Which city suffered a 'May Blitz' in 1941 – over a week of continuous night bombing destroying a large part of the Central Library, damaging the museum and art gallery and causing the explosion of an ammunition ship destroying the entire dock in which it lay?

13. The name of Herbert Morrison is commonly associated with which disastrous event of 6th May 1937?

Answers see page 291

Pattern Poser

Find a number that could replace the question mark. Each side represents a number under 10.

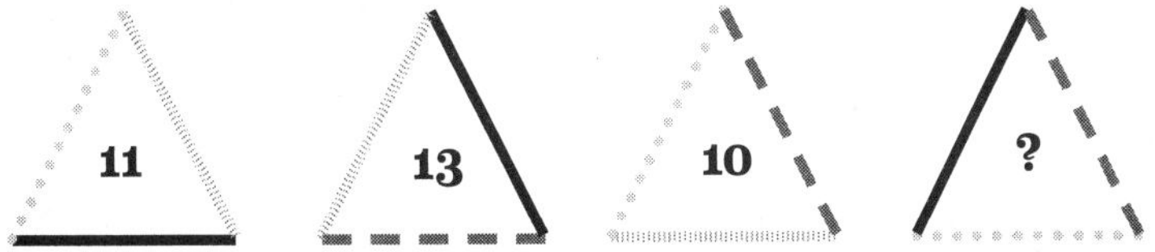

Answer see page 291

1. Who delivered the 'sceptered isle' speech in Shakespeare?

2. Shakespeare's *Othello* is set primarily on which island?

3. Which play by Shakespeare is also the name of a work by Chaucer (roughly speaking)?

4. What is the name of the Duke of Athens in Shakespeare's *A Midsummer Night's Dream*?

5. At the end of *The Tempest* who is left alone on the island?

6. Which three Verdi operas were based on works of Shakespeare?

7. Which Shakespeare play centers on the confusion produced by two sets of twins?

8. Which Shakespearean character is to marry the suitor who correctly chooses from three caskets made from gold, silver, and lead, the one which contains her picture?

9. In the Shakespeare play which French town was Henry V attacking when he made the speech about fighting on St. Crispin's Day?

10. Which Shakespeare character has the most number of lines in total?

11. In which Shakespeare play does the eponymous hero die in the first half of the play?

12. Which Welshman is described by Shakespeare thus: 'In faith, he is a worthy gent exceedingly well read, and profited in strange concealments, valiant as a lion and wondrous affable, and as bountiful as the mines of India'?

13. Whose family was murdered by Macbeth?

14. *Pyramus and Thisbe* is a play staged within which Shakespeare play?

15. Which Earl was a major patron of Shakespeare?

16. It is often reported that Cervantes and Shakespeare died on the same day – this is incorrect, but what is the source of the confusion?

17. The saying about 'method in your madness' originates from which Shakespeare play?

18. What is the name of the Merchant of Venice?

19. Prokofiev's *Dance of Knights* is connected with which Shakespeare play?

20. Who was Hamlet talking to when he made his 'poor Yorik' speech?

Answers see page 291

1. What was the former name of the US state of Washington prior to statehood?

2. In which American state is Kansas City?

3. At the Four Corners Monument in America, you can be in four states simultaneously. Which four states?

4. An Act of 1854, which removed a previous Northern boundary to slavery, was named after two potential states. Name one.

5. The Mason-Dixon Line separates which two states?

6. Who became Governor of California in 1998?

7. Excluding Hawaii, where is the southernmost point of the United States, specifically?

8. In which state is Fort Knox?

9. Which American state is being described: according to its founder, he originally wanted to call it New Wales, because of the large Welsh influence there, but was prevailed upon to use another name which still showed a Welsh influence (according to him)?

10. In which American state is Brown University?

11. Which novel by George Sands shares its name with an American state?

12. What is the capital of the smallest state in America?

13. Which American state is particularly connected with the Seminole Indian tribe?

14. *Gone With the Wind* was set in which state?

15. Which is the only American state where there are no coyotes?

16. In what year did California pass to the United States?

17. Which is the most northerly state to have incorporated territory ceded by Mexico to the USA after the war of 1848?

18. The Green Mountain Boys were an American fighting unit from which state?

19. According to the song, which American state wants RD Taylor?

20. Barack Obama, pictured here in his official Senate portrait, was elected a senator for which state?

Answers see page 292

1. Who sang the theme tune to the film *From Russia with Love*?

2. 'Tara's Theme' can be heard in which film?

3. What is the full name of the composer of the first piece of classical music to be heard in the film *2001: A Space Odyssey*?

4. Who wrote the music for the *The Bounty* – a film about the mutiny with Anthony Hopkins and Mel Gibson?

5. Which native American sang the theme tune to the film *Soldier Blue*?

6. Stubby Kaye and Nat King Cole provided the musical accompaniment to which Jane Fonda film?

7. Who wrote the theme tune to the film *The Pink Panther*?

8. On the flip side of 'I was born under a Wandering Star' by Lee Marvin, who sang another song from *Paint Your Wagon*?

9. Who both appeared in and sang the theme tune to the Sidney Poitier film *To Sir With Love*?

10. The music for the 1953 film *Genevieve* was provided by Larry Adler, an American. What had caused him to move to Britain?

11. Which music group consists of Sharon, Jim, Andrea and Caroline and first came to notice in the 1990 film *The Commitments*?

12. Who wrote the music for films such as *633 Squadron* and *Those Magnificent Men in Their Flying Machines*?

13. *The Force of Destiny,* which provided the theme tune for the film *Jean de Florette,* was written by the man pictured here. What is his name?

Answers see page 292

Sum Puzzle

Can you unravel the reasoning behind these diagrams and find the missing shape?

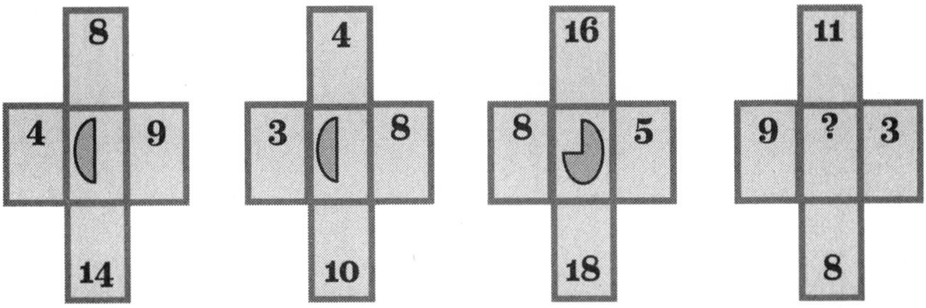

Answer see page 292

1. What is the official nickname of New York State?

2. What was the nickname of Friedrich I, who reigned from 1152–1190?

3. Which musician has the nickname *Slowhand*?

4. By what nickname is Henri Charrière better known?

5. Which group were named after a nickname given to Charlie Parker?

6. Which book features a teacher who has the nickname 'Pow-Wow'?

7. The name of which emperor was given as a nickname to one of the guards at Colditz?

8. Which squadron has the nickname 'The Dambusters'?

9. What was the nickname of Robert Stroud?

10. Which personality from the Soviet Union was usually known by a pseudonym which meant 'the Hammer'?

11. What pseudonym was adopted by Jean Francois Gravelet who lived in the 19th century and had started out as an acrobat when he was about six years old?

12. Who wrote under the pseudonym of Currer Bell?

13. The real name of actor Michael Keaton is the same as another actor. What is this name?

14. What was the real name of Miss Bluebell, organizer of the Bluebell Girls?

Answers see page 292

Puzzle Around

What number should replace the question mark?

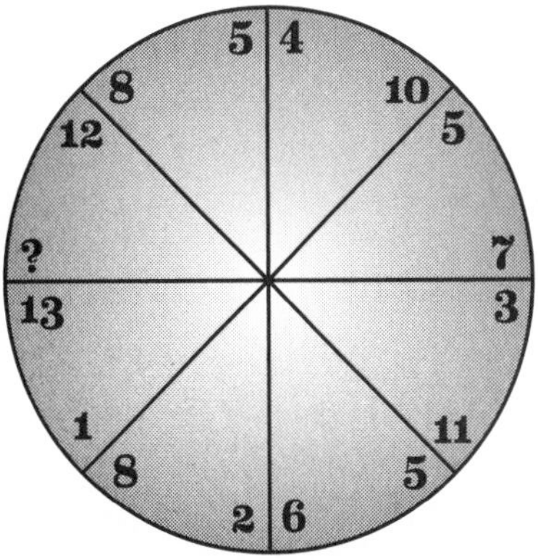

Answer see page 292

Odd One Out

Can you work out which is the odd number out in this circle?

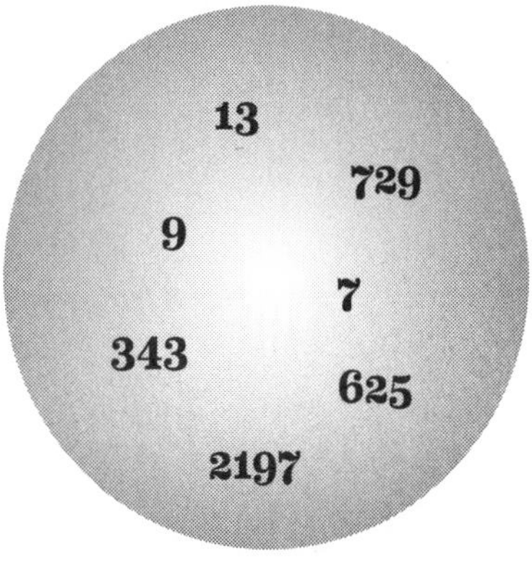

Answer see page 293

1. What property of the planet Jupiter did Galileo use to support the idea of a sun-centered planetary system?

2. Who discovered the real nature of the rings of Saturn?

3. Titania and Oberon are the largest moons of Uranus. The fourth and fifth largest are named after characters from which other Shakespearean play?

4. What was the primary role of the Magellan space mission?

5. Of all the appearances of Halley's Comet within the last 1,000 years, in which year was it brightest?

6. Which dormant volcano in Hawaii is home to several major telescopes?

7. Which constellation appears on the Australian flag?

8. How did Friedrich Bessel finally prove in 1838 that the Sun is at the center of the planetary system?

9. Which space probe has the same name as a district of London?

10. In astronomy, what is a TLP?

11. Mozart's 41st Symphony appears to be named after which heavenly body?

12. Which zodiacal constellation has a different name in astronomy to that in astrology?

13. Which animal is associated with the Northern Cross?

14. The Russian space probe 'Vega' visited which two bodies?

15. What does a radio astronomer call a neutron star?

16. Who was Luther referring to when he said: 'this fool wishes to reverse the entire science of astronomy, but sacred scripture tells us that Joshua commanded the Sun to stand still, and not the Earth'?

17. Which college was named in 1879 in honour of a female mathematician and astronomer?

18. John Flamsteed was the first Astronomer Royal. Who was the second?

19. Which eclipsing binary star is in the head of Medusa in the constellation Perseus?

20. The constellation Cassiopeia is shaped like which letter of the alphabet?

Answers see page 293

1. In which Olympics did Johnny Weissmuller win 3 medals?

2. Which was the first Olympics to be televised?

3. In the 1948 Olympics, who almost lapped all the other competitors in the 10,000 metres?

4. Why was the winner of the 1904 Olympic marathon disqualified?

5. What is the longest distance you would have to swim in an Olympic swimming event?

6. When was the first women's marathon in the Olympic Games?

7. Who won the 200 metres gold medal at the 1968 Olympics?

8. Who won a gold medal for swimming in the Olympics in 1932, and later portrayed Tarzan and Flash Gordon in films?

9. The old Olympic Stadium of 1896 in Athens was used in the 2004 Olympics for which athletic event?

10. The 1912 Olympics – who won both the pentathlon and decathlon?

11. Which Swedish skater won the figure skating at the 1908 London Olympics?

12. Which Finnish runner won both the 5,000 metres and the 10,000 metres at the 1972 Munich Olympics?

13. Eddie the Eagle made his name at the 1988 Olympics in which location?

14. Name two of the events in which Jesse Owens (pictured) won gold at the 1936 Olympics.

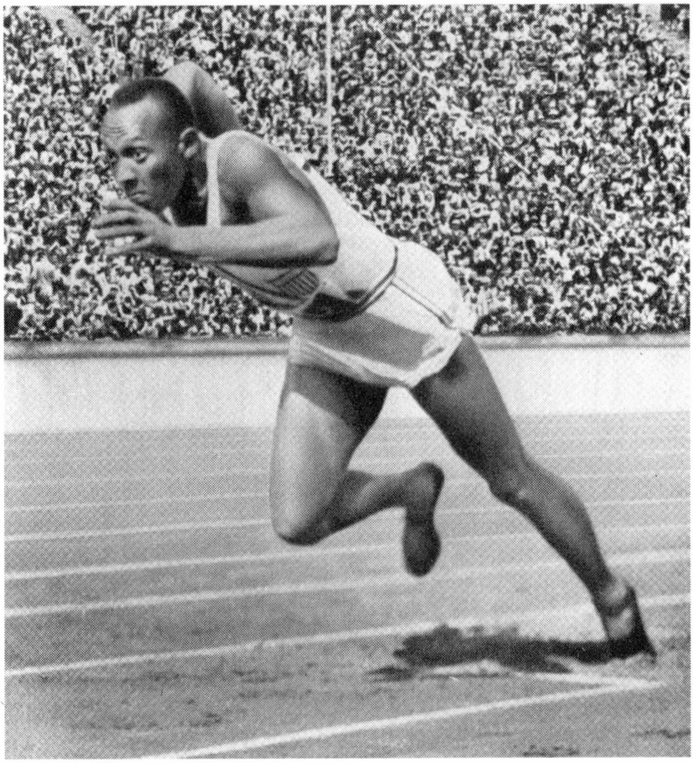

Answers see page 293

Missing Number

Can you work out the relationships between the numbers, and what number should replace the question mark?

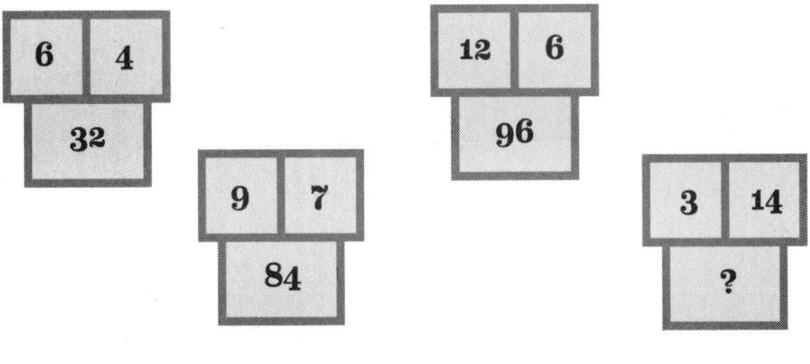

Answer see page 293

1. Who wrote the fiction book *Appassionata,* featuring the character of Abigail?

2. Who wrote *The Condition of the Working Class in England*?

3. Who wrote the book *i de Bello Gallico*?

4. Who wrote the book *The Children of the New Forest*?

5. Who wrote the original story of *Carmen* which Bizet turned into an opera?

6. Who wrote *Henry Esmond,* a story about England in around 1700 at the time of the later Stuart dynasty?

7. Who wrote the *History of the Peloponnesian War*?

8. Who wrote the novel *The Phantom of the Opera*?

9. Who wrote the *The Anthem of Doomed Youth*?

10. Who wrote the short story *Queen of Spades* about an officer who seeks to learn the secrets of playing cards?

Puzzle Around

What number should replace the question mark?

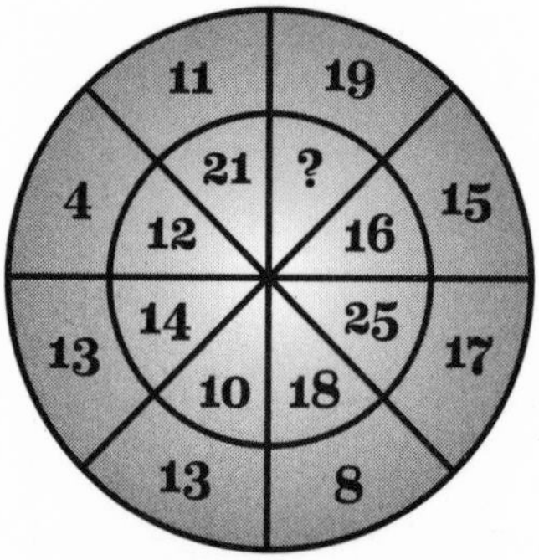

Answer see page 294

11. Who wrote the words for 'Hark the Herald Angels Sing'?

12. Who wrote the book on which the film *Murder She Said* was based?

13. Who (pictured here) wrote the poems called *Pisan Cantos* when he was being detained near that city?

Answers see page 293

Symbol Value

Each shape in this diagram has a value. Work out the values to discover what number should replace the question mark.

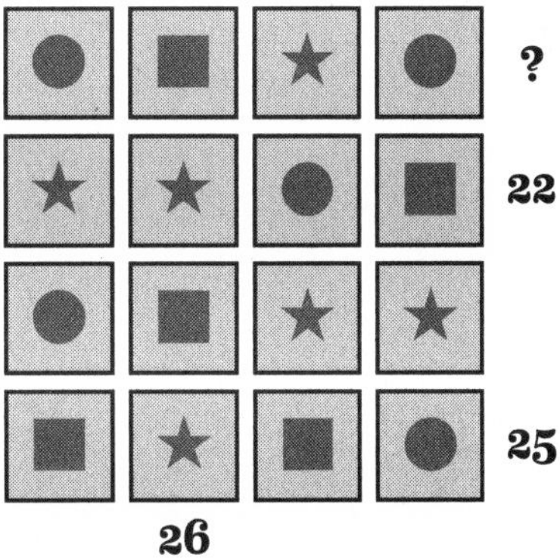

Answer see page 294

1. Kurt Masur was the conductor of which German orchestra for 26 years?

2. The fourth act of the 'Marriage of Figaro' starts with a search for what type of object?

3. Which composer returned to the Soviet Union in 1936, and died around the same time as Stalin?

4. Who composed the Leningrad Symphony?

5. Which composer, born in 1833, received much encouragement and assistance from Robert and Clara Schumann?

6. In 1915, the architect Walter Gropius married the widow of which composer?

7. Which composer was involved with George Sands (pictured) from 1836–49?

8. What was the name of Mozart's wife?

9. Which conductor from Buenos Aires and was beaten to the post of Chief Conductor of the Berlin Philharmonic by Simon Rattle in 1999?

10. When Schubert was buried in Vienna,was he was buried almost alongside which other composer?

11. Scheherazade was the subject of which composer's Symphonic Suite Opus No. 35?

12. With which composer do you associate the name of Von Meck?

13. What name is given to Haydn's 94th Symphony by virtue of a sudden fortissimo chord?

Answers see page 294

Square Solution

Find a number that could replace the question mark. Each shade represents a number under 10.

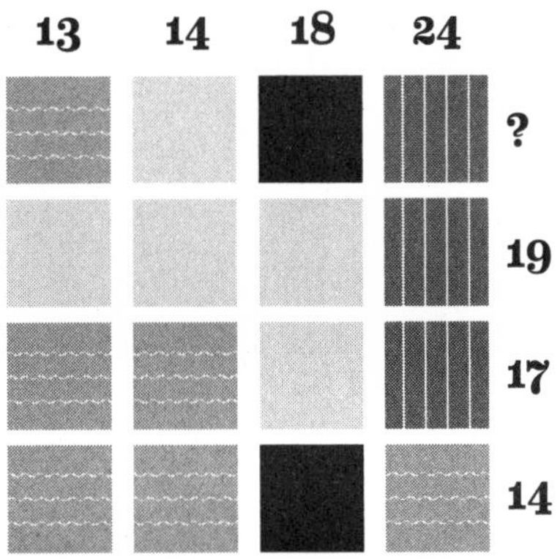

Answer see page 294

Cog Query

If the black arrow pulls in the direction indicated, will the load rise or fall?

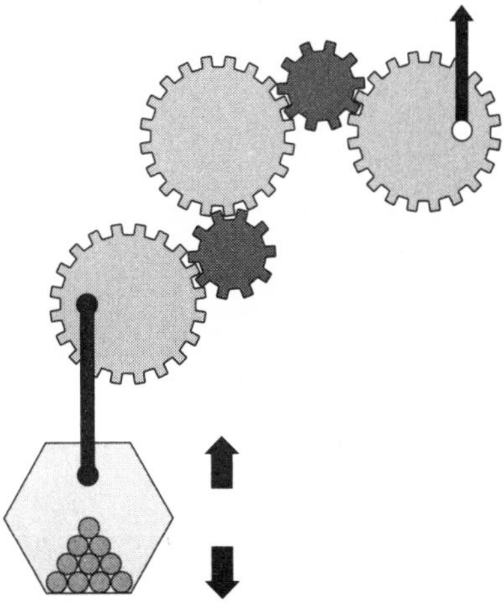

Answer see page 294

1. What word beginning with 'A' describes the process of heating a metal to a certain temperature for a period of time in order to reduce internal stresses and increase its ductility?

2. The Louisiana French word 'bayou' is derived from the language of which native American tribe?

3. Friction in a fluid is known by what term?

4. The word 'pulchritude' refers to what quality?

5. What word could be a bird, dog, runner or aircraft?

6. The internet word 'Wikipedia' derives its first syllables from which language?

7. What single word is used to describe a locomotive with the wheel arrangement 4-6-2?

8. Which word starting with 'H' describes our current inter-glacial period following on from the Pleistocene?

9. Which three-letter word can be used to describe 105 Pascals?

10. The word 'sabotage' stems ultimately from which item of clothing?

11. Which six-letter word of Latin origin indicates that the word or phrase occurs repeatedly in a work?

12. What is the Russian word for reconstruction?

13. The name of which barbarian tribe entered the English language as a byword for mindless destruction?

14. What word beginning with 'c' is used in the South of England to describe a deep fissure in the wall of a cliff?

15. The geographical name Weald stems from an old English word meaning what?

16. The word 'parchment' is derived from the name of which city?

17. What one word can describe a line of verse written in iambic hexameter?

18. Which tree has a name derived from the old word for book, by virtue of the fact that its wood was originally used to write on?

19. Which word beginning with 'd' is an alternative name for the Hedge Sparrow?

20. The word 'menhir', used to describe standing stones such as the ones shown here, comes from which language?

Answers see page 294

1. Which battle took place north of Hawaii in June 1942?

2. On 13th July 1977, which city was blacked out for the whole night?

3. The former Vice-Chancellor of Germany, Jürgen Möllemann died in June 2003, presumed to be by suicide. How did he die?

4. Which hotel was blown up by the Irgun in July 1946?

5. Who was the victim of a mutiny in June 1611 while searching for the North West Passage and cast adrift, never to be seen again?

6. Which strategic Normandy town was originally due to be captured on D-Day itself, but was only actually captured during the period of 9-20 July?

7. In June 2008, Florence revoked the death penalty they had passed on which person several centuries ago?

8. Which comet collided with Jupiter in July 1994?

9. Who, in June 2003, became the General Secretary of the Trade Unions Congress?

10. The capture of which fortress on the Mississippi River in July 1863 helped establish the reputation of Ulysses S. Grant?

11. Where did a strange event occur on June 14th 1947 which inspired a story about five aliens dying in a crash?

12. In July 2010, which area of Spain became the first to outlaw bull-fighting?

13. Which writer was involved in a fatal train crash in June 1865, when his carriage was left at a perilous angle over a bridge? He wrote a postscript about the incident in his next book and the incident is generally assumed to have permanently affected his health.

14. Which mountain, pictured, was first climbed in July 1954?

15. What is the popular name given to the United Nations Monetary and Financial Conference that took place July 1-22, 1944?

16. The day of 6th June 1944 was designated by the letter 'D' in the English-speaking world. What letter was used in France?

17. Which comet was hit by an American probe in July 2005?

18. Where did the G8 conference of July 2001 take place, at which a demonstrator was killed by two shots from the police?

19. Which battle of 4th June, 1859, near Milan, gave its name to one of the first aniline dyes to be discovered and thus to its colour?

20. Where did William Wallace suffer a major defeat in July 1298?

Answers see page 294

1. Which Hollywood actor fought as a bomber pilot during World War II, and eventually rose to the rank of Brigadier-General in the United States Air Force?

2. Which British writer was in Le Touquet when the Second World War broke out and spent most of the war in Berlin?

3. What was the name of the Russian counter-espionage organization operating during World War II which was directly under the control of Stalin from 1943 to 1946?

4. In which action of World War II were the names 'Achilles' and 'Ajax' important?

5. Between invading Czechoslovakia and invading Poland, Hitler also annexed land from which other country?

6. What popular name is normally given to the flying boat known officially as the Hughes Hercules, which originated during the Second World War?

7. Who was the Australian Prime Minister at the outbreak of World War II and later served a second term as Prime Minister for 17 years?

8. Which World War II aircraft was named after a pioneer of the United States Air Force?

9. Which Italian building, founded in 529, was destroyed by the Lombards in 590, again by the Saracens in 884, and yet again by an earthquake in 1349. It was also destroyed during World War II?

10. Which ravine in the Ukraine was the site of full-scale massacres in the Second World War, its name meaning '(old) womens' ravine' in translation?

11. Which native American language was used by the Americans during the war to transmit messages?

12. What name is given to that part of the Normandy coast that formed the bulk of the Juno and Sword beaches during World War II?

13. How did the North African Desert War of World War II have its origins?

Answers see page 295

Cycle Logical

Four cyclists are taking part in a race. The number of each rider and his cycling time are related to each other. Can you work out the number of the last cyclist?

No. 9

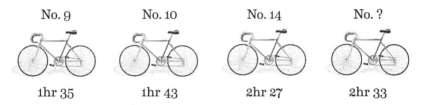

1hr 35

No. 10

1hr 43

No. 14

2hr 27

No. ?

2hr 33

Answer see page 295

1. Which Egyptian pharoah assumed power under the name of Amenhotep IV in 1379 BC and initiated the Amarna period?

2. Who killed his friend Cleitus in a drunken rage?

3. In ancient Egypt, royal wives were buried in which valley close to the Valley of Kings?

4. What name is given to the standard written language in Ancient Egypt from the 7th century BC onwards, a name also borne by the script used to write the language?

5. Which of Alexander's generals assumed power in Egypt?

6. When Julius Caesar met Cleopatra for the first time, he had actually gone to Egypt in pursuit of which person?

7. With which athletic event do you associate the ancient Greek Pheidippides?

8. Which Athenian orator remonstrated against Philip of Macedonia in his Phillipics, and was still opposing the Macedonians after the death of Alexander the Great?

9. At the beginning of the Persian attack on Greece in 480 BC, Leonidas and his Spartans made a stand at which pass?

10. Agamemnon came from which part of Greece?

11. Which historian hailed from Halicarnassus and told of the conflicts between Greeks and Persians?

12. The Greeks gave what name to the city partly occupied nowadays by Karnak and Luxor?

13. What word starting with 'Z' denotes high structures in Mesopotamia?

14. Who was the Persian Emperor at the time of the Battle of Marathon?

15. Which capital city lies close to the site of the ancient city of Memphis?

16. The Gordian Knot carried the legend that anyone who unravelled the knot would go on to rule Asia. How did Alexander the Great manage to 'unravel' the knot?

17. Where was Cleopatra's Needle, specifically, before it was transported to London?

18. Who discovered the tomb of Hatshepsut, a female pharaoh who ruled in her own right?

19. Which major Mesopotamian city was destroyed in 612 BC?

20. A 12-metre high statue of which deity once adorned the interior of the Parthenon?

Answers see page 295

1. Why was the Cavern nightclub demolished?

2. David was preceded by whom as King of Israel?

3. The National Theatre of Ireland is also known by what other name?

4. What type of animal is a Sea Leopard?

5. Which former Algerian goalkeeper won the 1957 Nobel Prize for Literature?

6. The name 'Reeperbahn' allegedly stems from which occupation which was originally carried out in the area?

7. What letter was omitted from Napoleon's original forename to make the one we know him by?

8. Winter Banana, Knobby Russett and Blenheim Orange are types of what?

9. In Scandinavia what does SAS stand for?

10. To whom was Sue Townsend referring when she remarked: 'What is Adrian Mole doing as a Conservative MP'

11. The Trojan War – who was the wife of Hector?

12. What is the full name of the German Formula 1 driver who drove for Williams in 2004?

13. Who sang: 'If you're going to San Francisco, be sure to wear a flower in your hair'?

14. What is the Falkirk triangle famous (or infamous) for?

15. Who was the Frenchman who created the characters featured in *The Magic Roundabout*?

16. This is the highest peak in America. What is its name?

17. Which French dish originating from Nice is made from aubergines and green peppers in a tomato sauce?

18. May Anning of Lyme Regis became well-known for finding what type of objects?

19. Etta Place was a confederate of which duo?

20. Why was Laocoon killed (by a snake or serpent)?

Answers see page 295

Square Solution

Can you find the missing number?

6		3	4		8	5		3	6		2
	11			**8**			**20**			**?**	
4		2	3		7	2		6	1		4

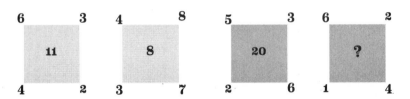

Answer see page 296

1. Which group did Ringo Starr leave to join the Beatles?

2. The Beatles recorded originally for which EMI-owned label?

3. The 1968 album called simply *The Beatles* is commonly known by what name because of its colour?

4. What type of apple is used as a logo for the Beatles' record company?

5. The Beatles returned to Hamburg in 1962 to play at which new venue run by Horst Fascher?

6. What is the largest coastal town on the Isle of Wight and has a name that has allowed transport firms to invoke a Beatles song?

7. Which early satire on the Beatles featured Neil Innes?

8. Which song by the Beatles was seemingly inspired originally as a reaction to the ideas on immigration expressed by Enoch Powell?

9. What is the name of the area of Central Park, pictured here, dedicated as a memorial to John Lennon?

10. When John Lennon's boyhood home at Menlove Avenue, Liverpool came on the market, it was bought by whom?

11. What popular name, derived from a Beatles song, was given to the early humanoid which was found by paleontologists in Ethiopia in 1974?

12. Who did Ringo Starr replace in the Beatles?

13. Which Beatles song features bits of *La Marseillaise*?

14. Which was the first British number one achieved by Paul McCartney, or his band, after he had left the Beatles?

15. Which actor, usually more associated with situation comedy, had a role in the Beatles film *A Hard Day's Night* playing Paul's grandfather?

Answers see page 296

Missing Number

Can you work out the logic behind this square and find the missing number?

24	?	21
22		45
5	38	17

Answer see page 296

Take Time

Can you work out, for each amount of time specified, whether you have to go forward or backwards to get from the time on the top clock to the time on the bottom clock?

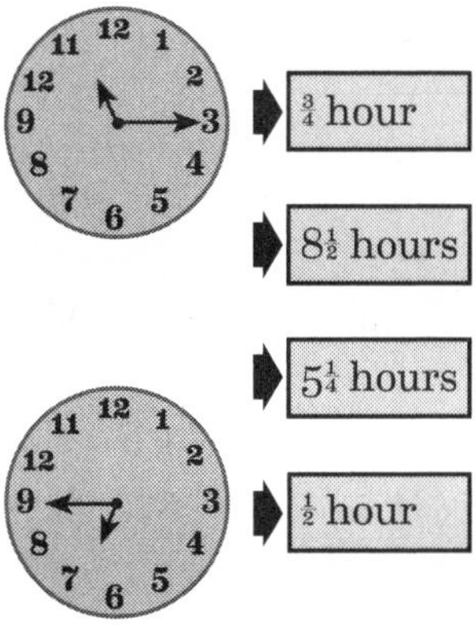

Answer see page 296

1. Which is the lowest commissioned rank in the US Navy, a name which, in Britain, denotes a flag?

2. Who composed the music used for the German national anthem?

3. Within two years either way, when was the requirement for an automobile to be preceded by a person with a red flag abolished?

4. The national anthem of which European country complains about the behavior of the Spanish, e.g - 'Pillaged by roving hands. O that the Spaniards rape thee'?

5. The German flag consists of three stripes. Which other European country has a flag consisting of three stripes of the same colours?

6. The colours of a Pizza Margherita are intended to represent what?

7. Which native American was one of the soldiers who raised the American flag over Iwo Jima in a famous photograph by Joe Rosenthal?

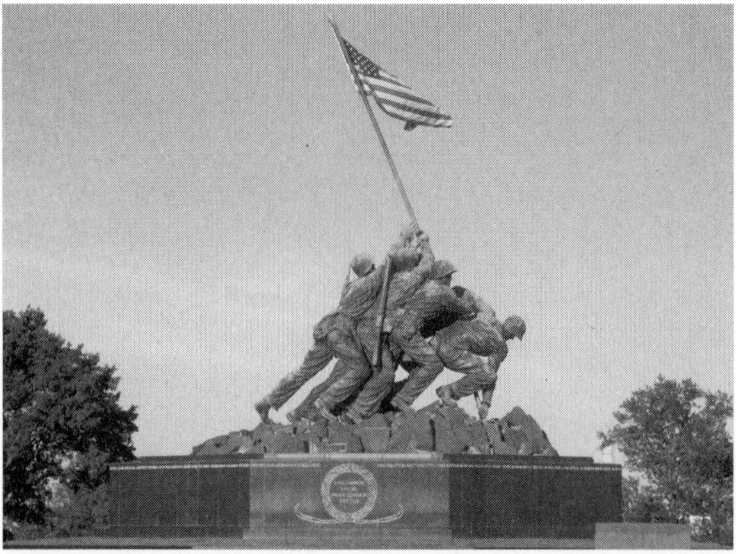

8. The 1977 vote for the new Australian national anthem was won by 'Advance Australia Fair'. What came second?

9. Which country's flag features a wheel called the Chakra at its center?

10. The flag of which American state portrays a genuine grouping of stars?

11. 'The Soldier's Song' is the national anthem of which country?

12. 'The Red Flag' is sung to the tune of which German carol?

13. The anthem 'Ode to Joy' is based on which work of music?

14. Which country has a Kalashnikov on its flag?

15. The current American national anthem was originally written during the British bombardment of which city?

Answers see page 306

Card Challenge

If you know that the answer forms a well-known sequence, can you work out how much each shape is worth?

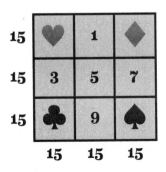

15	♥	1	♦
15	3	5	7
15	♣	9	♠
	15	15	15

Answer see page 296

Pattern Poser

Find a number that could replace the question mark. Each shade represents a number under 10.

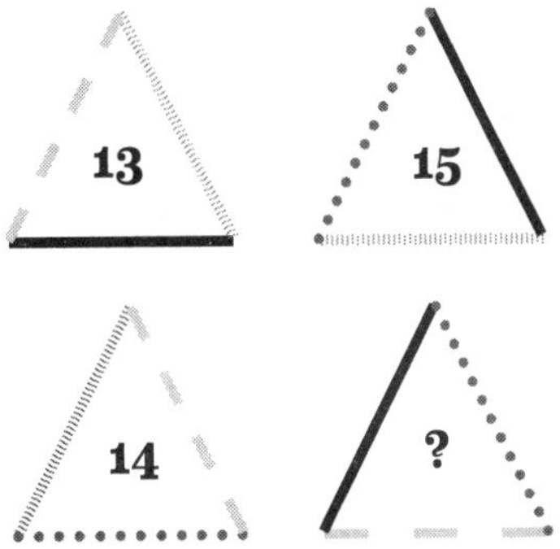

Answer see page 296

1. Who was the youngest daughter of Empress Maria Theresa of Austria, being born in 1755?

2. The actress Isabella Rossellini is the daughter of which other actress?

3. Who was the daughter of Oedipus who angered the King of Thebes by burying her brother and was entombed alive as punishment?

4. Which singer was the subject of the film *The Coal Miner's Daughter*?

5. What was the name of Karl Marx's youngest daughter?

6. A daughter of the first Bourbon King of France was married to which King of England?

7. Which of his daughters did Agamemnon sacrifice to the Gods on Aulis, on his way to the Trojan War (in some versions she is saved from sacrifice)?

8. The daughter of Franz Liszt married which other composer?

9. Which actress is the eldest daughter of Tony Curtis and Janet Leigh?

10. Who became an organist at the Marienkirche in Lubeck in 1688? Both Handel and Bach visited him there hoping to succeed him but were put off by the stipulation that they had to marry his daughter.

11. Which English queen was the daughter of Ferdinand and Isabella of Spain?

12. The singer Jackie Dankworth is the daughter of which other singer?

13. Emmeline Pankhurst had three daughters (two are pictured with her) who also involved themselves in the Suffragette movement. Name two of them.

Answers see page 296

Missing Number

Can you work out the relationships between the numbers, and what number should replace the question mark?

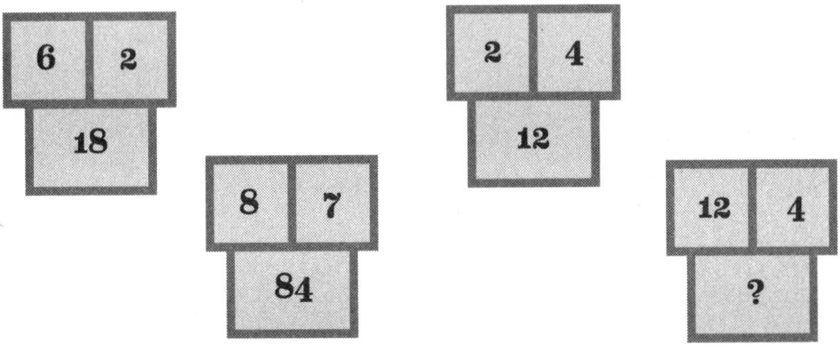

Answer see page 297

1. In which country is the Horn of Africa?

2. Until 2011 what was the largest state in Africa by area?

3. The enclave of Cabinda belongs to which country?

4. Which is Africa's second-largest producer of gold?

5. BOSS is/was the secret police of which country?

6. In which present day country was the former African state of Benin?

7. Where is the Okavango Delta, pictured here?

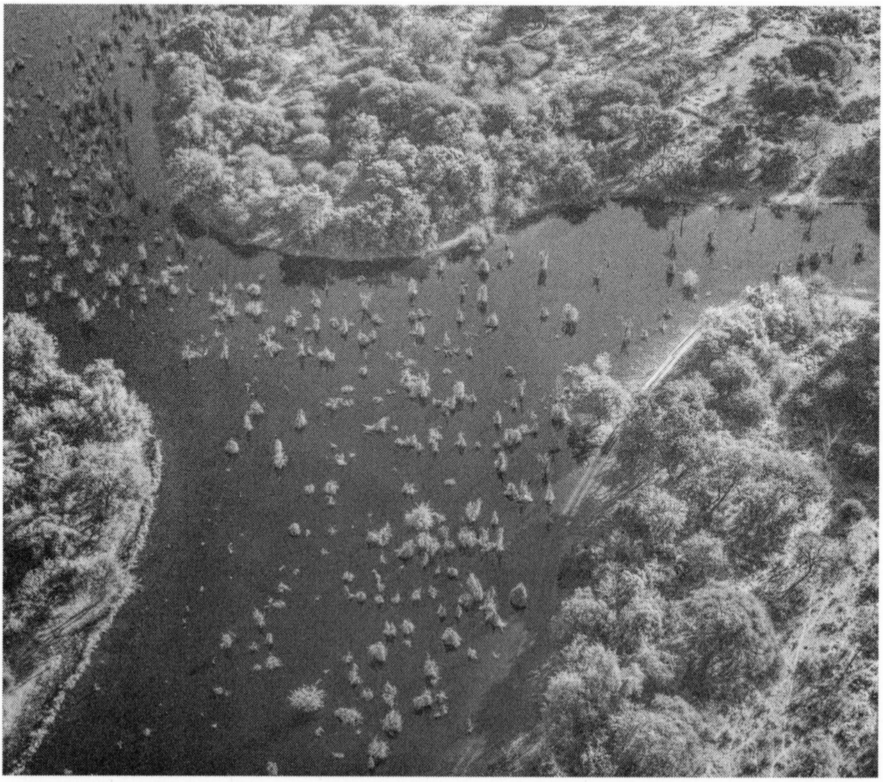

8. The Dinka live in which country?

9. Which country is completely enclosed by South Africa?

10. Troops from which country overthrew the government of Idi Amin?

11. Named after a former German Chancellor, the Caprivi Strip can be found where?

12. The city of Beira is in which country?

13. Which British colony in Africa achieved independence in 1957?

Answers see page 297

All Square

Which piece can be put with the top one to make a perfect square?

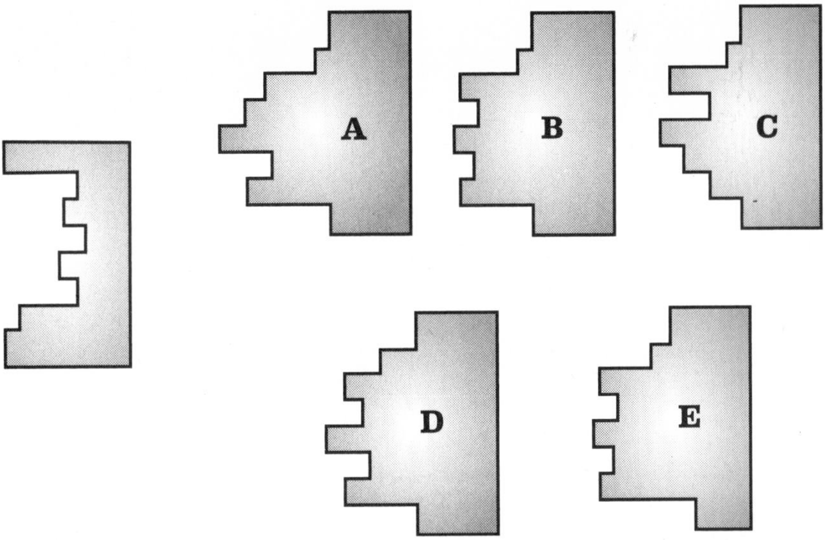

Answer see page 297

1. *Midnight's Children* by Salman Rushdie relates to midnight on 14th and 15th August 1947. What happened on this date?

2. On 27th September 2008, what did Zhai Zhigang do specifically that only the USA and USSR had done before?

3. Which Russian submarine was lost in the Barents Sea in August 2000?

4. In September 1191 Richard I captured which city?

5. Which European country became a member of the United Nations on 10th September 2002?

6. On what date in 1973 did the Chilean Army overthrow President Allende?

7. What was the name of the group that carried out the attack on Israeli athletes at the Munich Olympics in 1972?

8. What German-sounding name is given to the format size adopted by The Guardian in September 2005?

9. Why did nothing happen in England on 10th September 1752?

10. Who was the female hijacker who was unsuccessful in hijacking an Amsterdam to New York plane in September 1970, resulting in the plane landing in London?

11. In August 2010, a stretch of about 100 kilometres of which canal was closed because of drought?

12. Which battle of 3rd September 1651 was played out between Scottish troops under Charles Stuart and Parliamentary forces?

13. Which song became well-known when Radio Belgrade started regularly transmitting it at a set time from August 1941 onwards?

14. Which naval battle took place on 10th September 1813 between the victorious Americans under Commander Oliver Perry and the defeated British under Commodore Robert Barclay?

15. In September 1529, a Muslim army under the pictured Suleiman I was at the gates of which European city?

Answers see page 297

Puzzle Around
Can you work out the reasoning behind this wheel and replace the question mark with a number?

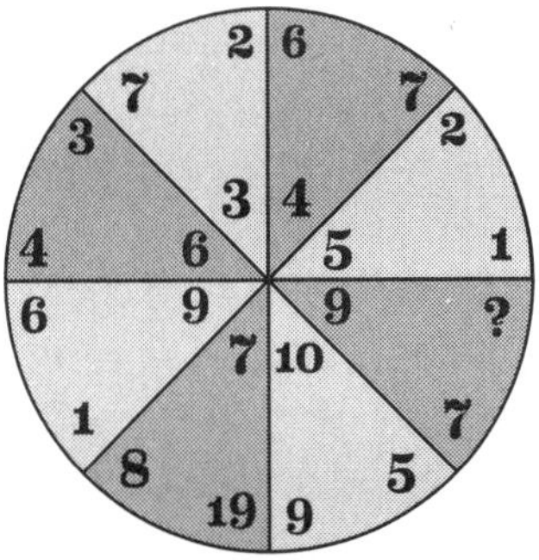

Answer see page 297

1. Julia Gillard, prime minister of Australia, was born in which town or city?

2. Who was the Russian prime minister at the time the Bolshevik Revolution broke out?

3. Caetano was the prime minister of which country before he was overthrown by a military coup?

4. Which former Italian prime minister was sentenced to 14 years in prison for corruption although he remained exiled in Tunisia rather than serving this punishment?

5. Who was prime minister of the Cape Colony at the time of the unsuccessful Jameson Raid which was intended to cause an uprising against the Boers in the Transvaal?

6. Jacques Santer was prime minister of which country?

7. Which French prime minister once claimed that one in four Englishmen was a homosexual?

8. Who was a commander of Boer guerilla forces during the Boer War, but became prime minister of South Africa in 1919, and again in the 1940s?

9. Which former French prime minister was sent to Buchenwald during the Second World War?

10. Who succeeded Menachem Begin as prime minister of Israel?

11. Which Australian prime minister withdrew Australian troops from Vietnam?

12. Who was the Iranian prime minister who nationalized the Anglo-Iranian Oil Company and was eventually overthrown by Winston Churchill and the Americans?

13. Georgi Dimitrioff (seen here), who was tried and acquitted of causing the Reichstag fire in 1933, later became prime minister of which country?

Answers see page 297

Sum Circles

Can you find the missing number that fits into the sector of the last wheel?

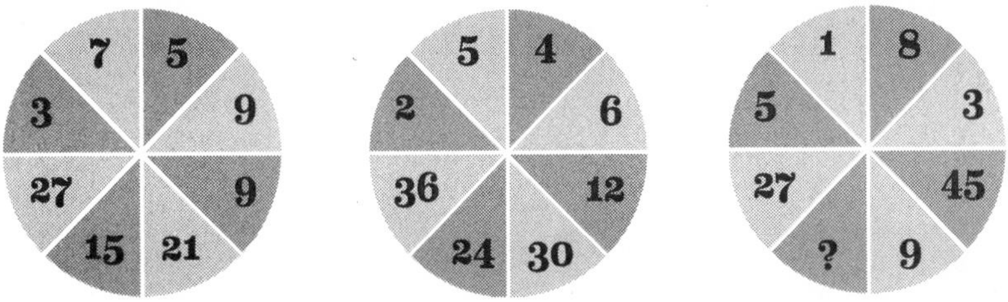

Answer see page 298

1. Which penguin is found only off South Africa, and is also known as the Black-Footed Penguin?

2. What type of animal is a Zebra Danio?

3. Which animal is primarily responsible for clearing algae from rocks (and whose absence is therefore particularly noticeable after oil spills)?

4. In what physical form did Dracula enter Britain?

5. Which animal does Shelley refer to as *Blithe Spirit*?

6. What do you call a young whale?

7. The duck (with Latin name *Spatula elypedta*) pictured here gets its name because of the shape of its bill? What type is it?

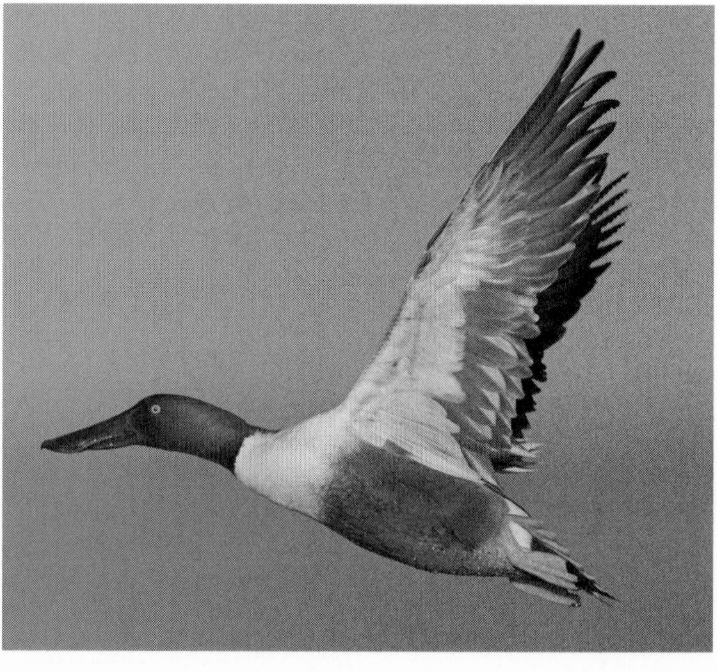

8. Apart from the tiger, which animal occurs in Sumatran, Javan and Indian varieties?

9. Which animal is the emblem of Bacardi Rum?

10. What is the main visual difference between true seals and sea lions?

11. Which type of animal was collected by Darwin in his youth?

12. In what does a hare live?

13. What type of animal is an 'Ara'?

Answers see page 298

Rectangle Assembly

Which of the surrounding shapes fits exactly onto the middle piece to make a rectangular block?

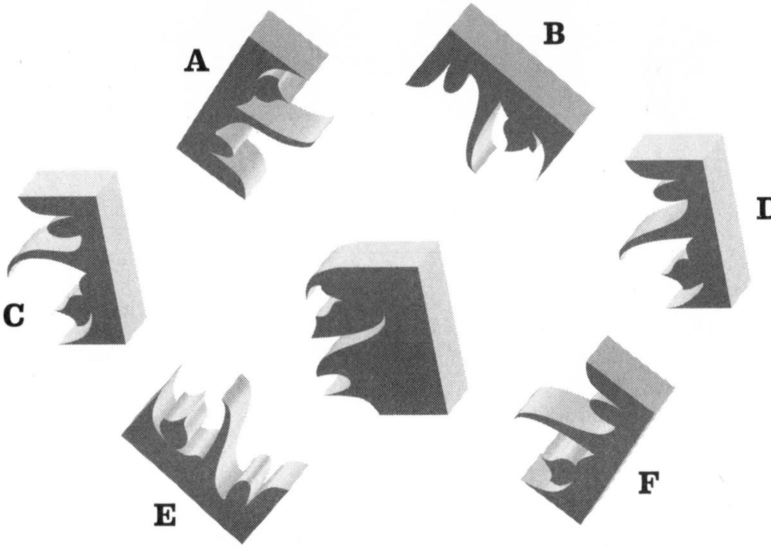

Answer see page 298

1. Which 1938 film directed by Sergei Eisenstein relates an incident from the year 1242?

2. Who was the director of the film *Kes* about a young lad who 'adopts' a kestrel?

3. Which film-maker celebrated her 100th birthday in 2002, after surviving a helicopter crash in Africa at the age of 98?

4. A still-existing film set north of Almeiria in Southern Spain has been used for several films, but was constructed by Sergio Leone originally for which film?

5. Who had his directing career effectively wrecked when dismissed from a Gloria Swanson film, but nevertheless played alongside her in the film *Sunset Boulevard*?

6. *Oh! What a Lovely War* was adapted for the stage in 1963 by which director?

7. Who made the award-winning film *The Silent World* in 1956, concerning the underwater world?

8. The 2009 film *The Concert* directed by the Romanian Radu Mihaileanu is mainly delivered in which two languages?

9. Who was the director of the film *Spartacus* along with Anthony Mann?

10. Who was the aptly named director of the film *Kidnapped* starring Peter O'Toole and Peter Finch?

11. What was the surname of father Pierre Auguste, a painter, and son Jean, a film director?

12. A trilogy of films by Krzysztof Kieslowski is named after which three colours?

13. Which German film of the silent era tells ostensibly of a mad director of an insane asylum, although at the end we learn that it is the narrator who is actually an inmate of the asylum and the tale is his fantasy?

Answers see page 298

Odd One Out

What is the odd number out?

19 **53** **23**
11
17 **91** **41**

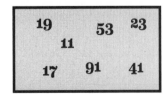

Answer see page 298

1. St Valery, which was the point of embarkation for William the Conqueror's invasion of England, lies at the mouth of which river?

2. In which river did the Pied Piper drown the rats?

3. Which ship was built for the Confederate Navy on the River Mersey, and sunk in an engagement with a United States ship off Cherbourg?

4. The River Bug forms the border between which two countries, for part of its course?

5. Which Mediterranean island sounds like a German river, although the two are spelled differently?

6. The old part of Tunis is described by a name which is also the name of a river on the Isle of Wight. What is it?

7. Which is the longest river in Switzerland?

8. Chateau Gaillard on the River Seine was commissioned originally by which King?

9. Which river, which gave its name to two battles of World War I, enters the Seine just downstream of Paris, adjacent to Vincennes?

10. Which city lies at the confluence of the Tanaro and Borbera rivers in Piedmont and is the capital of the same-named province which is known for a special type of wine?

11. What name is given to a section of the valley of the River Düssel, about 15 km east of Düsseldorf. It was named after a clergyman but is better known nowadays for an archaeological discovery?

12. Which river, whose tributaries include the Fiddich, runs thru one of the most important whisky areas of Scotland, and enters the sea east of Elgin?

13. What was invented by Giovanni Maria Farina, an Italian who came to reside in Köln (Cologne) by virtue of circumstances following from Cologne's restrictive control of the River Rhine?

14. Which river is formed by the confluence of the Trent and the Ouse?

15. Which town lies within a loop of the River Severn, and has an English Bridge and a Welsh Bridge?

16. The Kama is the chief tributary of which river?

17. Which river separates County Antrim and County Derry?

18. What is the second-longest river in Italy?

19. Which town lies at the mouth of both the Dhoo River and the Glass River?

20. The iron bridge shown below in present-day Ironbridge spans which river?

Answers see page 298

1. Southern Comfort is flavored with which fruit?

2. The German Reinheitsgebot of 1516 sets quality standards for which commodity?

3. What is the chemical name of the type of alcohol found in beers and spirits?

4. Which drink similar to root beer (or the same as root beer, depending on your point of view) is produced from the roots of a woody member of the plant kingdom from South America, which receives its name from the Spanish for 'small brambled vine'?

5. Which cocktail consists of rum, coconut milk and crushed pineapple?

6. What spirit is distilled from beer?

7. Which wine is flavored with herbs like cinchona and nutmeg?

8. How many German wine regions are there?

9. The town of Chablis is known for making wine from which type of grapes?

10. What word describes the headspace in a barrel of wine caused by loss of wine through the wood?

11. The term 'wine-dark sea' comes from which work of literature?

12. How many liters are there in a beer barrel?

13. Which expression has the following definitions (among others): a) the second full moon in a month with two full moons and b) a cocktail made from curacao and gin?

14. Geneva schnapps is a form of what alcoholic drink?

15. The makers of Pernod also manufacture which similar aniseed-flavored drink which is much more popular in France?

16. Which Hungarian drink was the cause of a dispute involving Baron Munchausen, a dispute which nearly cost him his life?

17. What is both a drink and an island South of Skye?

18. Which brand of drink has a name derived from the Gaelic for 'the drink that satisfies'?

19. Liebfraumilch was originally wine produced in the vineyards around the Liebfraukirche in which German town?

20. Which cocktail, pictured, was seemingly invented in Raffles Hotel and contains gin, cherry brandy and in its original recipe had a foamy top formed by the addition of pineapples?

Answers see page 298

1. Which book and film is centered on Brookfield School?

2. Who traveled throughout Britain in the 1720s and recounted his experiences in book form?

3. Which clergyman famously converted from the Anglican Church to Catholicism and wrote *The Dream of Gerontius*?

4. What reason does the writer Craig Brown give for making a point of working in his pyjamas up to midday?

5. Which writer is particularly associated with the Grand Hotel in the Normandy resort of Cabourg?

6. Which famous writer and critic was also a Professor of English and Comparative Studies at the University of Warwick?

7. Which writer, pictured below, was married to the pictured Frieda von Richthofen, a distant relative of the Red Baron?

8. In which town did the real 'James Herriot' have his veterinary practice?

9. What writer lived at Newstead Abbey, Nottinghamshire?

10. Which French writer spent 1898 in Britain after being accused of libel in France?

11. Which writer published his *Ready and Easy Way to Establish a Free Commonwealth* just prior to 1660? After 1660 he was under some threat of death, deeply in debt and found his books being burned in some quarters.

12. Which book by George Orwell was originally called *The Confessions of a Dishwasher*?

13. The book *Heart of Darkness* is based on Conrad's experiences in which country?

Answers see page 299

Odd One Out

Which of the following is the odd one out?

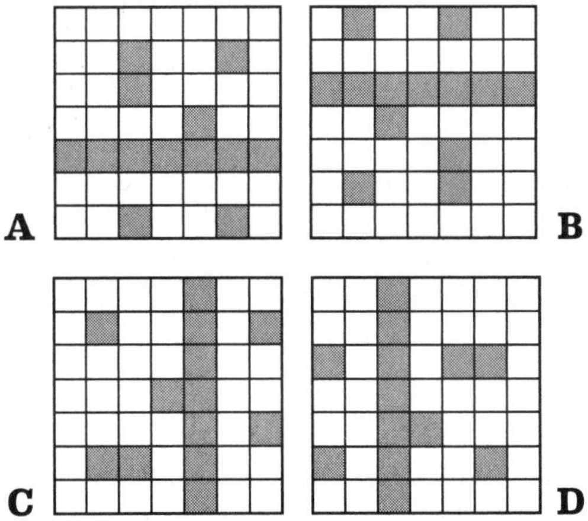

Answer see page 299

1. Which sporting trophy depicted the goddess Nike and was stolen in 1983, never to be seen again?

2. The film *Cool Runnings* was inspired by which specific events of the Olympic Games in Calgary in 1988?

3. What one word is a more common name for underwater hockey?

4. How many periods does an ice hockey match have, and how long is each period?

5. The rules of which game were formulated at McGill University in the 1870s?

6. Jackie Robinson became the first black person to play Major League Baseball when he turned out for which club?

7. The Lord Derby Cup is a major French trophy awarded in which sport?

8. In which team sport does the goalkeeper have to wear a red/white or red/dark quartered cap?

9. What did Charles Miller introduce into Sao Paulo towards the end of the 19th century?

10. The outer part of a football used in professional games tends to be made of a pattern of which two geometric shapes?

11. Which two countries waged the so-called ‘Football War’ of 1969?

12. What event of 1954 is known to the Germans as ‘The Miracle of Bern’?

13. *This Sporting Life* by David Storey concerns, indirectly, which sport?

15. The Stanley Cup is a competition in which sport?

14. In the German language, what is the difference between the word 'Fussball' and the word 'Football'?

Answers see page 299

Weigh-in

Each horse carries a weight handicap. Can you work out the number of the fourth horse?

No. 4

15kg

No. 7

29kg

No. 3

14kg

No. ?

24kg

Answer see page 299

1. Which beach formed by longshore drift stretches for 16 km westward of the Isle of Portland?

2. When were the Germans ejected from the Channel Islands at the end of World War II?

3. In which TV program did Tracy Island feature?

4. On which island is Holyhead?

5. Which small island, with an area of a couple of square kilometres, lies south of the Isle of Man?

6. In Robert Louis Stevenson's *Treasure Island* we hear of the Sea Cook. Who or what does this refer to?

7. Which island off Poole was the site of the birth of the Boy Scout movement?

8. What is the title of the Bill Bryson book which appeared in 1997, relating his travels around Britain?

9. Which is the most northerly of the Channel Islands?

10. Who achieved national celebrity after her exploits in saving several passengers of the stricken Forfarshire off the Farne Islands in 1838?

11. From 1852 onwards, Victor Hugo sought exile in British territory. Where exactly?

12. Which island was claimed by England in 1583 although it only became secure as a British possession as a result of the Treaty of Utrecht in 1713, having previously been also widely settled by the French?

13. Tobermory, seen here, lies on which island?

Answers see page 299

Odd One Out

Which of the following is the odd one out?

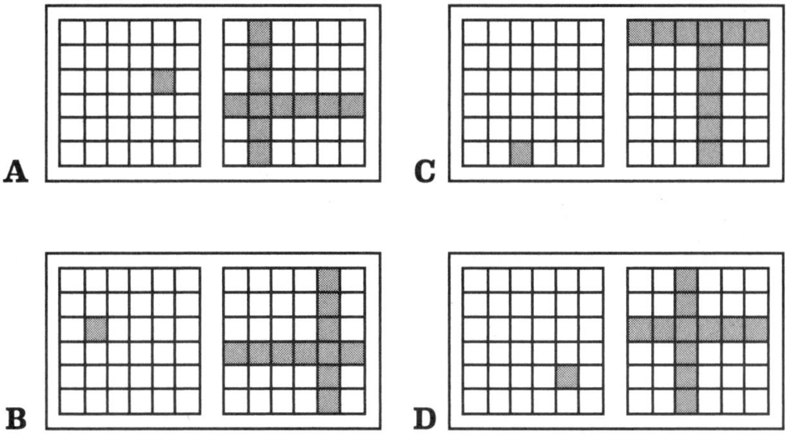

Answer see page 300

1. Who translated the *Arabian Nights* and *Kama Sutra* into English?

2. What is the translation of 'Fledermaus'?

3. Henry VIII introduced an English language bible into churches – who was the main translator of this bible, who had produced an English language bible in 1525?

4. Translated into English, what did the abbreviation KGB stand for?

5. Jean Francois Champollion carried out a famous work of translation (or deciphering) on what?

6. Which word associated with the government of Mikhail Gorbachev, shown here, is generally translated as 'openness'?

7. Which port was sung about in French by Jacques Brel and in an English 'translation' by David Bowie?

8. The Landsker is a line dividing which two languages?

9. Who wrote the book which tends to be translated as *In Search of Lost Time*?

10. Which liquid has a name which is a corruption of a phrase meaning, in translation, something like 'the best' or 'the finest'?

11. What is normally chanted in a foreign language, but in English translation starts off with 'There is going to be a fight between us. May it mean death to you and life to us'?

12. At which event was simultaneous translation used for the first time in a major way?

13. What is the translation of *Moulin Rouge*?

Answers see page 300

Triangulation

Can you find the number to go at the bottom of triangle D?

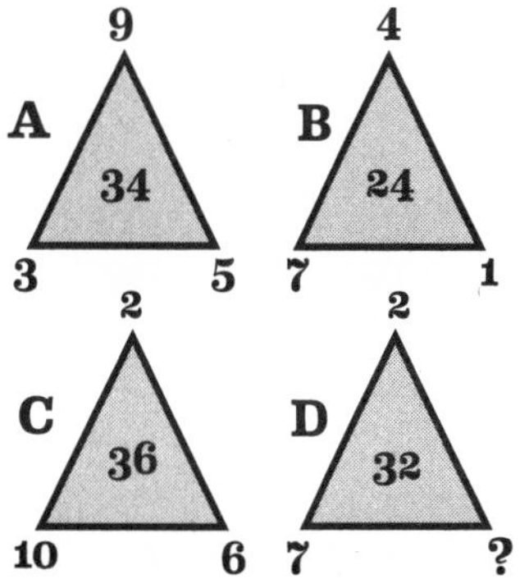

Answer see page 300

Clock Wise

Can you work out the pattern of the clocks and say what the time on clock 4 should be?

Answer see page 300

1. The Council of Constance of 1414–1418 dealt with which issue?

2. Who commissioned the Old St. Peters Basilica over which the current St. Peters in the Vatican is built?

3. Pope Gregory XIII's 'Te Deum' mass of 1572 controversially celebrated which event?

4. Who was the Holy Roman Emperor who traveled to do penance to Pope Gregory VII at Canossa?

5. In 1406, Owain Glyndwr agreed to which specific request of Charles VI of France in relation to allegiance to the pope?

6. Which pope commissioned Michaelangelo to paint the Sistine Chapel, who painted the image shown here?

7. What was the civil forename of Pope Alexander VI, a member of the Borgia family?

8. What is the 'civilian' name of Pope Benedict 16th?

9. Why is the Sistine Chapel so named?

10. The ancient town of Alba Longa was possibly on a site where which current Papal residence is now situated?

11. During the Great Schism, where was the base of the alternative Pope to the one at Rome?

12. Which hill of Rome got its name because it was formerly a base for soothsayers?

13. Who was Pope during the Second World War?

Answers see page 300

Pattern Poser
Can you work out which square would follow squares 1–4 below?

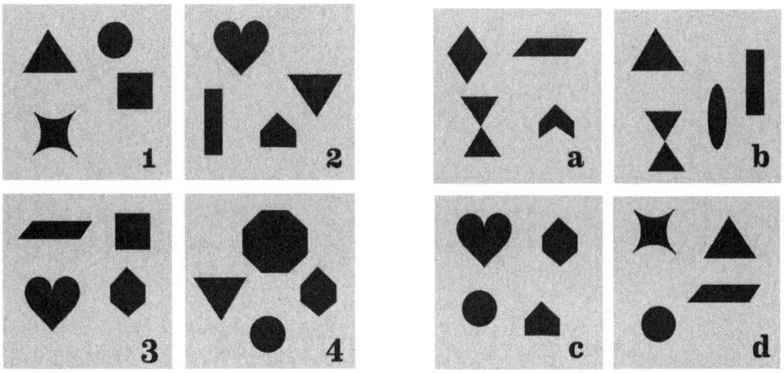

Answer see page 300

1. Which was the first German city to be captured by American forces in 1944 – on 21st October?

2. Which Prime Minister was overthrown by the October Revolution in Russia?

3. Which forgery became a major discussion point of the October 1924 election?

4. In which Italian village, was there a tragic collapse of a school in late October 2002?

5. Who became Prime Minister of Hungary in October 1956, and was overthrown by the Russians soon after?

6. The National Day of Spain takes place on 12th October, in memory of which event?

7. What name is given to a rebellion by miners on the Ballarat goldfields in Victoria, Australia from October to December 1854?

8. Which journalist from Novaya Gazeta was assassinated in October 2006?

9. Which battle raged from 16-19 October 1813, resulting in a decisive defeat for Napoleon?

10. The 1973 Middle East War of October 6-26 is often named after which regular event?

11. In November 885, the Vikings settled in for what was to be a long and unsuccessful siege of which city? They withdrew in the following October after being confronted with troops from the Holy Roman Empire.

12. During October – November 1962, China was engaged in a military conflict against which country?

13. The Reuben James was a destroyer sunk by a German submarine on 30th October 1941. Which navy did it belong to?

Answers see page 300

Squared Up

In this diagram, starting from the bottom of the diamond and working in a clockwise direction, the four basic mathematical signs (+, –, x, ÷) have been omitted. Your task is to restore them so that the calculation, with the answer in the middle, is correct. Use all four symbols. Bodmas does not apply.

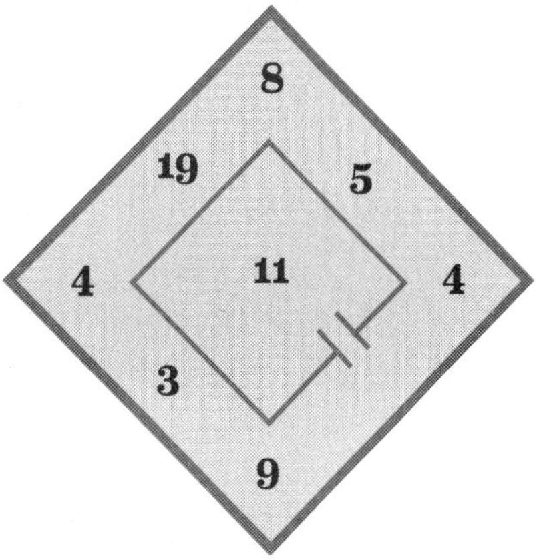

Answer see page 300

1. What name is used in America for a Mediterranean type of area with a name derived from the Spanish for 'scrub-oak'?

2. In 1963, a small area of which American city was transferred to Mexico?

3. Which American national passenger rail company was set up in 1971?

4. Whereas a carat is a weight of 20 mg for precious stones, with respect to gold it is a measure of purity. How does America seemingly attempt to reduce the confusion to a certain extent, in comparison with Britain?

5. Which company was described by Fortune magazine as America's most innovative company, in every year from 1996 to 2000?

6. In 1999, which American zoo managed to get the pictured Giant Panda Bai Yun to breed?

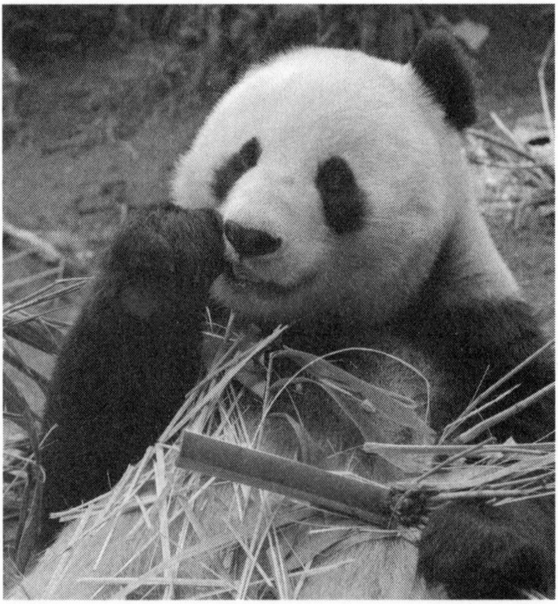

7. Within 10 years either way, when were elections introduced for the American Senate?

8. What was the effect of the Treaty of Tordesillas?

9. Jakob Boehm was a miller who played a part in the creation of Bourbon whiskey. What is the Americanized version of his name?

10. Which American General attempted to sell the plans of West Point to the British?

11. In which ship did John Cabot become, in 1497, the first European to reach the American mainland since the Vikings?

12. What is known in America and some English regions as a Pollywog?

13. Which company, more usually associated with 19th. Century America, still exists as a banking concern and handles transfers from the Paypal internet site, for example?

Answers see page 301

Time Travel

This clock was correct at midnight (A), but began to lose 3.75 minutes per hour from that moment. It stopped half an hour ago (B – 7.30 pm), having run for less than 24 hours. What is the correct time now?

A 

midnight

B 

p.m.

Answer see page 301

1. In the Sherlock Holmes story 'The Speckled Band', what is the speckled band?

2. Pierluigi Collina is a well-known name in which occupation?

3. Jack Griffin was known as what in a HG Wells story?

4. Which county uses/used a Red Kite as its symbol (the Red Kite being a bird)?

5. With respect to mobile phones, what does SIM stand for?

6. Who wrote *Mary Poppins*?

7. Emmer is an early form of what?

8. Which French region gets its name because it is 'where the land comes to an end'?

9. On a western ranch, what does a wrangler do?

10. In which town can you view the Seamen's Bethel (1832), a chapel described by Herman Melville in his novel ***Moby-Dick***?

11. Indira Gandhi was assassinated on her way to be interviewed by whom?

12. In the story by Hans Christian Andersen, what did the mermaid trade in order to become human?

13. What designation meaning 'Southern Ape' was given to an early hominoid?

14. Rudolf Nureyev defected while in which country?

15. Who wrote the book *A Dialogue Concerning the Two Chief World Systems*?

16. Before automation, which lighthouse used to be situated at Britain's northern inhabited extremity (this does not necessarily mean the extremity of the mainland)?

17. What caused Dr. David Livingstone's left arm to become unusable?

18. Both the oldest and second-oldest prisons in California were used to stage Johnny Cash concerts. What is the second-oldest?

19. Sleeping Beauty's Castle in Disneyland is based on this real-life castle. What is its name?

20. What is the collective noun for a group of flying geese?

Answers see page 301

1. Which sporting trophy is made from melted-down rupees?

2. The French gold coin called a Louis was continued after the Revolution as a 20-franc coin under what name?

3. Why do non-circular coins always have an odd number of sides?

4. Which British coin was introduced in 1849 and named ultimately after an Italian city?

5. Which is the most-visited tourist attraction in France and featured on a 20 franc coin of 1992?

6. What is the currency of the West Indies island of Guadeloupe?

7. State the two colours of the one-Euro coin, and explain how they are arranged?

8. Which word for a tithe in French reminds of a non-French coin?

9. For what reason were the words 'Decus et Tutamen' imprinted onto British coinage?

10. Prior to decimalization in 1957, an Indian rupee was split into which unit equal to one-sixteenth of a rupee?

11. Who wrote a story about an American stranded in London who comes into the temporary possession of a 1 million pound note?

12. Which currency was used in France prior to the franc of 1799?

13. Guilders were the currency in the southern part of which country until replaced in 1875?

14. What is the currency in the Philippines?

Answers see page 301

Shape Shift

Use logic to find which shape has the greatest perimeter.

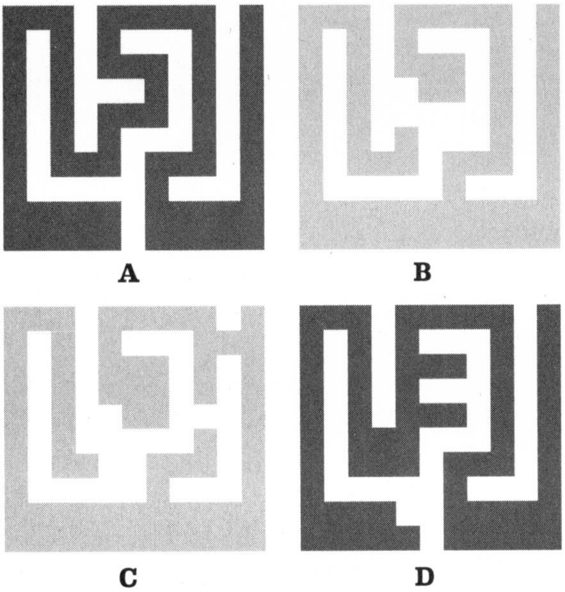

Answer see page 301

1. Who is the anti-hero of the *Beggars Opera* and *The Threepenny Opera*?

2. What expression would be used in opera to describe an adult male who sings in an alto, mezzo or soprano range, who can take on the roles formerly sung by castrato singers?

3. Hugo von Hoffmansthal was the librettist for which opera composer?

4. Which major opera has connections with the opening of the Suez Canal?

5. Who was appointed the conductor of the Vienna Court Opera in 1897?

6. Which musical work by Beethoven became the name of a book by Tolstoy, this book then spawning an opera of the same name?

7. Who wrote the original libretto for Bernstein's opera based on Voltaire's *Candide*?

8. Which Alban Berg opera has the same name as the stage name adopted by Marie Lawrie?

9. In which opera does a character commit suicide after having blindfolded her baby?

10. Who wrote the opera *Hansel and Gretel*?

11. Which Bizet opera is set in Ceylon?

12. Arnold Schönberg wrote an opera about which two biblical brothers?

13. The opera *Billy Budd* is based on the work of which author, pictured opposite?

Answers see page 301

Clock Wise

Can you work out which number the missing hand on the last of these strange clocks should point to?

Answer see page 302

1. Which starfish, scientific name *Acanthaster planci*, was noted to be causing damage in the Red Sea in 1998-2003?

2. What do you call a young whale?

3. What sort of fish is an Arbroath Smokie?

4. What are the young of sharks called?

5. What are Skipjack and Yellowfin?

6. Which fish wreaked havoc on the existing ecology of Lake Victoria after it was introduced there in the 1950s/60s?

7. Which whales received their name because they were ideal for hunting?

8. What is a Lessepian migration, named after the engineer who constructed the Suez canal?

9. What is a Beluga?

10. Which is the second largest fish in the ocean?

11. What is a Cichlid?

12. What type of fish gives its name to Schubert's *Piano Quintet D667*?

13. Which fish has the Latin name *Betta Splendens*?

14. What name is given to a juvenile salmon, that is just preparing to enter the ocean for the first time?

Answers see page 302

Square Assembly

Arrange the pieces to form a 5x5 square where the numbers read the same horizontally and vertically. What will the finished square look like?

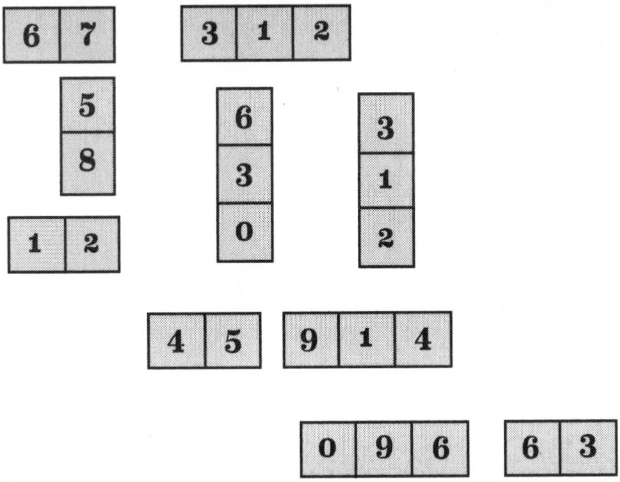

Answer see page 302

1. Who won Nobel Prizes in both Physics and Chemistry?

2. Which Nobel Prize winner caused controversy in 2006 by admitting that he had been a member of the SS?

3. Pablo Neruda, winner of the Nobel Prize for Literature in 1971, hailed from which country?

4. Which South African won the 1984 Nobel Peace Prize?

5. Name two Irish writers who have won the Nobel Prize for Literature?

6. Who was awarded the first Nobel Prize for Physics for his work investigating the rays which were subsequently named after him?

7. Who was awarded a Nobel Prize in 1918, despite having produced poison gas for use in the World War?

8. *Combat* was a clandestine newspaper of the French Resistance. Two of its editors later became winners of the Nobel Prize for Literature – name one.

9. Which President of Israel received a Nobel prize in 1994?

10. Name one of the two Irish women who were jointly awarded the Nobel Peace Prize in 1976?

11. Who was awarded the Nobel Prize in 1921 for his work in Quantum Theory?

12. Who was awarded the Nobel Peace Prize in 1975 for his efforts in trying to obtain a nuclear test-ban treaty, although he himself had been a leading light in hydrogen bomb developments?

13. Which Nobel Prize winner was married five times and had a daughter with his last wife when he was 84 years old?

14. Which Russian Nobel Prize winner, pictured here, had worked with Rutherford in Cambridge but after attending a scientific conference in the USSR in 1934 was refused permission to leave the country again?

15. Name one of the two scientists who shared the 1945 Nobel Prize with Fleming for discovering Penicillin?

Answers see page 302

Odd One Out

Which one of the following numbers is the odd one out?

50 31 24 68 18

Answer see page 302

1. Where in Wales do you mostly see the words 'Dynion' and 'Merched'?

2. Which Welshman sacked Panama City in 1671?

3. The type of Neolithic tomb which are referred to as dolmens in England, are known by what name in Wales?

4. Which riots took place in Wales during the period 1839-1843?

5. Which American singer appeared in the film *Proud Valley* set in the Welsh mining valleys?

6. The engine used to power the VC10 aircraft had the name of a Welsh river. Which one?

7. Name the Welsh town that is picture below and has a funicular railway?

8. Which mountain is named after a Welshman who became Surveyor General of India in the nineteenth century?

9. Who was the only Welsh king to reign over all of Wales?

10. Which battle of about AD 616 between Northumbria and a couple of Welsh kingdoms is often stated as the event which separated the Celts in present-day Wales from those in the North of Britain?

11. The tragic story of which poet formed the basis of the first Welsh Language film to be nominated for the Foreign-Language Oscar in Hollywood?

12. Which Welsh town was called Segontium by the Romans?

13. What is the smallest cathedral in North Wales?

Answers see page 302

Pattern Poser

Find a number that could replace the question mark. Each pattern represents a number under 10.

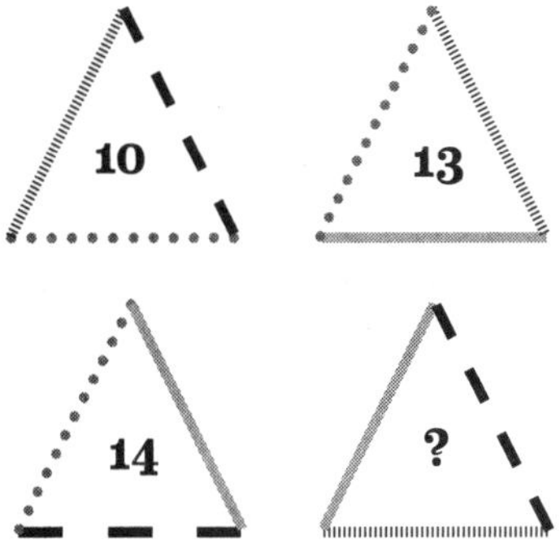

Answer see page 303

Stacked

Can you work out what number should replace the question mark in this diagram?

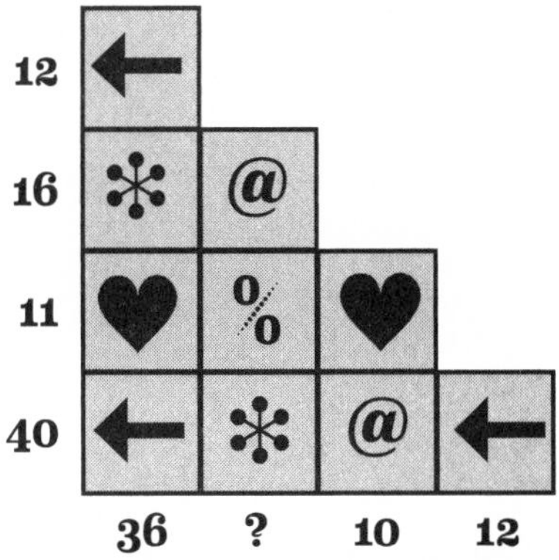

Answer see page 303

1. Which musical work of 1728 was a parody of Handel and corrupt London society?

2. From which musical does the song 'You'll never walk alone' come?

3. Which musical was 'composed' by George Wright and Robert Forrest, with music based on the Polovtsian Dances by Borodin?

4. Who is the daughter of Fantine in *Les Misérables*?

5. The Cole Porter song 'Too Darn Hot' features in which musical?

6. In which story do we meet Mr George Banks of 17 Cherrytree Lane?

7. When Chechen rebels took over the Dubrovka in Moscow in 2003, what musical was being staged at the time?

8. 'Dream the impossible dream' comes from which musical?

9. What is the name of the female singer in *Cabaret* who was portrayed by Liza Minnelli in the film?

10. Ira Gershwin's first name is short for what?

11. The song 'If I ruled the world' comes from which musical?

12. What was the last musical written by Rodgers and Hammerstein?

13. Which impresario built the pictured Savoy Theatre to present Gilbert and Sullivan operas?

Answers see page 303

1. Who painted *Les Demoiselles d'Avignon*?

2. Which Parisian railway station was the subject of a series of paintings by Monet in 1876/7?

3. Who painted *The Madonna of the Goldfinch* of 1505 in which the influences of Leonardo da Vinci are apparently evident?

4. Ford Madox Brown was loosely associated with which artistic movement?

5. Which painting was recovered in Florence in 1913, after being stolen two years beforehand?

6. A painting of a steam train by Turner from 1844 carries an eight word title. The last four words are 'The Great Western Railway'. Ignoring the word 'and', what are the other three words?

7. *The Anatomy Lesson of Dr. Nicolaes Tulp* is a painting by whom?

8. Which ship had a tragic history, providing the subject of a painting by Theodore Gericault?

9. What is the traditional name for the painting which depicts the Company of Captain Frans Banning Cocq?

10. Who painted *Le Déjeuner sur l'herbe*?

11. What popular name is given to Raphael's painting in the Stanza della Segnature in Rome?

12. Who painted *The Persistence of Memory*?

13. Which painting is known officially as *Arrangement in Black and Grey No. 1*?

14. Millais' painting *Lorenzo and Isabella* is based on a poem by Keats which itself is based on a story by which author?

15. Which Van Gogh painting of 1889 features the Moon over Saint Remy?

16. Turner's painting *Snow Storm* (to give the name in short) depicts which historic event?

17. Which building is shown in Constable's painting *The Hay Wain*?

18. Who painted the picture entitled *Manchester City v Sheffield United*?

19. Where is the painting by Giotto that allegedly shows Halley's Comet, a painting that lead to the name *Giotto* being given to a space probe to investigate the comet?

20. The painting *Impression, Sunrise,* which gave the Impressionists their name, shows a scene from which town or city?

Answers see page 303

1. One of the longest-lasting dispute in the industrial history of Britain endured from November 1900 until November 1903, in which industry?

2. Which battle of 2nd December 1805 confirmed France's hegemony over Europe?

3. After the Revolution of 7th November 1917, which former school gained central importance as headquarters of the Bolshevik Party?

4. In December 1989, who was elected chairman of the Czech Federal Assembly?

5. Napoleon's coup of November 9/10 1799 took place in which month of the French Revolutionary Calendar?

6. Which battle (or massacre) took place on December 29th 1890, two weeks after Sitting Bull had been killed by the Americans?

7. Which ship famously sank on 25th November 1120?

8. The murder of which Bolshevik leader in December 1934, pictured below with him, provided a major pretext for Stalin's purges?

9. In December 1939, the Graf Spee entered which port for repairs?

10. Which city was attacked on 13th November 1940 as part of Operation Moonlight Sonata?

11. Who was the French Interior Minister at the time of the riots in late December 2005?

12. When is the Feast of Stephen?

13. An observation of a solar eclipse in November 1919 by the likes of Arthur Eddington has been commonly stated (inaccurately) as providing proof for which major theory?

14. What was the cargo carried by the *Tricolor* when it sank on 14th December 2002 in the English Channel (where it was subsequently hit by two other ships)?

15. Which group from the North East of England played their farewell concert in November 2003?

Answers see page 303

Missing Number

Can you unravel the reasoning behind this square and replace the question mark with a number?

3	6	3	5
4	15	11	1
3	?	15	5
1	6	7	2

Answer see page 303

Odd One Out

Can you work out the reasoning behind this puzzle and find the odd number out?

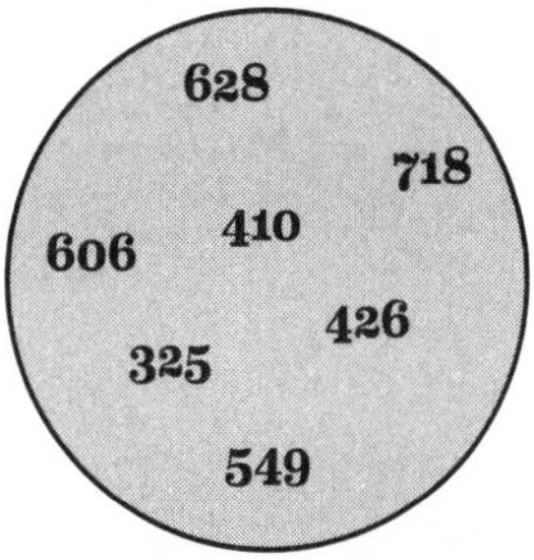

Answer see page 304

1. The murder of Cassetti forms the basis of which book?

2. What is the name of the Leonard Wibberley book about a country that declares war on the United States?

3. Which work of fiction mentions the existence of a book by Emmanuel Greenstein which is full of heresies?

4. In Alex Haley's book what new name is forced on Kunta Kinte in America?

5. Which book features Billy Pilgrim who experienced the horrors of the bombing of Dresden as well as being abducted by aliens and displayed in a zoo on their home planet?

6. What is the name of the pig in the book *Charlotte's Web*?

7. The title of the book *Cry the Beloved Country* refers to which country?

8. Which book is subtitled *The Sacred and Profane Memories of Captain Charles Ryder*?

9. William of Baskerville features as a character in which book?

10. Whose first novel was called *Nausea* , achieving great acclaim, including a nomination as the book of the first half of the twentieth century?

11. Which Shakespearian character utters the words 'brave new world' which were later used as the title of a book?

12. Lynne Reid Banks wrote about what type of room?

13. The picture shows the leader of the leader of the Seeonee wolf pack in *The Jungle Book,* who is driven out to hunt alone when he becomes too old. What is his name?

Answers see page 304

1. How can a sailor use the pole star to calculate latitude?

2. Who is the person credited with being the first to recognize the Milky Way was actually composed of stars?

3. In which constellation is the Andromeda galaxy?

4. The number of constellations in the sky is equal to the number of keys on a standard piano. What number?

5. What constellation is sometimes referred to as 'The Teapot'?

6. The constellation of 'Lynx', adjacent to the Great Bear, was invented by Johannes Hevelius. It gets its name not because it looks like a lynx but why?

7. The rising of which star indicated to the ancient Egyptians that the Nile was just about to flood?

8. What is the fifth-brightest star in the sky, and the brightest to be permanently in the Northern Sky (or nearly so, depending where you are)?

9. The Pole Star is in which constellation?

10. Which extremely large star has a red colour and has a name which seems to mean 'rival of Mars' (i.e. Mars the planet)?

11. The Southern constellations were created fairly recently and are generally not named after any inherent shape that they might have. How did the constellation of 'Mensa' come to receive its name?

12. What is the analog of longitude in astronomy?

13. Which two satellite galaxies of the Milky Way are named after this Portuguese sailor?

Answers see page 304

Make Up

Which of the following cubes cannot be made from this layout?

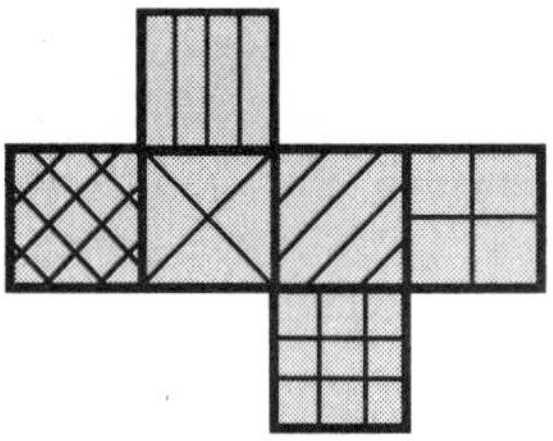

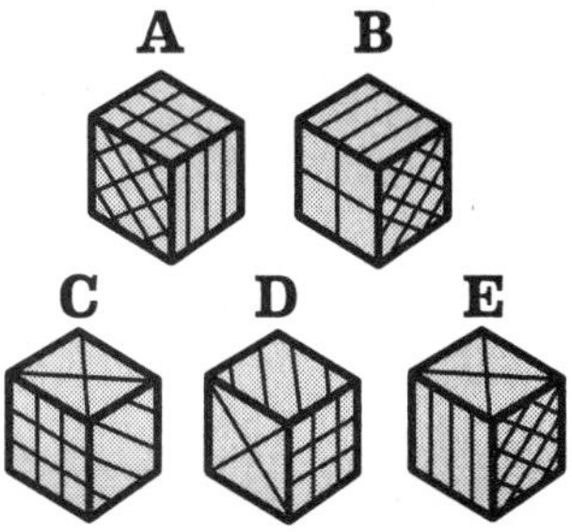

Answer see page 304

1. What is the derivation of the word 'carnival'?

2. What is the name of the white starchy endosperm of durum wheat from which traditional pasta is made?

3. What is the main difference between a Shepherd's Pie and a Cottage Pie?

4. 'Genuine' salami is distinguished from the more usual variety by containing the meat of which animal?

5. A European PDO (Protected Designation of Origin) is intended to protect the geographical integrity of certain products, e.g. Parma ham can only come from Parma and Champagne only from Champagne. Which British product covered by a PDO is unusual in that the place mentioned in its name actually lies outside the area in which the product can be legally made?

6. From which country does Chicken Tikka Masala originate?

7. Kasha is what sort of foodstuff?

8. Which food crop has varieties called Stockdale Arrow and Crimson Crown and is associated with Yorkshire?

9. Which country is the main producer of maple syrup?

10. According to Clemens Forell in his book relating his escape from a Siberian prison camp, what is the one food that prisoners esteem highly both while in prison and after they are released?

11. What is Blue Vinny?

12. Although nowadays mostly made from cows' milk, Mozzarella cheese was originally made from the milk of which animal?

13. Until 1968, the Egg Marketing Board placed what symbol on eggs as a sign of approval?

Answers see page 305

Timed Puzzle

The clocks move in a special way. What time should come next?

Answer see page 305

1. Which mathematician do you especially associate with the town of Syracruse in Sicily?

2. How many bridges did the city of Königsberg possess, leading to the mathematical problem known as the Königsberg Problem?

3. Which mathematical theorem was the subject of a popular book by Simon Singh?

4. What shape is the Gaussian Distribution?

5. What is a diamond shape known as to a mathematician?

6. In Mathematics, what do you call a segment shaped like a piece of pie marked out on a circle (ie a shape with sides of two radii and a bit of the circumference)?

7. What concept is denoted by a horizontal eight?

8. When De Valera set up the Institute of Advanced Studies in 1939, he incurred the memory of which famous Irish mathematician at the inauguration ceremony?

9. What is the more well-known name (beginning with F) of the mathematician Leonardo of Pisa?

10. How do you calculate the average known as the median?

11. What does SOHCAHTOA denote in Mathematics?

12. What number do you get when you divide the length of a piece of A4 paper by its width?

13. Sudoku is really just a more complicated form of what type of square introduced by the Swiss mathematician Leohard Euler in the 18th century?

Answers see page 305

Odd One Out

There is a logic to the patterns in these squares but one does not fit. Can you find the odd one out?

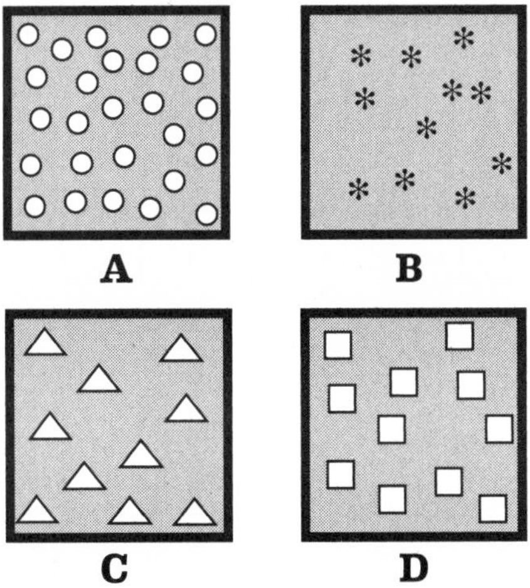

Answer see page 305

1. The last album of which singer was called *Tropical Brainstorm*?

2. Jacqueline du Pré famously played which instrument?

3. Who christened his daughter 'Moon Unit'?

4. Luciano Pavarotti hailed from which Italian town or city?

5. Manuel and the Music of Mountains was a stage name used by which bandleader?

6. What was the name of Robert Schumann's wife, depicted here, who was a well-known musician in her own right?

7. Which country singer is the sister of Loretta Lynn?

8. Which singer had the hits 'Girl Don't Come' and 'Long Live Love'?

9. The song 'Edelweiss' from the *Sound of Music* provided a hit for which British singer?

10. What instrument did Django Rheinhardt play?

11. Which Greek singer represented Luxembourg in the 1963 Eurovision Song Contest, singing in the French language?

12. Which bandleader led the Tijuana Brass?

13. Freddie Mercury was accompanied by which opera singer in rendering the song 'Barcelona'?

Answers see page 305

Squared Up

Each symbol in the square below represents a number. Can you find out how much the question mark is worth?

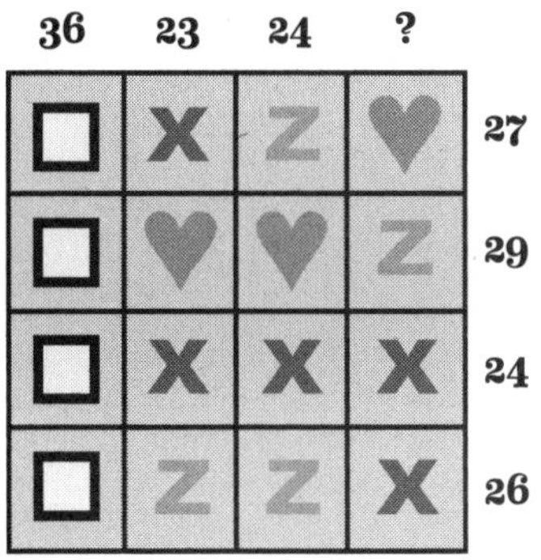

Answer see page 305

Triangulation

The four triangles are linked by a simple mathematical formula. Can you discover what it is and then find the odd one out?

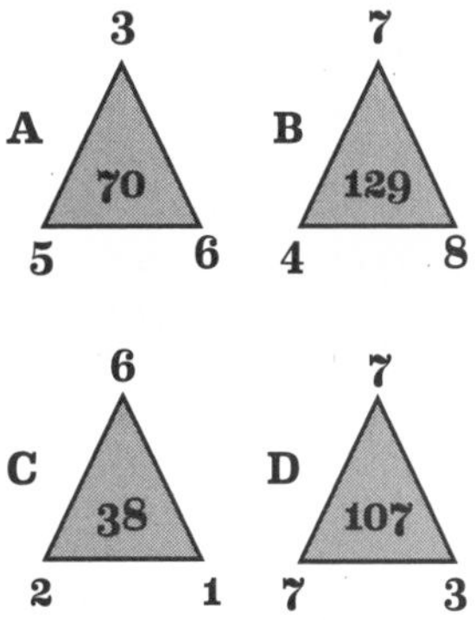

Answer see page 305

1. In the film ***Fort Apache***, who played the role of Colonel Thursday?

2. What is the derivation of the name 'Shrove Tuesday'?

3. Who was the author of the 1958 book *Saturday Night and Sunday Morning*?

4. Which Sunday paper was set up supporting the Chartists in 1850, passed into the hands of the Co-op movement and lasted until 1962, by which time it was known as the Sunday Citizen?

5. Tony Kay was banned from football because of a betting scandal in 1964. Name one of the two clubs he played for.

6. How is the date of Easter calculated?

7. The Christian festival of Maundy Thursday celebrates what?

8. Which Australian horse race is always held on the first Tuesday in November?

9. *Staying Alive* was the sequel to which film?

10. Who carried out an enquiry in 1972 into the Bloody Sunday events that year in Derry?

11. What is French for 'Tuesday'?

12. What name was given to 19th October 1987 in economic circles?

13. Which type of cake, pictured opposite, is traditionally associated with Mothering Sunday?

Answers see page 305

Total Mystery

Can you work out what number should replace the question mark to follow the rules of the other wheels?

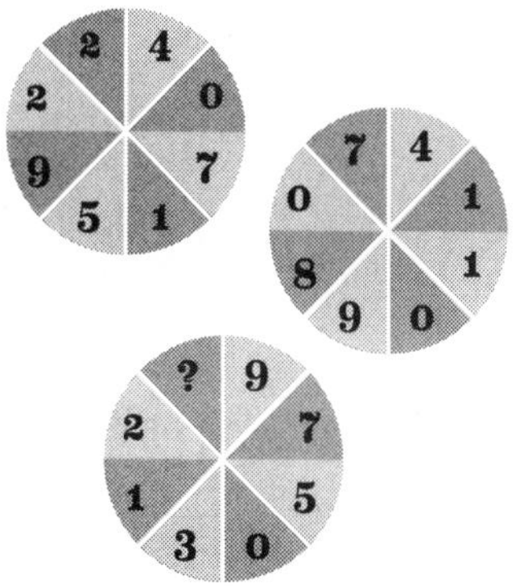

Answer see page 305

Number Pattern

What number continues this sequence, and why?

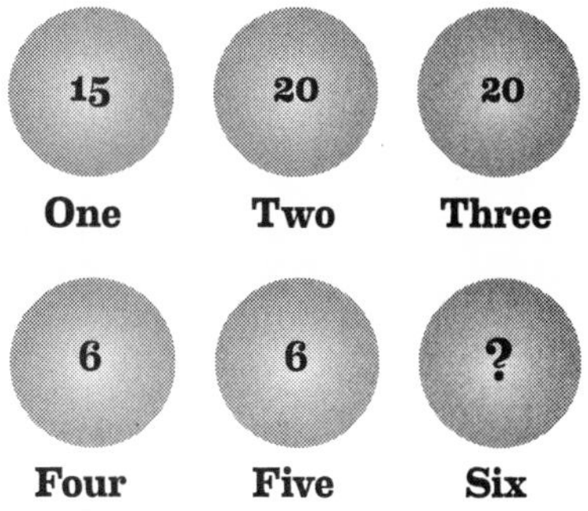

Answer see page 306

1. Which author married a woman in 1928 with the same forename as himself?

2. Under what other name is the author Barbara Vine known?

3. Which author developed an excellent knowledge of poisons while working in a hospital in Torquay?

4. The author C.S. Lewis came from which part of the world?

5. Which author initiated the phrase 'Vanity Fair'?

6. Robert Markham was a pen name of which author?

7. Which author recalled problems entering South Africa originally because she was actually born in Persia, although at a later date she appears to have been refused entry for political reasons?

8. Which author was the daughter of Leslie Stephens, the editor of *The Dictionary of National Biography*?

9. Winifred Holtby wrote a book about which non-existent district of Yorkshire?

10. Eastwood in Nottinghamshire is particularly associated with which author?

11. Which author has a Birthplace Museum in Portsmouth, despite the fact that he only lived in Portsmouth until he was 3 years old?

12. Who wrote *The Vindication of the Rights of Women*?

13. Platform $9\frac{3}{4}$, from which you can catch a train to Hogwarts, is in which station?

Answers see page 306

Boxed In

This figure has been partially filled with numbers according to a system. Can you work out the logic of the system and replace the question mark with a number?

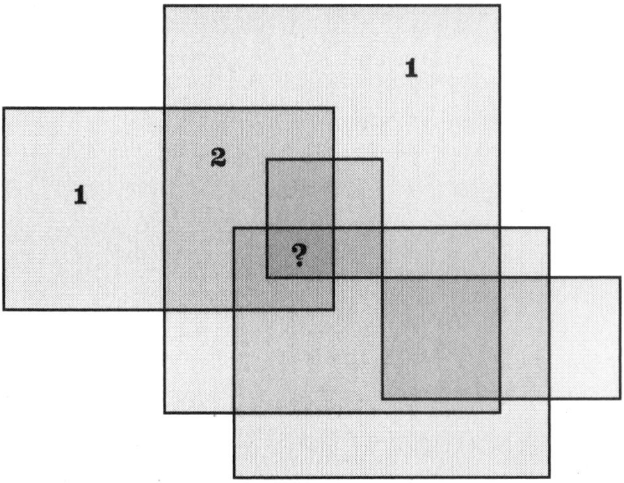

Answer see page 306

1. The rivers Garonne and Dordogne merge to form what?

2. Which playwright who shares his name with a river in Berlin premiered a play called *Leaving* in 2008?

3. On entering the River Rhine from the sea in the time before the arrival of railway bridges, which town/city had the first bridge across the river?

4. Which river in South America gets its name from a Spanish word for 'silver'?

5. The aircraft which ditched in the Hudson River in 2009 belonged to which airline?

6. In 1907, crowds gathered in large numbers on the River Mersey to watch which large new liner set off on its maiden voyage, Liverpool landing stage having been altered to accommodate its great length?

7. The wind known as the Mistral flows down which river valley?

8. On which river does Prague lie?

9. What is the longest river contained wholly in England?

10. Which two rivers meet at the Shatt-al-Arab?

11. Who was the producer of the Ike and Tina Turner song 'River Deep, Mountain High'?

12. Hanoi lies on which river?

13. Which work of fiction has a scene where two dogs enter Suffolk by crossing the River Stour at Sudbury?

14. Which road stretches from the Moscow Station in St. Petersburg to the River Neva?

15. The eastern delta of the River Niger flows into which Bight?

16. Harper's Ferry, where John Brown made his raid in 1859 and which was a strategic point during the Civil War, lies at the confluence of the Potomac and which other river?

17. Which river separates Canada and western New York state?

18. Enoch Powell's so-called 'rivers of blood' speech, gets its title via a quote he borrowed from which classical work of literature?

19. Which river draining the Lammermuir Hills, and a tributary of the Tweed, has the same name as a comedy character on TV?

20. Who was the boatman, seen here, who ferried the dead across the River Styx?

Answers see page 306

1. The song 'Whistle While You Work' comes from which film?

2. Which singer sang the theme tune and also appeared in Sam Peckinpah's 1973 film about Billy the Kid?

3. Who appeared in the film *The Misfits*, the screenplay being written by her husband?

4. Which Liverpool group of the 60s was named after a John Wayne film?

5. Which film has Rufus T. Firefly in charge of the country of Freedonia?

6. The events which are related in the film *Mississippi Burning* took place in a town with the same name as a large city in America. What was its name?

7. Which film starts off with Clint Eastwood as a preacher who endures a murder attempt?

8. Who was the director of the documentary *Bowling for Columbine*?

9. Charlie Chaplin first appeared on the screen in 1913 in a film made by which company?

10. Which story by Richard Matheson was adapted for TV by Stephen Spielberg?

11. Which film of 1944 features Peter Lorre as Dr. Einstein?

12. Who became a 'dream pair' in Hollywood after the 1935 film *Captain Blood* and consequently made several other films together?

13. Which building is taken over by criminals in the film *Die Hard*?

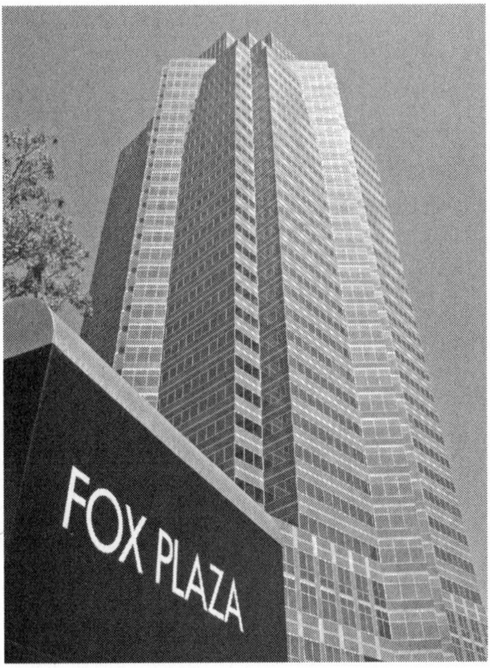

Answers see page 306

Triangulation

Can you work out the reasoning behind the triangles in this sequence and replace the question mark with a number?

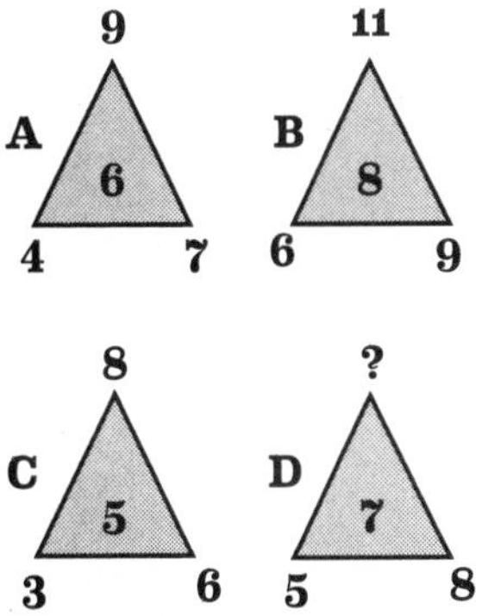

Answer see page 306

Missing Number

What number should replace the question mark?

3	1	4	2	7
5	6	6	5	0
7	8	9	6	9
1	9	4	1	5
2	6	?	2	5

Answer see page 307

1. Which Moscow football team was taken over by the secret police, the name also being subsequently used by other secret-police-run clubs in Eastern Europe?

2. Which play was an enormous success for the Moscow Arts Theatre in the theatre's first year, despite being a major flop when it was first staged in St. Petersburg six years beforehand?

3. The Russian rouble is divided into 100 what?

4. The name of which area of London has indirectly passed into the Russian language as the word for a railway station?

5. Prior to the revolution, Russians had a name day each year, which was possibly more important than their birthday. What was a name day specifically?

6. Sailors on which Russian ship mutinied in the Black Sea in 1905?

7. Sasha is a short form of which Russian name?

8. St. Petersburg was built at the head of which river?

9. Which Russian player was World Chess Champion from 1969-1972?

10. What is the name of the principal city of Siberia which lies where the Trans-Siberian Railway crosses the River Ob?

11. What is the name given to the time in the westernmost time zone of Russia?

12. Originally serving with Ivan the Terrible, who became czar of Russia from 1598-1605? His reign occurring during the so-called 'Time of Troubles', which ended with the accession of a Romanov in 1613.

13. What is the present-day name of Stalingrad?

14. The Russian dish Borsch is made from what?

15. Who was Russian foreign minister at the end of the Second World War?

16. Russian Caravan is a variety of which grocery item?

17. What was the name of the first woman to become Empress of Russia, in 1710?

18. Which 1972 Russian film, based on a story of Stanislav Lem, was remade by Hollywood in 2002?

19. What is the name of the sub-arctic region of Russia permanently forested with coniferous trees?

20. What's the name of this fortress, which was built in 1703 and is the oldest building in St. Petersburg?

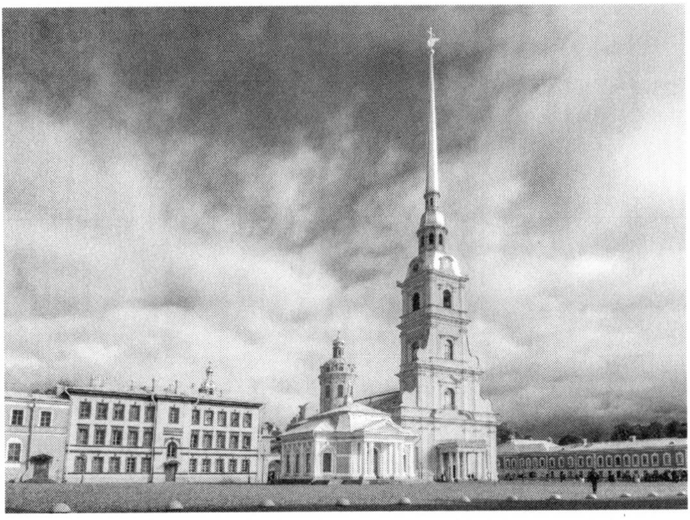

Answers see page 307

1. Which three countries were sometimes known as the 'ABC Powers' in the early 20th century?

2. What type of plant is a Cereus?

3. Why had Yul Brynner shaved his head originally, thus producing his trademark look?

4. Which line, or barrier, was established by the United Nations to divide Nicosia?

5. Who was the voice of Mr Magoo?

6. Why did Belgium skip Christmas in 1582?

7. The IWW was an American trade union of the early 20th. Century. What do the initials stand for?

8. Which type of tiger is the largest?

9. What is Frankenstein's forename?

10. Joy Division transformed into which group?

11. Which George Eliot novel is set during the General Election of 1832?

12. In which work can we read about the 'traitors' Judas, Brutus and Cassius being frozen into ice at the Earth's very center?

13. Sean Connery received his only Oscar for which film?

14. Which company introduced Babycham?

15. Which was the first Sherlock Holmes story to be published after he was 'killed' off in 1893?

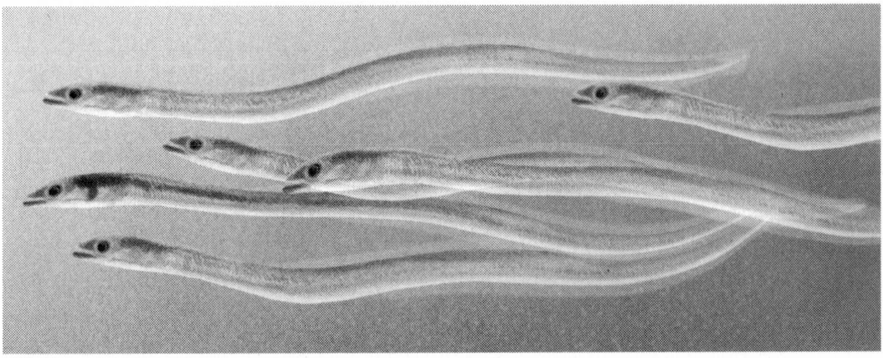

16. What is a young eel called?

17. 'Los Lobos' means what in English?

18. What had happened to Gregor Samsa when he woke up one morning?

19. Mick Talbot and Paul Weller formed the nucleus of which music group?

20. Which was the only French possession left to England at the end of the Hundred Years War?

Answers see page 307

Take Time

Can you work out, for each amount of time specified, whether you have to go forward or backward to get from the time on the top clock to the time on the bottom clock?

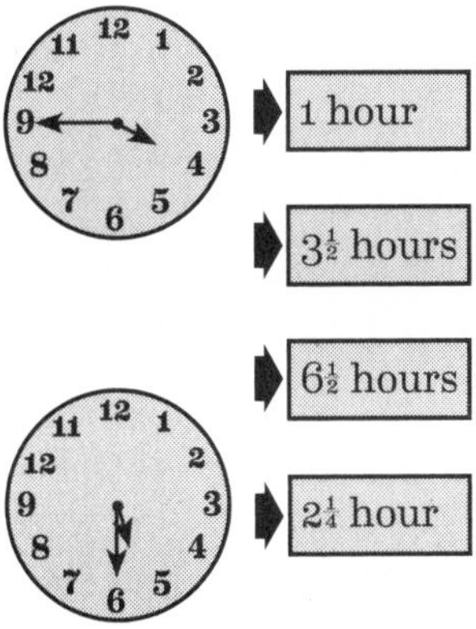

Answer see page 307

1. Which bird can swim the fastest?

2. What feature defines an animal as a bird?

3. Which is the only European bird to have gone extinct during the previous millennium?

4. The Greenshank and Redshank are types of bird, but what does the word 'shank' refer to?

5. Up to 90% of the world population of the bird known scientifically as *Puffinus puffinus* nest and breed in Britain, on islands like Skomer. What is its common name?

6. The town of Arundel in Sussex allegedly has a name derived from the French word for which bird?

7. An eagle carrying a hammer and sickle is the emblem of which country?

8. Which bird has three varieties – Brown, Great Spotted and Little Spotted?

9. In the same way that blackbirds are a type of thrush, condors are examples of which wider type of bird?

10. The small helicopter, the Flettner 282, used by Germany during the Second World War was named after which bird?

11. 'My heart aches and a drowsy numbness pains my sense' – which bird is being referred to?

12. What type of bird engages in a mating procedure called a 'lek'?

13. The word 'halcyon' originally made reference to what type of bird?

14. Which bird has the scientific name *Passer domesticus*?

15. On one of his voyages, Sinbad's ship is sunk by boulders dropped by which type of bird?

16. Which bird has a name derived from the Anglo-Saxon for 'White Arse'?

17. Which sea bird with the latin name of Larus canus is one of the less-frequently seen birds around the British coasts?

18. What is a rockhopper?

19. The name of Lundy Island derives from an Old Norse expression meaning what?

20. The flightless and extinct bird pictured here, the Moa, inhabited which part of the world?

Answers see page 307

1. How can you tell whether an egg is fresh by placing it in water?

2. Which street in York was occupied by meat traders in the Middle Ages, and was described by Pevsner as 'over-restored and twee'?

3. Who wrote *The Jungle* describing the terrible conditions in the American meat industry?

4. Which country produces Jarlsberg cheese?

5. What does a Gala Pie contain at its center, apart from meat?

6. The practice of pannage involves the letting loose of pigs to eat what?

7. A Cheese and Ham Toastie would usually be known by what name in France?

8. Wheat is a member of which botanical family?

9. The name of which type of meat is also used to describe junk e-mail on the internet?

10. What has varieties of Cabaret, Victoria and Marquis?

11. Which sheep's cheese comes from the South of France where it is aged in caves near Combalou?

12. A cantaloupe is a what?

13. What is a langoustine?

Answers see page 308

Make Up

Can you spot the cube that cannot be made from the layout below?

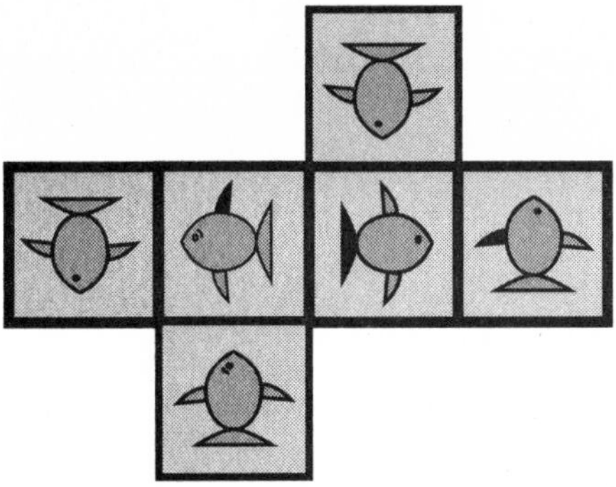

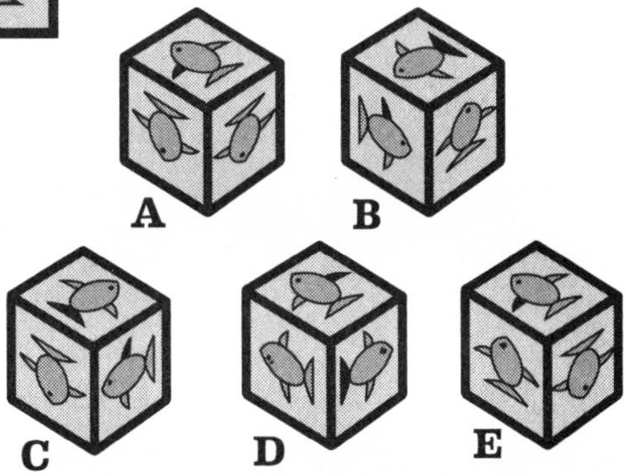

Answer see page 308

1. Which city is named after the wife of William IV?

2. The name of which New Zealand city is the Gaelic name for a Scottish city?

3. What is both the French word for straits and the name of a large city?

4. When Palestine was split into Israel and Judah, Jerusalem was the capital of Judah - which city was the capital of Israel?

5. From 1889 until 1977, the Orient Express connected which two cities?

6. Which Indian city was the site of an extremely major chemical factory disaster?

7. Who is usually credited with the founding of Salt Lake City?

8. Which city in Iran suffered a major earthquake in 2003?

9. As it is most commonly understood in America, the Metroplex is the name of a region dominated by two particular cities. Name one.

10. The four statues of horses that adorn San Marco Square in Venice were stolen by Venice from which city?

11. Tel Aviv was originally a suburb of which city?

12. What is the largest city in South America?

13. The streets of the original Monopoly boards were based on which town or city?

14. Sachertorte originates in which city?

15. Which town lies at the confluence of the Klondike and Yukon?

16. Which city has a center based on a grid plan, with street names like A2, L3, M2 etc. The central avenue leads away from the baroque palace, blocks on one side of this avenue being numbered clockwise, and the blocks on the other side being numbered counter-clockwise?

17. Which 16th Century English bible was named after a European city?

18. In the song, where is the House of the Rising Sun?

19. Which group of people founded Puerto Madryn in Argentina?

20. In which Texan city is this building (the Alamo)?

Answers see page 308

1. Which Prussian military leader in the wars against Napoleon had a battleship named after him which was sunk on Boxing Day 1943?

2. Which liner sank in New York while it was being fitted out as a troop carrier?

3. Which four-engined bomber of World War II was manufactured by Handley Page?

4. In 1953 which aircraft became the first non-American design to be adopted by the United States Air Force since World War I?

5. Which advisor of Catherine the Great is better known because of the Battleship named after him?

6. What popular name was given to the B-17 aircraft, seen in action here?

7. What new name was given to the Eurofighter aircraft?

8. Name one of the three types of V-Bomber.

9. Which fighter aircraft was the first with the ability to accompany bombers all the way on their missions over Germany?

10. Which was the RAF's first monoplane fighter?

11. Britain's first nuclear-missile submarine was equipped with what type of nuclear missiles?

12. Name one of the first two jet aircraft to enter RAF service?

13. What was the name of the South Korean Naval ship that sunk mysteriously in 2010 (also the name of a city in Korea)?

Answers see page 308

Squared Up

The shades represent four numbers under 10, and each square shows a multiplication. What number replaces the question mark?

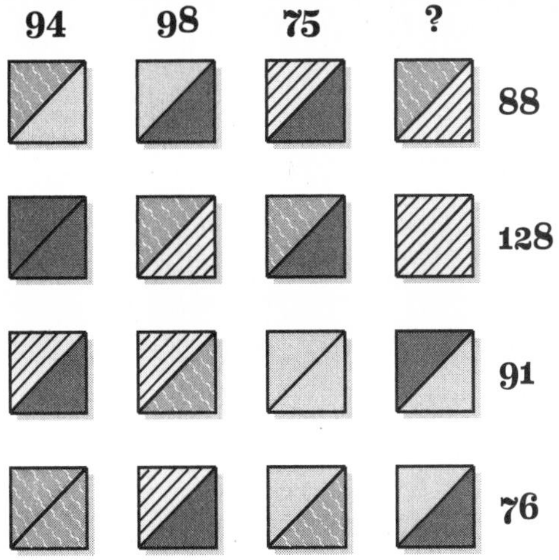

Answer see page 308

1. Lew Wallace, who was governor of New Mexico in the time of Billy the Kid, wrote which famous book?

2. Which district of the town of Poole in Dorset shares its name with a fictional kingdom introduced in the work of an Irish writer, published in 1726?

3. George Sand wrote about *A Winter In* ... where?

4. Which book by Jerome K. Jerome tells of a trio engaged in a cycling holiday around Germany?

5. Chaucer received the inspiration for his 'Troilus and Crsiyde' from the works of which other writer?

6. Which writer used the name 'Gotham' to refer to New York in an 1809 story featuring Dietrich Knickerbocker?

7. Which book tells the story of David Powlett-Jones, a teacher at Bamfylde school?

8. Which book by Graham Greene tells the story of a vacuum-cleaner salesman who is mistaken for a spy?

9. Hemingway wrote about *The Snows of* ... where?

10. Which fictional author of detective novels and acquaintance of Lord Peter Wimsey received much publicity for her books by virtue of being charged with murder?

11. Pushkin wrote a story about a Bronze Horseman that comes to life. The Bronze Horseman is a statue of which person?

12. Pierre Boulle is a French writer who wrote the book now known in English translation as 'The Planet of the Apes'. Which of his other books was filmed in 1957 with Alec Guinness in a leading role?

13. What is the name of the relatively barren plateau region in South-Central Spain (pictured here) which became famous because of a book of 1605?

Answers see page 309

Triangle Logic

What number should replace the question mark?

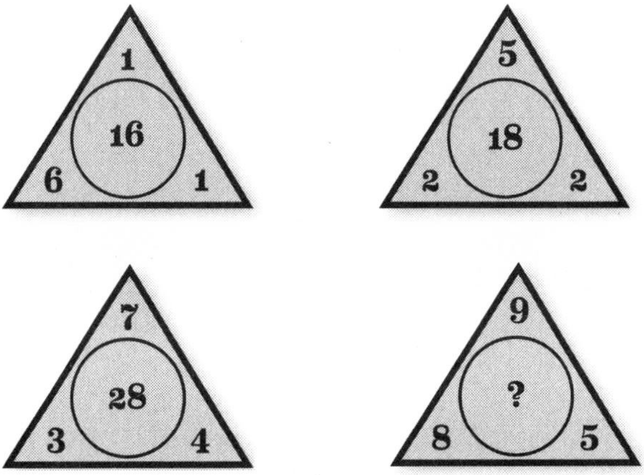

Answer see page 309

1. The band Jefferson Airplane 'reappeared' under what name when releasing an album which was nominated for a Hugo Award?

2. Who was the drummer in Cream?

3. Two members of the Zombies pop group were instrumental in forming which later rock group?

4. A 1970 album was entitled *The Who Live at* ...where?

5. Which group bemoaned 'The taxman's taken all my dough and left me in my stately home'?

6. Bob Dylan's 'Mr. Tambourine Man' was made into a hit by who?

7. What name is shared by a founder of the American Navy (pictured here) and a member of a famous British rock group?

8. Which album has a cover depicting a black and white representation of the Hindenburg exploding?

9. Jerry Garcia, who died in 1995, was a member of which band for 30 years?

10. Which group is named after a character in *David Copperfield*?

11. What was the former name of Marc Bolan's group T.Rex?

12. Of which band was Peter Green a co-founder, although its name actually referred to other co-founders?

13. Paul Kossof became a member of which band in 1968?

Answers see page 309

Make Up

Can you spot the cube that cannot be made from the layout below?

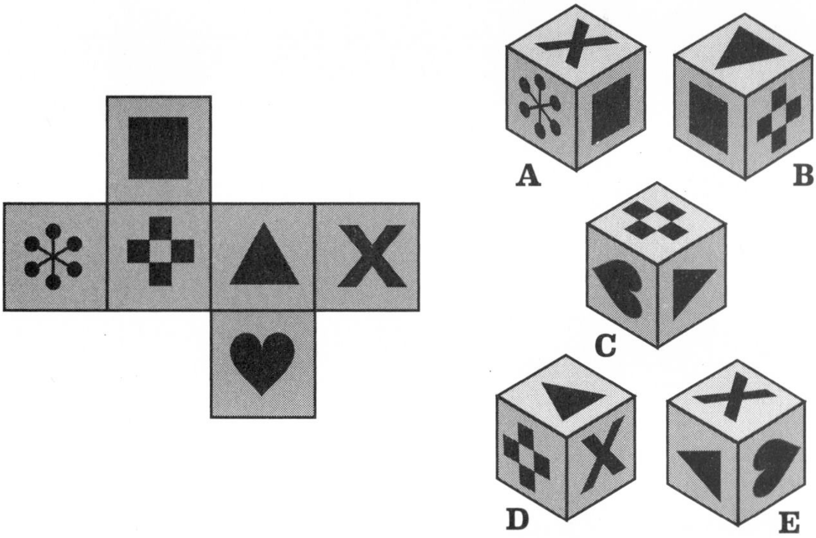

Answer see page 309

1. The word *martinet* is the word for which animal in the French language?

2. What is the German word for satellite, which is also the name of a German car?

3. The slang words used in the book A Clockwork Orange e.g. '*droogs*', '*horrorshow*', '*moloka*', '*ptitza*' are based on what European language?

4. Which biblical name has entered the French language as the word for the youngest child in a family?

5. The word *Ombudsman* comes from which language?

6. Which English word is derived from the Nordic word 'Jarl'?

7. What is the French word for 'grape', a word that has a slightly different meaning in English?

8. Which fuel derives its name from the Greek word for coal?

9. What is the Spanish word for fox, a word that is better known to most people as the name assumed by a fictional hero?

10. Modern French words like 'cadeau' and 'velours' stem from which earlier form of French?

11. What is the Welsh word for waterfall, which gives a town in Mid-Wales its name?

12. What is the Russian word for 'lion', as well as being a Russian forename?

13. Which French phrase meaning 'dead-pledge' or 'dead-security' has passed into English as a single word with a broadly similar meaning?

14. What word connects an aircraft and the place where Louis XVI was executed?

15. Which island derives its name from the Spanish word for pelicans?

16. What is the basic meaning of the word 'baguette' in French?

17. The London district of Vauxhall has possibly indirectly entered the Russian language as the word for what (Hint: the word has a transport connection)?

18. The word 'Slalom' comes from which language?

19. Which word beginning with P is another name for the game of boules?

20. What is both the name of a town and the Spanish word for the pictured fruit?

Answers see page 309

1. Gilgamesh was a character in the religious myths of which civilization?

2. What is the name of the 'Island (or Land) of the Dead' in Finnish legend, (Hint – its best-known name begins with the letter T)?

3. According to Greek mythology, who set up the rocks of Gibraltar and Ceuta?

4. The quotation 'One swallow doesn't make a summer' stems from which source?

5. In Greek mythology, what was the name of the river of forgetfulness in the underworld?

6. The documentary film *White Wilderness* perpetuated a myth about which particular animal?

7. Who got rid of Grendel (pictured here)?

8. According to legend, who was the Habsburg bailiff who forced Wilhelm Tell to shoot an apple off his son's head?

9. Under what name does Robin Hood appear in Walter Scott's *Ivanhoe*?

10. In Norse mythology what is Ragnarok?

11. The German writer Clemens Brentano claimed to have created what legend in his novel of 1802, *Godwi*?

12. The *Red Book of Hergest* and the *White Book of Rhydderch* were the sources for which set of tales?

13. Which Etruscan king, according to popular legend, came to the aid of Tarquin, the last King of Rome, and was opposed by Horatio and two colleagues before a bridge leading to Rome (the true history is a bit different)?

Answers see page 309

Make Up

Can you spot the cube that cannot be made from the layout below?

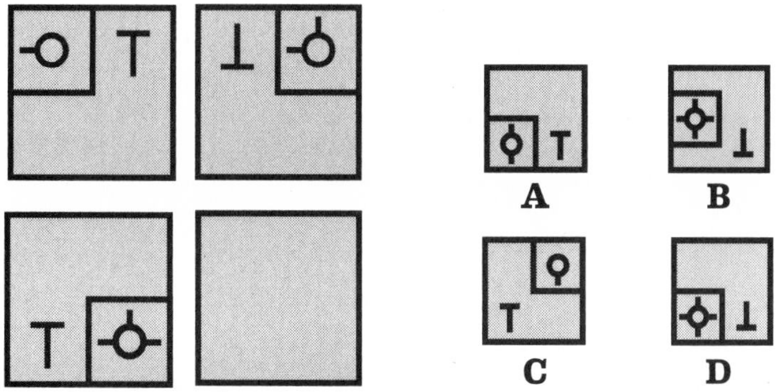

Answer see page 310

1. Alec Guinness once portrayed eight members of which family?

2. The shop used for the Hugh Grant film *Notting Hill* is actually situated in which road?

3. In the film *The Full Monty*, which song famously produced some synchronized 'dancing' in the dole queue?

4. 'Infamy, infamy, there've all got it in for me' is a classic line from *Carry on Cleo* but it first appeared in a work by which comedy-writing duo?

5. In the 1973 film *The Wicker Man*, who portrayed the policeman who eventually became the victim?

6. Which railway (pictured here) experienced an enormous increase in its fortunes when it was chosen as the location for Lionel Jeffries' film *The Railway Children*?

7. In *The Spy Who Came in from the Cold*, who played Alec Leamas?

8. Which Oscar-winning film met with a total lack of co-operation from Cambridge University and had some its scenes filmed in a sporting venue in the vicinity of Birkenhead?

9. In which film do we hear about the Self-Preservation Society?

10. After EMI backed out, who stepped in and provided the financial backing for the Monty Python film *Life of Brian*?

11. 'Broadsword to Danny Boy' is a line from which film?

12. The film *Looking for Eric* features a character called Eric and which other real-life 'Eric'?

13. Who appeared regularly on *That Was the Week That Was*, as well as having a small part in the film Alfie?

Answers see page 310

Squared Up

In this diagram, starting from the top of the diamond, four basic mathematical signs (+, –, x, ÷) have been omitted. Your task is to restore them so that the calculation, with the answer in the middle, is correct. Use all four symbols. Bodmas does not apply.

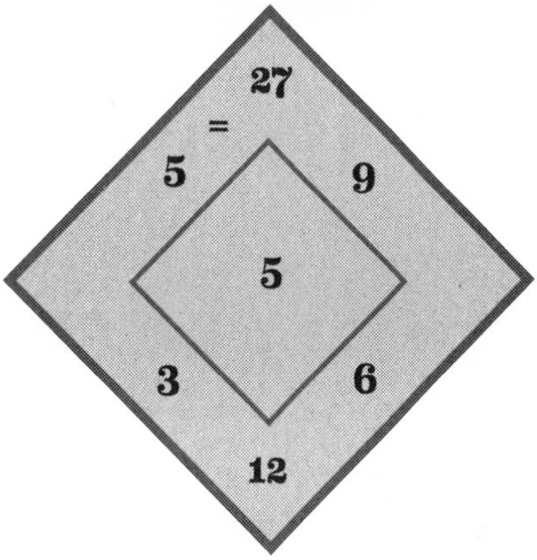

Answer see page 310

1. What name is used to describe hurricanes in the Indian Ocean?

2. Where would you be able to sail on a boat called The Maid of the Mist?

3. Which gulf joins the Red Sea and The Indian Ocean?

4. What name is commonly given to the swampy areas left behind where the Mississippi has changed course?

5. Which island in the Chagos Archipelago in the Indian Ocean was evacuated in the 1960s to make way for an American military base?

6. At which falls (seen here in real life) did Sherlock Homes disappear, presumed dead?

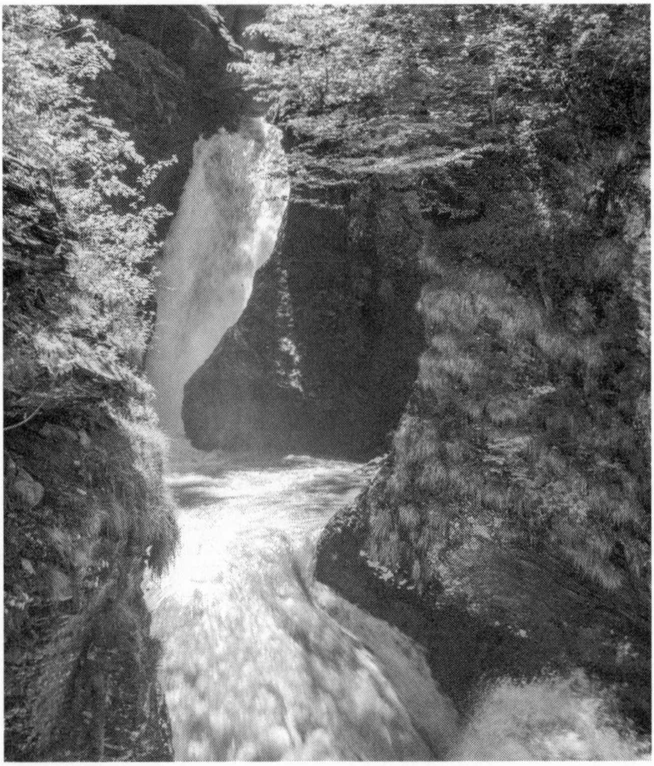

7. In which country is the Mekong Delta?

8. In which country is the Great Slave Lake?

9. Who gave the Pacific Ocean its name?

10. Which 10-km-long reservoir lies just south of the Scottish border?

11. Christmas Island in the Indian Ocean belongs to which country?

12. What is the largest lake in Britain?

13. Which important shipping lane is about 800 km long, connecting the Indian Ocean with the South China Sea?

Answers see page 310

Puzzle Around

Can you work out the pattern of numbers in this circle, and find the missing number?

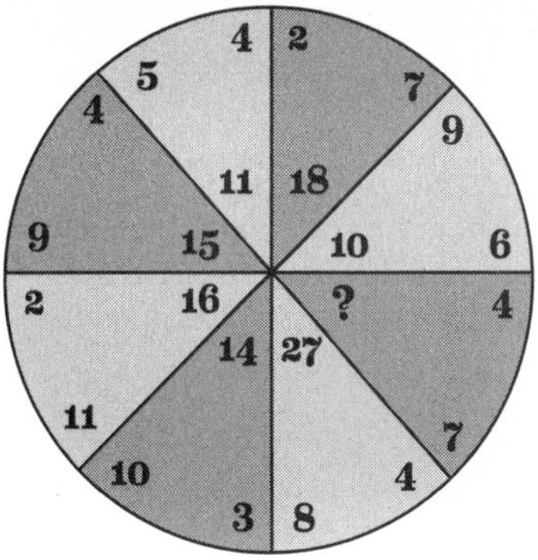

Answer see page 310

Shapes

Can you find a number that logically fits below the 7?

Answer see page 310

1. What is the name of the strong tidal current to the south of the Lofoten Islands off Northern Norway?

2. Which island is also the name of an Internet programming language?

3. In the 1960s, British troops were sent to which West Indian island which had broken away and declared in-dependence?

4. Which island lies South of Elba, about halfway between Corsica and Italy, and has a name which is actually well-known?

5. Gerald Durrell's autobiographical book *My Family and Other Animals* relates a story of his childhood on which Mediterranean island?

6. Which island with a population of about quarter of a million has a name which means 'wood' in Portuguese?

7. In 1794, British troops were sent to try to suppress a slave uprising on which island (unsuccessfully, as it turned out)?

8. Which islands were named by Pliny the Elder because of the large number of dogs there?

9. Spanish Town is the former capital of which island?

10. Which island was named around 1600 in honour of the current stadtholder or chief magistrate of the Netherlands?

11. The First Punic War was largely centered around and on which island?

12. Which area of Brooklyn has a name derived from Dutch which seems to be making reference to the rabbits which once used to be endemic there?

13. The action of *Anne of Green Gables*, illustrated above, takes place in which Canadian province?

Answers see page 310

1. Which is considered to be Germany's oldest city, founded by the Romans 2000 years ago, and later the birthplace of Karl Marx?

2. What is the town of Wolfsburg famous for?

3. The German speaking area of Eupen is situated in which country?

4. Why was the German mark introduced in 1875?

5. In which city is there a University which is still known by its old German name of Albertina?

6. Where did most of the German Navy scuttle itself after the First World War?

7. The type of grape known in Germany as Spätburgunder is also known in Austria, Switzerland, Hungary and the former Yugoslavia by names which implies it comes from Burgundy. It is indeed much cultivated in Burgundy, but what is it called there?

8. Which master criminal was played by the German actor Gert Fröbe?

9. Which East German club was expelled from the German Football League in 1995?

10. The name of the German company MAN is actually an abbreviation, two initials indicating cities or towns – name one.

11. Otto von Guericke, who did experiments on atmospheric pressure, was a Burgermeister of which German city?

12. What is a Harzer Roller which was commonly to be found in the coal mines of the Harz region of Germany?

13. Who built the 'Adler', pictured here, an early locomotive on Germany's first railway line between Nurnberg and Furth?

Answers see page 311

Far From Home?

On this strange signpost how far should it be to Aberdeen?

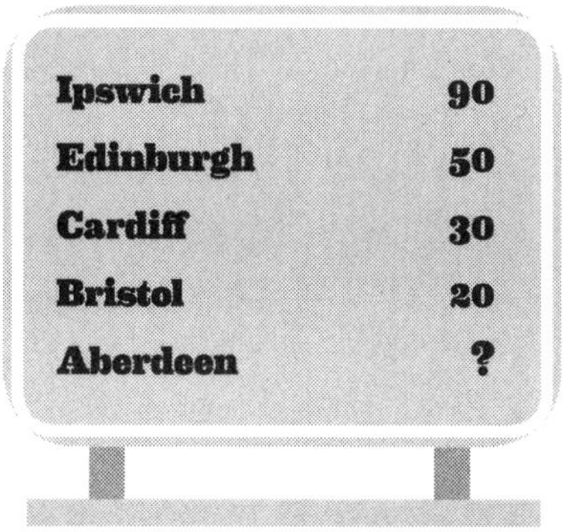

Answer see page 311

Grid Challenge

Can you unravel the reasoning behind this grid and work out which face should replace the question mark?

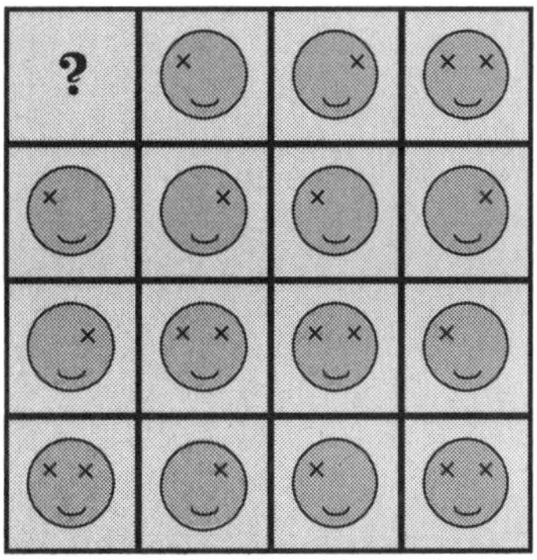

Answer see page 311

1. The game called Sphairistike is possibly an early ancestor of which modern sport?

2. What did Gertrude Enderle famously do in 1926?

3. Which present-day sporting event claims an indirect connection with the Dreyfus Affair?

4. What is the order of swimming strokes in the individual medley, starting from the first?

5. Which two boxers fought each other in 1936 and 1938, with one win each, the latter bout being a world championship match in Yankee Stadium?

6. Cycle races in which two countries form, with the Tour de France, the top three races in the sport in Europe?

7. In the Tour de France, who wears a white shirt with red spots?

What do these astronauts all have in common?

A

B

C

D

E

Answer at the back of this section

These are all paintings by James Abbott McNeill Whistler. Which one caused art critic John Ruskin to remark that the artist was 'flinging a paint pot into the public's face', a remark which offended Whistler so much that he unsuccessfully sued Ruskin in court?

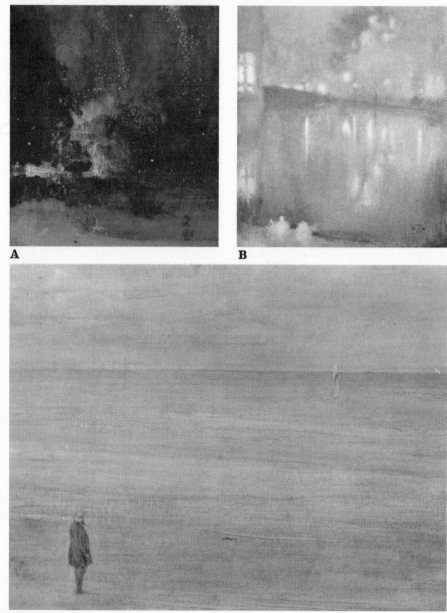

A

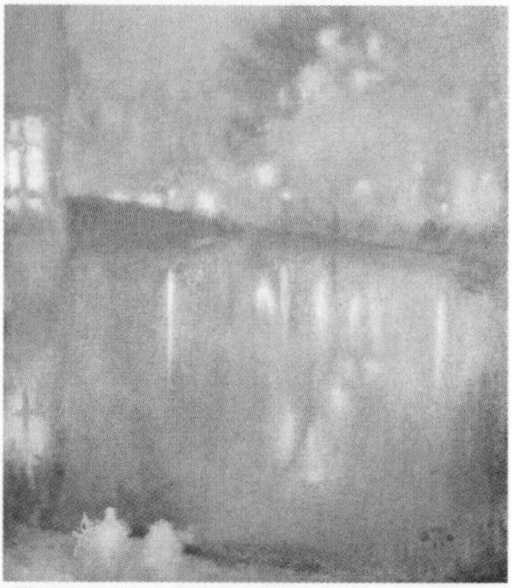

B

C

D

E

Answer at the back of this section

Identify each type of bridge and rank them in order of when they were finished.

A

B

C

D

E

Answer at the back of this section

What do each of these flags have in common?

A

B

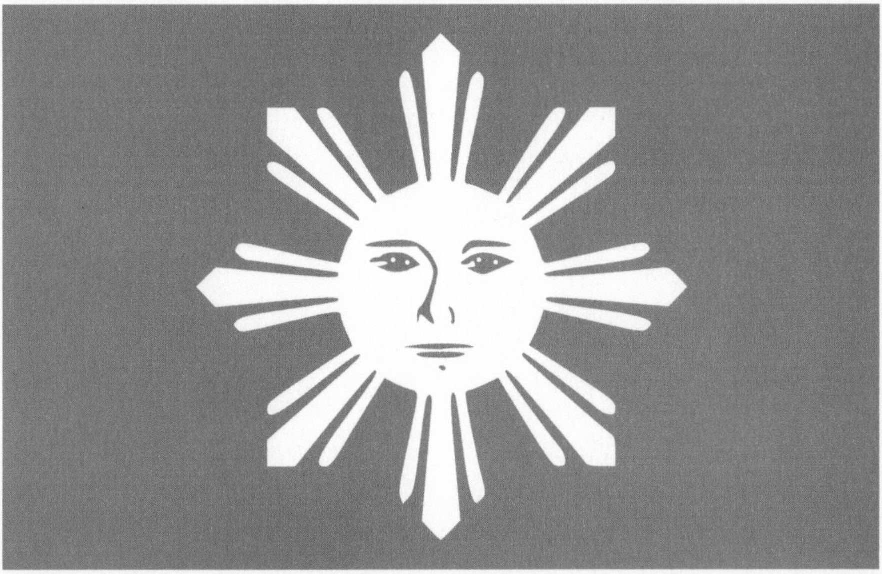

C

D

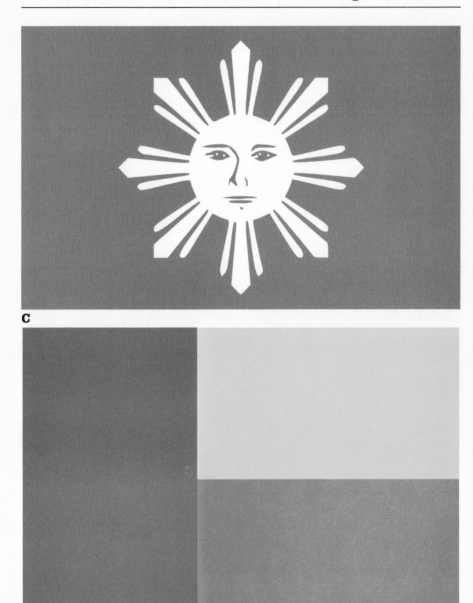

Answer at the back of this section

Identify each pictured Roman emperor and arrange them in order of the year they started their reign.

A

B

C

D

E

Answer at the back of this section

Identify each painting and work out what connects the four artists.

A

B

C

D

Answer at the back of this section

Identify all of the pictured Romantic poets. Rank them in order of how old they were when they died, starting with the youngest.

A

B

C

D

E

Answer at the back of this section

Identify each of these space rovers.

A

B

C

D

E

Answer at the back of this section

Answers

Astronauts

Each astronaut was the first person from their country to fly in space (a: Marc Garneau from Canada, b: Sigmund Jähn from Germany, c: Claude Nicollier from Switzerland, d: Akiyama Toyohiro from Japan and e: Georgi Ivanov from Bulgaria)

Whistler and Ruskin

a., Nocturne in Black and Gold: The Falling Rocket

Notable Bridges

a: Brooklyn Bridge (Hybrid cable-stayed/suspension, 1883), e: Forth Bridge (Cantilever, 1890), b: Tower Bridge (combined bascule and suspension, 1894), d: Sydney Harbour Bridge (through arch, 1932), c: Golden Gate Bridge (suspension, 1937)

Flags of the World

They represent states which no longer exist and that were independent for less than a year:

The Third Republic of Acre (a) lasted nine months, the Republic of Formosa (b) lasted five months, the Republic of Biak-na-Bato (c) lasted just over a month and the Republic of Benin (d) lasted only a day.

Roman Emperors

b: Caesar Augustus (27 BC, although Augustus himself dated it from 23 BC), d: Tiberius (AD 14), a: Caligula (AD 37), e: Claudius (AD 41), c: Nero (AD 54)

Artists and Religion

a: Charlotte Salomon, b: Camille Pissarro, c: Chaim Soutine, d: Marc Chagall

All of the artists were Jewish.

Romantic Poets

a: John Keats (25), e: Percy Bysshe Shelley (29), c: Lord Byron (36), b: Robert Burns (37), d: William Wordworth (80)

Space Rovers

a: Yutu, b: Curiosity, c: Sojourner (belonging to the Mars Pathfinder spacecraft), d: Lunokhod 1, e: Lunar Roving Vehicle (LRV)

8. Which female tennis competition ran from 1923 to 1989 when it was abandoned?

9. Which East German won female figure skating gold in both the 1984 and 1988 Winter Olympics?

10. Which three events constitute a triathlon?

11. Which ice skater was involved in a dispute with Tonya Harding in 1994?

12. Who was the British cyclist who died in 1967 while ascending Mont Ventoux in the Tour de France

13. Anita Lonsbrough is a famous name in which sport?

14. The conservation of which physical property explains why ice-skaters speed up when they bring their arms in whilst spinning?

15. Which tennis player was stabbed in Hamburg by a spectator?

Answers see page 311

Odd Ones Out

Can you identify which of the following sets of numbers is the odd one out?

A

313	454	262
695	727	

B

4	8	10
32	64	128

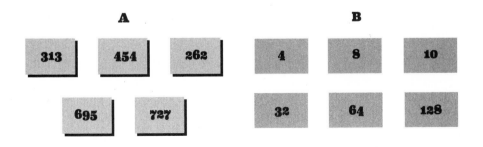

Answer see page 311

1. Rutgers is the State University of which American state?

2. In 1976, who became, at the age of 32, the youngest ever governor of his particular American state?

3. Name two slave-owning states that fought with the Union, against the Confederacy, in the American Civil War?

4. Which was the first of the Confederate states to secede from the USA?

5. Elvis Presley was born in which American state?

6. The book 'Little House on the Prairie' is set in which American state?

7. In which state is Galveston?

8. Who was governor of Alabama from 1971 to 1979?

9. Which state was the fourteenth state to join the United States?

10. The Ozarks lie in which American state?

11. In which state is Dodge City?

12. The New York Jets and New York Giants play their games in which American state?

13. In which American state is the pictured monument?

Answers see page 311

Square Solution

Find a number that could replace the question mark. Each shade represents a number.

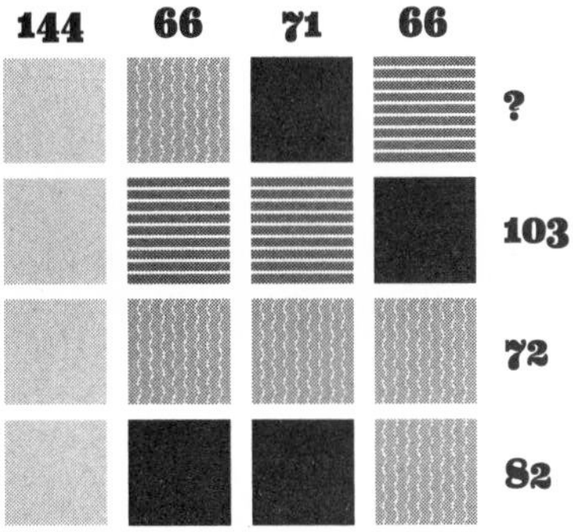

Answer see page 312

Line Up

What numbers replace the question marks?

4	7	4	9	5
8	5	1	3	6
3	7	6	?	?

Answer see page 312

1. Which type of tea is flavored with bergamot?

2. Pontefract Cakes are made from what?

3. Which coffee receives its name because its frothy milk head looked like a friar's cowl?

4. Gelato is a type of what?

5. Starbucks coffee shops are named after a character in which book?

6. What is the name of the type of sponge cake made famous by Marcel Proust and his declaration that they instantly reminded him of events in the past?

7. Which people were introduced by the British into Ceylon from India, in order to work the tea plantations?

8. Who wrote the advertising slogans 'Naughty but Nice' for cream cakes, and 'Irresistabubble' for Aero chocolate?

9. Nice biscuits, like the one pictured, are flavoured with which fruit?

10. Which port, about 80 km from Sao Paulo, is the world's leading coffee port?

11. Stracciatella is a name given to ice cream or yogurt containing pieces of what?

12. Name the ingredients of the drink called a St. Clements?

13. In 1732 Bach wrote a cantata named after which drink?

Answers see page 312

Make Up

Which of the following can be constructed using the shape below?

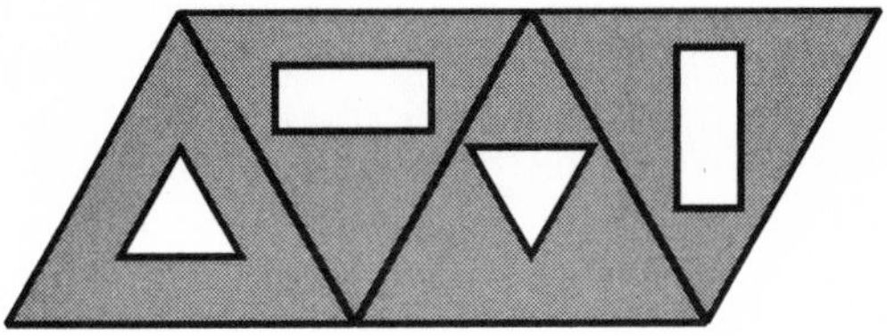

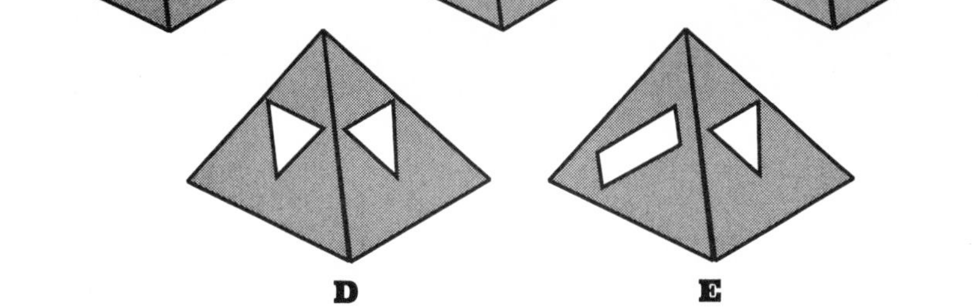

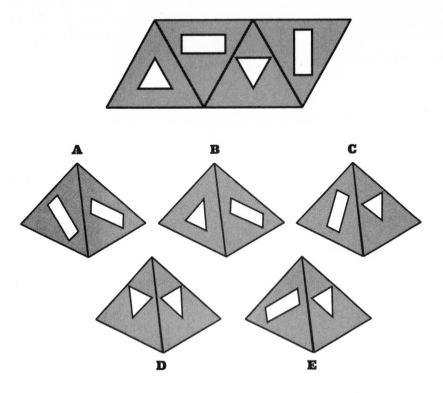

Answer see page 312

1. Which play starts with the words: 'To Begin at the Beginning'?

2. Who wrote: 'The owl and the pussycat went away in a beautiful pea-green car; in a nearby inn they had a gin, and a pound of caviar.'

3. Which character in an 18th century French play says the following: 'Just because you are a nobleman, you think you are a great genius. What have you done for such fortune? You took the trouble of being born and nothing else.'?

4. Which song begins with the words: 'I came upon a child of God'?

5. Who wrote: 'The boy stood on the burning deck. Twit.'?

6. 'All happy families are alike' are the first words of which work of fiction?

7. Which musical contains the lines: 'Everything's all right if you're all white in America'?

8. 'Arms, and the man' are the first words of which work (in a respected translation anyway)?

9. The words: 'to everything there is a season ... a time to weep, and a time to laugh' originate from where?

10. Which Neapolitan song starts with the following words in translation:

    What a beautiful thing is a sunny day,
    The air is serene after a storm
    The air's so fresh that it already feels like a celebration

11. Which song contains the lines: 'Nothing you can do that can't be done, Nothing you can sing that can't be sung'?

12. Who wrote: 'Was this the face that launched a thousand ships, and burned the topless towers of Ilium'?

13. 'Someone left the cake out in the rain' are words from which song about the pictured location?

Answers see page 312

Triangulation

The traingles below follow a certain logic. Can you discover what the question mark should be?

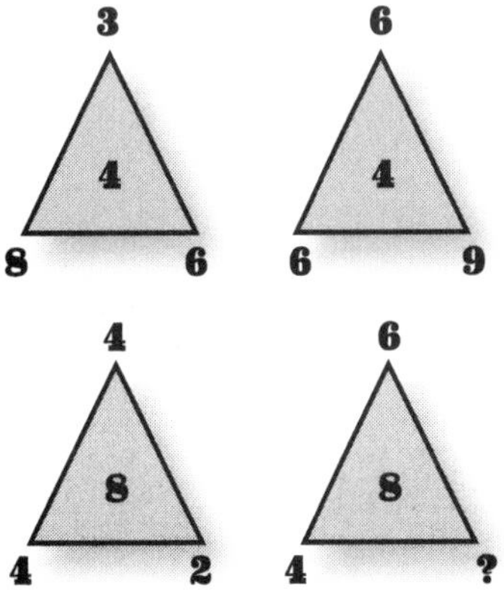

Answer see page 312

Watch this Space

Have a look at the strange watch faces below. Can you crack the logic that connects them and work out what time should be shown on the face of the fifth watch?

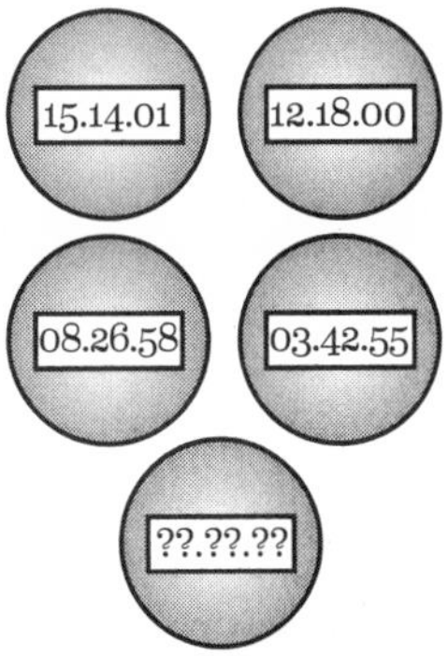

Answer see page 312

1. Which element was found in the Sun during an eclipse in 1868, before it was discovered on Earth?

2. Who was the first person to show that compressibility effects in a gas flow are not related directly to its velocity but rather to its relationship to the speed of sound?

3. Which dinosaur was discovered by Barnum Brown in 1902?

4. Thomas Young and Jean-Francois Champollion both had an interest in which object discovered in 1799?

5. Which city flourished in the Indus Valley region during the 3rd century BC and was re-discovered in 1922? It was excavated by Mortimer Wheeler from 1945 onwards.

6. What powerful explosive was not used extensively until Alfred Nobel used it to make dynamite?

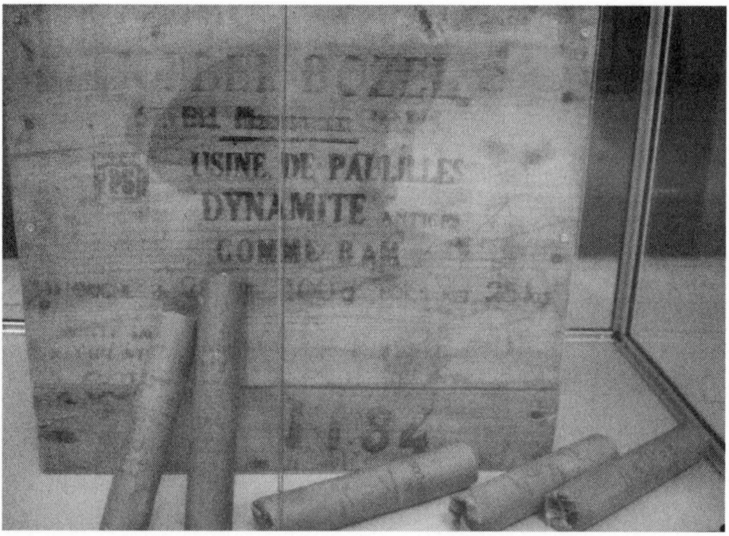

7. How did Salmonella get its name?

8. Who discovered the anesthetic properties of nitrous oxide?

9. Which invention by Trevor Bayliss has been taken on board by the South African government?

10. Erwin Schroedinger, who appears on an Austrian banknote, was a pioneer in which field, specifically?

11. Which British inventor independently invented the light bulb and consequently became involved in legal disputes with Edison?

12. Who was the author of the controversial book called, in English translation, *Revolutions of the Celestial Spheres,* which was only published at the end of his life?

13. Which residual forces between neutral molecules are named after a professor of physics at Amsterdam University?

Answers see page 312

Odd Ones Out

Which of the numbers in each set is the odd one out?

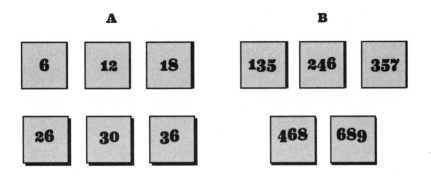

A			B		
6	**12**	**18**	**135**	**246**	**357**
26	**30**	**36**	**468**	**689**	

Answer see page 312

1. On which Pacific Island did the rule of the road change from right to left during 2009?

2. Which car was named after the person who founded Detroit in 1701?

3. The name of which type of car is also Latin for 'let it be done'?

4. Which city has a 7-km road, skirting the sea, called the Malecón?

5. Who was the worker in a plutonium factory in Oklahoma who died in a potentially-mysterious car crash in 1974?

6. What name was given to the sports car division of the Morris Car Company?

7. Which road originally marked the western border of the Roman conquests of Britain for a few decades after AD 43 (or maybe this road was built along the line of the former boundary)?

8. Which car company introduced the modern seat belt?

9. Billy Jo Spears sang the praises of which type of car specifically?

10. Which company owns the Skoda car company?

11. Which group had a hit with a record allegedly dedicated to the A555 motorway between Köln (Cologne) and Bonn?

12. Which car company was founded by August Horch. Since Horch was unable to use his own name for le-gal reasons, he used his own name translated into a different language?

13. What is the proper name for Spaghetti Junction, pictured opposite?

Answers see page 313

Square Solution

Can you work out the reasoning behind these squares and replace the question mark with a number?

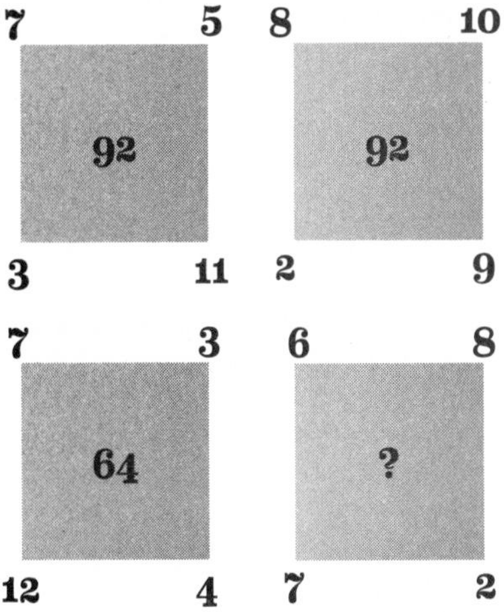

Answer see page 313

Puzzle Around

The values of the segments are 3 consecutive numbers under 10. The white segment is worth 7 and the sum of the segments equals 49. What do the grey and black segments equal?

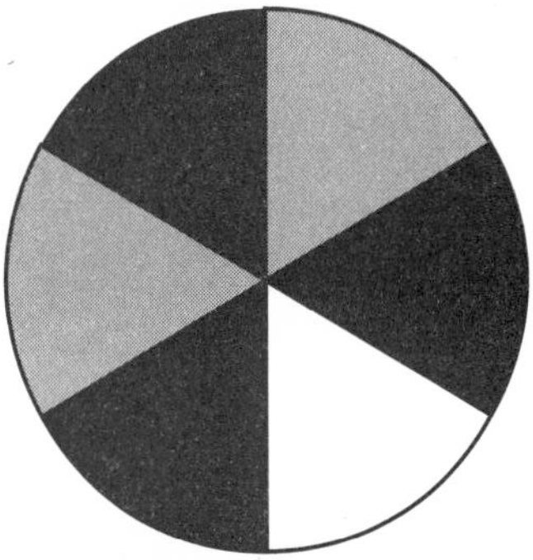

Answer see page 313

1. What was the last battle fought on English soil?

2. The Battle of Borodino took place in which country?

3. What was the last battle of the American War of Independence?

4. In which war did the Battle of Blenheim take place?

5. At which battle in 31 BC were Cleopatra and Mark Antony defeated by Augustus?

6. Which country lost the Battle of Tsushima?

7. What was the name used by the Confederates for the two battles of Bull Run?

8. Which battle was also known as Belle Alliance or Mont Saint Jean?

9. Which Irish king won the Battle of Clontarf of 1014?

10. Two battles – one a victory of Charles Martel over the Saracens, the other fought during the Hundred Years War – have the same name. What is it?

11. Who was Harold's brother who rebelled against him and was killed at the Battle of Stamford Bridge?

12. The Battle of Amphipolis of 422 BC was fought between whom?

13. Which Prussian General was defeated at the Battle of Ligny in 1815 but played a major part in the Battle of Waterloo?

14. Which alcoholic-sounding battle of 1777 in America did not go the Americans' way?

15. Which Scottish battle of 1054 resulted in a change of monarch?

16. The day before the battle of Trafalgar, the French accepted the surrender of the Austrian army in which Bavarian town?

17. Who had a vision before defeating Maxentius at the battle of Milvian Bridge?

18. Which river in Slovenia gave its name to 12 battles of the First World War, battles which form the background to Hemingway's book A Farewell to Arms?

19. The Battle of Zama took place during which war?

20. Which Confederate General, pictured here, was killed by his own troops at the Battle of Chancellorsville?

Answers see page 313

1. What type of aircraft was 'Jason', the aircraft in which Amy Johnson attempted to break the record for flying from Britain to Australia?

2. After leaving school, Stalin originally trained to follow which occupation?

3. What river is also known as the Hafren in one of the countries through which it flows?

4. Which is the only American country to appear on the United Nations's 'Least Developed Countries' list?

5. Altona, once the second-largest city in Denmark, has been reduced to being a suburb of which other city?

6. Which comedian set up the Establishment Club?

7. According to its Latin scientific name, which fruit is actually a Persian apple?

8. What unusual feature is possessed by the plant known as the Rose of Jericho?

9. Shingles is a recurrence of which childhood illness?

10. Which nebula in the Large Magellanic Cloud has a name beginning in T and alludes to an eight-legged creature?

11. When Hong Kong is referred to as Hong Kong S.A.R., what does S.A.R. stand for?

12. Which of the Mitford Sisters married Oswald Mosley?

13. What note has four times the length of a crochet?

14. Why is the highest peak in Australia named after a Pole?

15. What is a boomslang?

16. Joan, the daughter of King John married whom, establishing a line which would later take over the throne?

17. Which animal character is tricked by a fox into gathering together the ingredients of stuffing?

18. What was the name of the Paranoid Android?

19. You would use a 'Sicilian Defense' in which activity?

20. What is the surname of the Icelandic singer pictured below?

Answers see page 313

1. According to a poll run by the BBC's African Service, who was the African of the Millennium?

2. Which city in Queensland has the same name as a former colony in Africa?

3. Name one of the three main tribes in Nigeria?

4. Azania was a name planned by some to be the new name of which African country?

5. Which area of the Congo proclaimed itself an independent country 11 days after the Congo was itself granted independence by Belgium?

6. What was set up as the capital of the South African Republic in 1860?

7. Which Portuguese trader visited present-day Mozambique in 1544 and had a town named after him in the 18th century?

8. What is the name of the low-lying area, some of it be-low sea level, which is spread across Ethiopia, Somalia, Eritrea and Djbouti?

9. The Polisario movement fights for the independence of which land?

10. Which company was set up by Ernest Oppenheimer and became one of the world's largest companies via its interests in mining in Southern Africa?

11. Where was Fashoda, scene of an imperialist incident at the end of the Nineteenth Century?

12. Which country is sometimes currently referred to as 'The Rainbow Nation'?

13. What was the name of the first X-ray satellite, pictured here? It was launched off Kenya and was given the Swahili word for 'freedom'.

Answers see page 314

Triangle Teaser

Work out the three missing numbers in the third triangle.

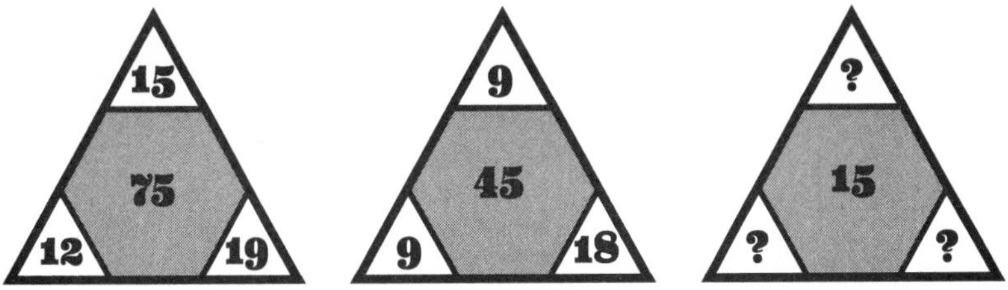

Answer see page 314

1. Which animal has a name in English which derives from the Spanish for 'the lizard'?

2. What is a Natterjack?

3. What animal has a named derived from the Greek for 'Earth Lion'?

4. Which is the world's largest lizard?

5. What type of animal is a hamadryad?

6. Chicxulub, site of the meteor strike currently believed by many to have caused the dinosaur extinction, is in which country?

7. What is the forename of Crocodile Dundee?

8. What is the name of Kermit's nephew?

9. In Australia, what type of animal is known as a 'saltie'?

10. Which poisonous lizard, one of only two in the world, lives in the deserts of Utah and Nevada, among other places?

11. What is a Gavial?

12. Which promontory contains a large amount of the type of rock called 'serpentine' which occurs nowhere else in England?

13. An Apatosaurus is the current name for a dinosaur previously known by what name?

Answers see page 314

Stars

Use six straight lines to divide the diagram into seven sections containing 1, 2, 3, 4, 5, 6, and 7 stars, respectively. The lines always touch one edge of the box, but not necessarily two.

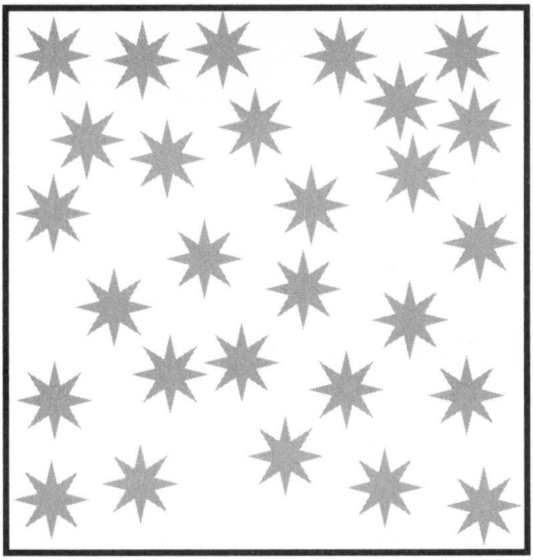

Answer see page 315

1. What does APB stand for?

2. In computing, what does ASCII stand for?

3. What does 'NICE' stand for, as in reports that the Nice Decade is coming to an end?

4. With respect to pensions, what does AVC stand for?

5. What does the 'K' in K-FOR stand for?

6. In a library what does the acronym OPAC stand for in full?

7. What does CCD stand for?

8. Computing – what does the abbreviation USB in USB cable stand for?

9. In banking, what does ATM stand for?

10. What does VHS stand for?

11. Certain rights of way are designated as being a BOAT. What does this stand for?

12. What does 'pH' mean, as in the scale indicating acidity/baseness?

13. What does FIFA stand for?

Answers see page 314

Odd Ones Out

Which is the odd one out?

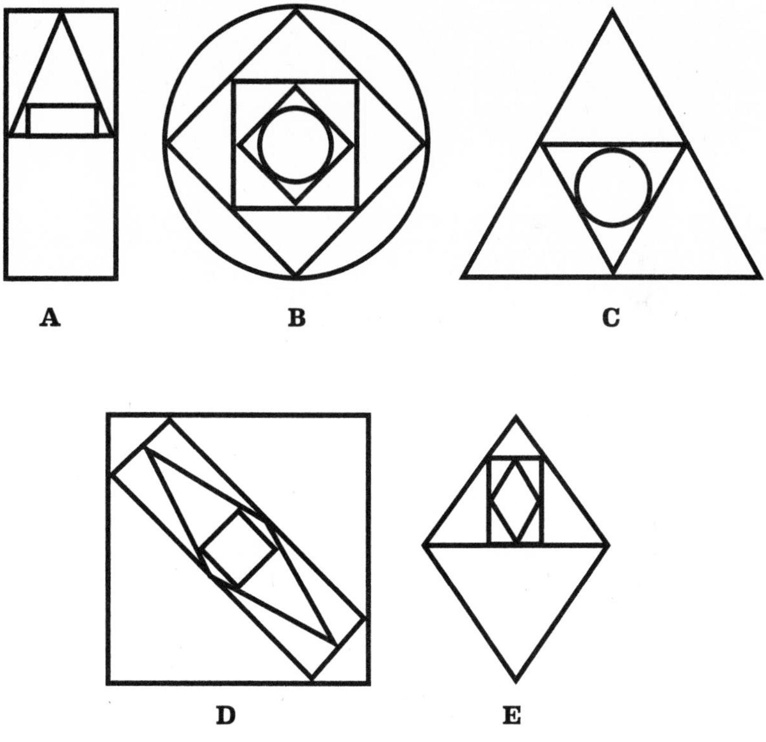

Answer see page 315

1. Who was the second president of the Weimar Republic?

2. Which surname was shared by the French Prime Minister at the time that French troops occupied the Ruhr, and a famous French mathematician?

3. Who was president of Mexico when Napoleon III invaded the country, an invasion which lead to the installation of the Austrian Maximilian?

4. Douglas Hyde was the first president of which country?

5. Which country has had a president called Sarney?

6. Golda Meir, prime minister of Israel, was born in which present-day country?

7. What was the forename of President Perón who was removed by a military coup in 1976?

8. Who was the first president of the French Second Republic?

9. In which country was a female elected head of state succeeded by another female elected head of state, for the first time?

10. Who was elected leader of Liberia in 1997?

11. Which president of Afghanistan was executed by the Taliban in 1996?

12. Who was the first president of Cyprus, remaining in office until 1975?

13. As pictured opposite, who was Grevy, the person who gave his name to Grevy's zebra?

Answers see page 315

Missing Number

Which two numbers should replace the question marks?

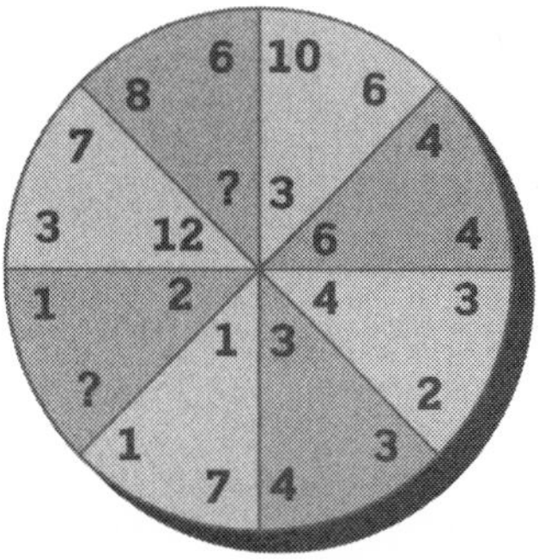

Answer see page 315

Symbol Value

Which two boxes in the diagram have similar contents?

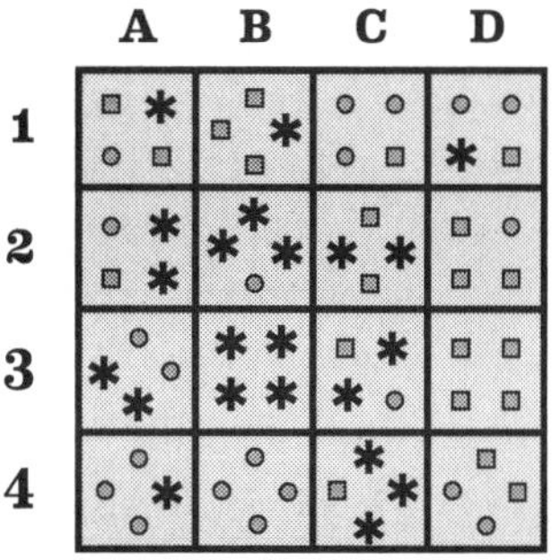

Answer see page 315

1. Which paper would you associate with CP Scott?

2. For what reason did Bruce Ismay incur the continual wrath of various newspapers, particularly those owned by Hearst?

3. Which paper was founded in 1912 and transferred to the ownership of Trades Union Congress in 1922?

4. The 'underground' magazine often referred to as IT, which was prosecuted during Edward Heath's premiership, was known as what under its full name?

5. Which political figure is a major shareholder in *Novaya Gazeta* and helped set the paper up in the first place?

6. In Evelyn Waugh's *Scoop*, William Boot worked for which paper?

7. Who was described by *Private Eye* magazine as 'The Bouncing Czech'?

8. Which daily paper has the same name as a term used to describe a particular planet of the solar system?

9. When the Russian Interior Minister, Pleve, was assassinated by a bomb thrown through the window of his moving coach in 1904, the *Chicago News* printed a contentious off-hand piece stating that the assailant should be tracked down as soon as possible and made to do what?

10. Name the journalist fired from the *New York Times* in 2003 for filing false stories?

11. Which press baron bought St. Donat's Castle in South Wales?

12. When was the *Guardian* newspaper founded and what was it called??

Neue Rheinische Zeitung.
Organ der Demokratie.

13. Who was the editor of the pictured 'Rheinische Zeitung' newspaper in 1843 when it was shut down by the Prussian Government?

Answers see page 315

Brain Twister

Which of the labelled shapes completes a diamond when fitted with the shape below?

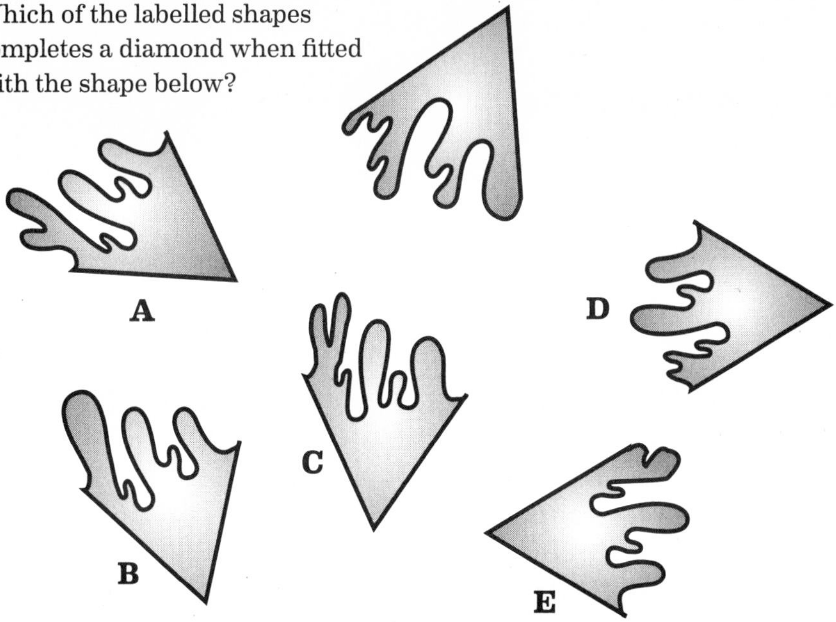

Answer see page 315

1. Which author was also an aeronautical engineer under his proper surname of Norway?

2. Who wrote *All Quiet on the Western Front*?

3. Which author was the elder brother of Thomas Mann?

4. What pen name was adopted by the author born as Alexei Peshkov?

5. Which Irish author was the business manager for English actor Sir Henry Irving, joining him in the management of the Lyceum Theatre?

6. Who was the author of the original book *The Phantom of the Opera*?

7. Simone de Beauvoir was the partner of which author?

8. Which author would you associate with Nora Barnacle?

9. Who was the author of the book 'Small is beautiful'?

10. The father of which author was the son of a Haitian slave but rose to become a General in the French Army at the age of 31?

11. Which Belgian author announced in 1933 that he was giving up writing, and set off for a short visit to Odessa?

12. What was the nationality by birth of the author of *The Scarlet Pimpernel*?

13. This illustration comes from *Birds of America*, which first appeared in 1827. Who created it?

Answers see page 315

1. Alan Bennett's *An Englishman Abroad.* Where exactly was 'abroad' in this play?

2. In which country is the play *Playboy of the Western World* set?

3. Nora Helmer is the heroine of which Ibsen play?

4. In the play *Danton's Death,* who is described as the 'lawyer from Arras'?

5. Which play features the character No-good Boyo?

6. The play *Copenhagen* by Michael Frayn deals with which subject?

7. In a play by Oscar Wilde, by what name was Algernon Moncrieff's Aunt Augusta known to most of the other characters?

8. Which story about a friendship between a slave and a wild animal was adapted into a play by George Bernard Shaw?

9. Who wrote the set of plays *The Norman Conquests*?

10. In Bertolt Brecht's play *Galileo* who is continually referred to as the 'burnt man'?

11. The musical *Boys from Syracruse* is based on which play?

12. According to Pierre Corneille's play *El Cid,* who is the father of El Cid?

13. The newspaper *Le Figaro* – under its name the paper always carries a quote by which playwright, pictured here?

Answers see page 316

Matchpoints

By taking away four matches from this diagram leave eight small squares.

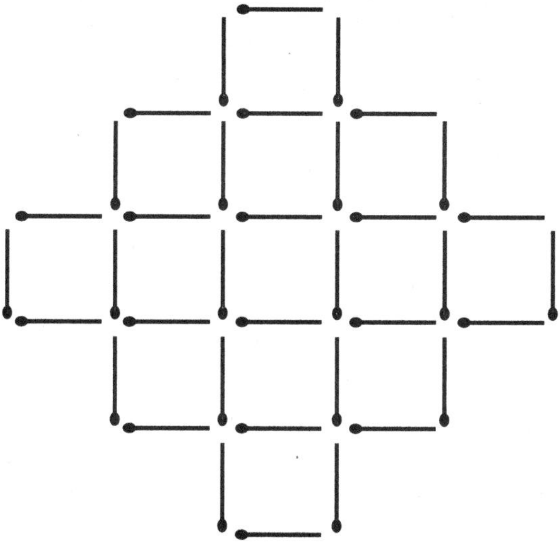

Answer see page 316

1. Who built the Menai Suspension Bridge?

2. In 1908, locomotive no 224 travelled over the Tay Bridge, the first time it had done this for about 30 years because the drivers had refused to take the engine over the bridge. What was the reasoning behind the drivers' attitude?

3. The Tyne Bridge has become one of the most inland nesting locations of which seabird?

4. Where is the most popular place in the world for committing suicide by falling from a height (i.e. place with the most incidents)?

5. Upstream of Arnhem, the Rhine splits into the Niederrhein and the Waal. The Allies failed to take Arnhem Bridge over the Niederrhein in Operation Market Garden, where was the bridge over the Waal that they did manage to capture

6. Which is the oldest bridge in Florence?

7. This is the Oresund bridge – which two countries are separated by it?

8. Which is the first bridge traversed by runners in the New York Marathon?

9. Where can you find the Ha'Penny Bridge?

10. Which British city has a name derived from an expression for 'place at a bridge'?

11. Leonardo drew up proposed designs for the Galata Bridge, and Michaelangelo was also asked to design the bridge. Which stretch of water is crossed by the Galata Bridge?

12. The Tacoma Narrows Bridge is famous for what event in 1940?

13. Who escaped over the Brig O'Doon (i.e. the old bridge over the Doon)?

Answers see page 316

Odd One Out

Why is D is the odd one out?

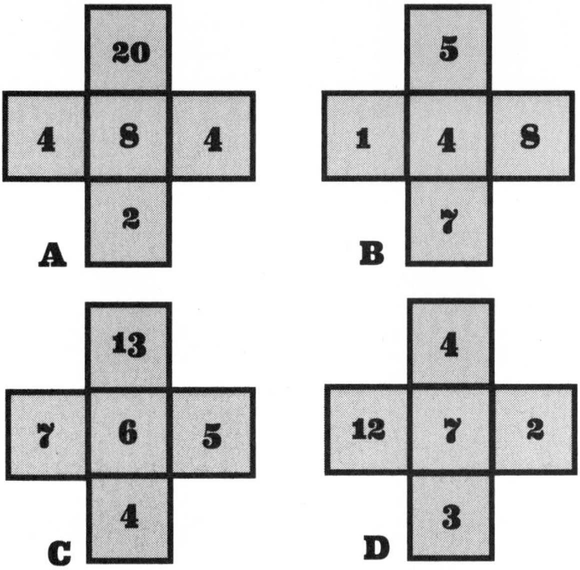

Answer see page 316

1. What name is shared by an Irish head of government and an Apollo astronaut?

2. Apart from James Lovell, name one of the other two astronauts on Apollo 13

3. Who was the commander of Apollo 14?

4. What was the name of the rocket which was intended to be launched by the USA as a response to Sputnik, but which exploded on the launch pad?

5. On which mission did three cosmonauts die?

6. At what time of year in 1968 was Apollo 8 orbiting the moon?

7. Which rocket powered the Apollo 11 mission into space?

Mensa uses a range of certified industry-standard IQ tests to analyse applicants. Great care is taken to ensure that these tests are standardized, and it is common for IQ tests to strongly feature abstract reasoning challenges. The tests that you will find in this section attempt to draw on some of the same types of abstract reasoning that you will encounter in IQ tests.

The goal here is to have fun, of course. Afterwards, if you're not already a member, why not get a practice test from Mensa and get an estimate of how you'd do at one of our supervised IQ tests?

Pick a Pattern

Which option A to E most accurately completes the pattern?

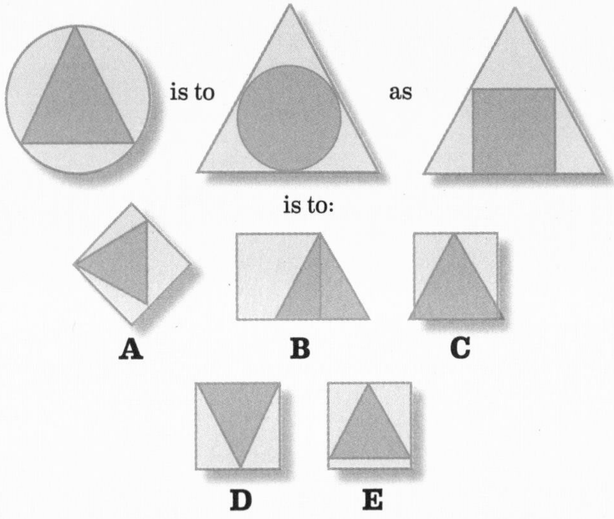

Triangle Teaser

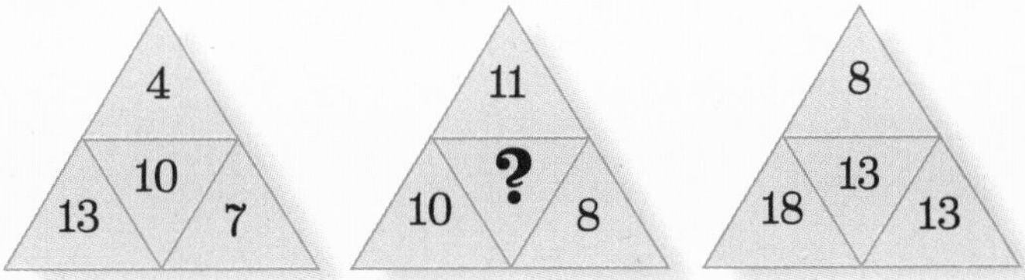

Answers at the back of this section

Hidden Pattern

Shade the cells in the grid below so that each row and column holds continuous lines of shaded cells of the lengths indicated by the numbers shown at the start of that row or column. Blocks are separated from others in the same row or column by at least one empty cell. A picture will emerge when the cells are shaded correctly.

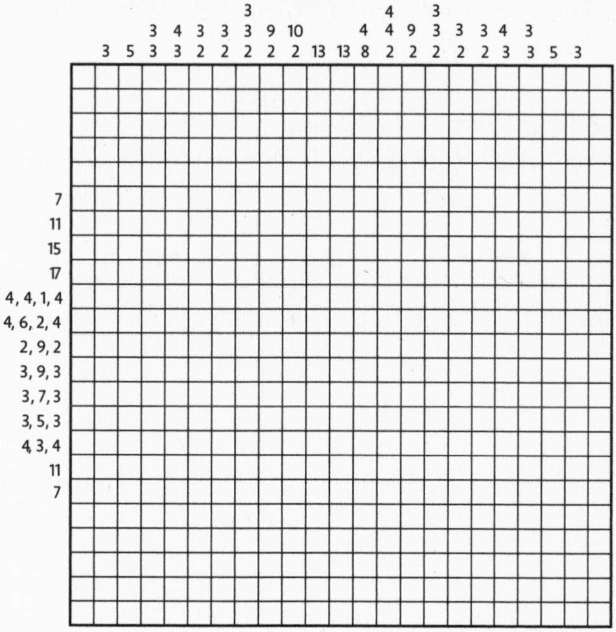

Sudoku Challenge

Complete the grid below so that every row, column, and 3x3 square each contains the digits 1-9 precisely once.

	3				5	8	9	
	8			4				
					7		5	2
		5					6	
4				6				1
	2					4		
2	6		8					
				1			8	
	4	8	9				3	

Tile Teaser

Complete the grid below so that each unbroken horizontal and vertical stretch of light cells sums to the total indicated in the cell to the left or above the stretch respectively. Each cell may contain only the digits 1–9, and no digit may be repeated in any given stretch of cells.

Off Balance

What number should replace the question mark to balance the beam?

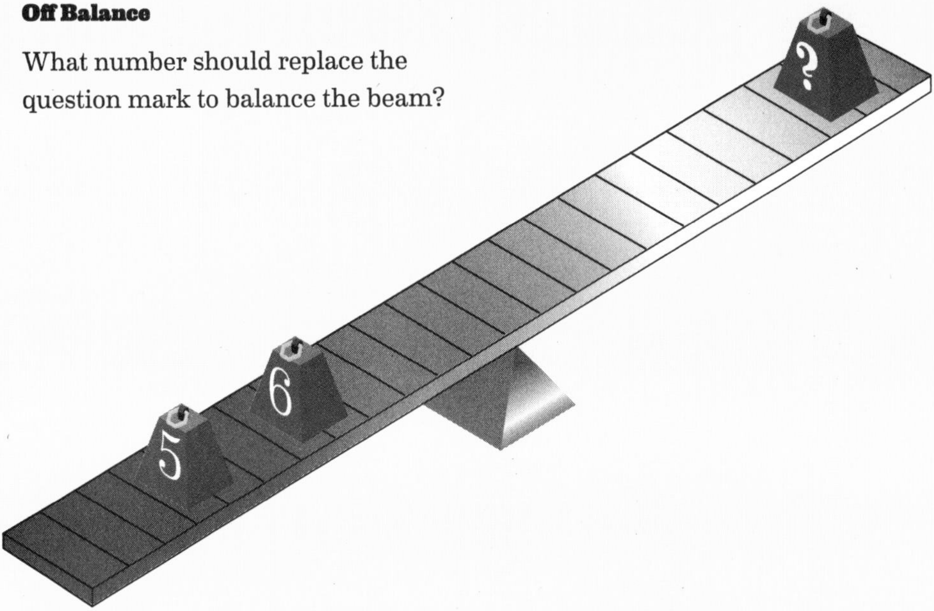

Answers at the back of this section

Find the Sign

Fill in the missing plus, minus, multiplication and division signs to make the equation below correct, performing all calculations strictly in the order they appear on the page.

28 38 41 5 6 5 = 55

Tricky Triangles

Use eleven straight lines to divide the field below into eight sections, each containing nine triangles, which must include at least one of each orientation of triangle.

Cube Crisis

Which of the cubes A to E cannot be made using the layout shown?

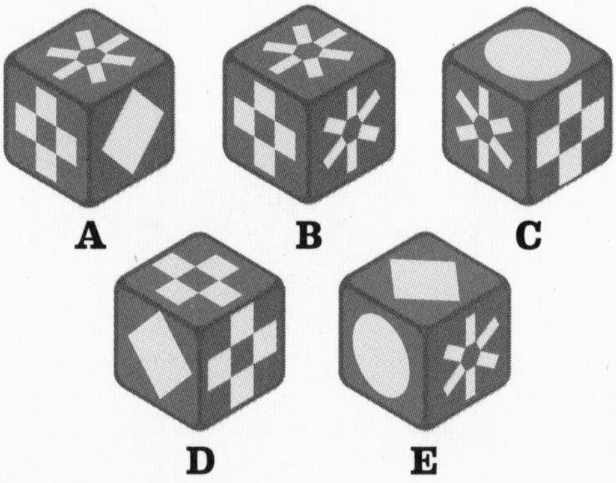

Pick the Shapes

Which option A to E most accurately completes the pattern?

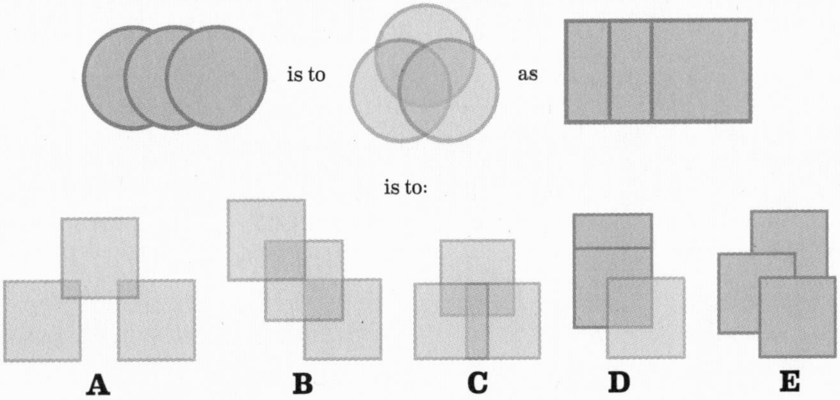

Crossword Numbers

Fit the numbers shown into the design to complete the grid.

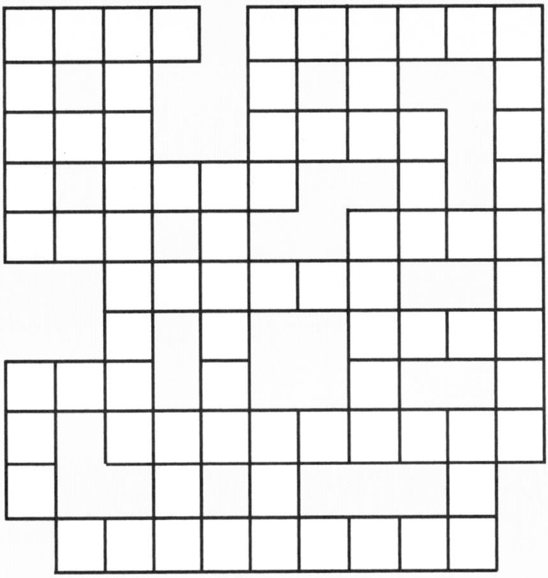

3 digits
187
434
471
478
495
792
814
851
875

4 digits
1662
2599
5917
7424
8113
9879

5 digits
16871
88584

6 digits
862098
902091
907063

9 digits
371837789
541484449
625278445
818354914

Answers at the back of this section

Battleship Hunt

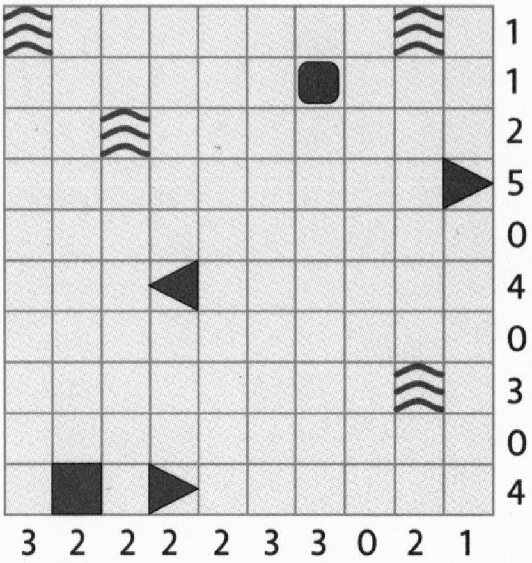

Ten vessels are hidden in the grid below, four one cell ships, three two-cell ships, two three-cell ships, and one four-cell ship. Ships are positioned horizontally or vertically. No two ships are immediately adjacent to each other, including diagonally. The numbers next to each row and column show the total number of ship segments in that line. Identify the exact locations of all ten vessels. Some ship segments and/or spaces of empty ocean are shown to assist you.

Shape Sums

In the grid below, how much is each symbol worth?

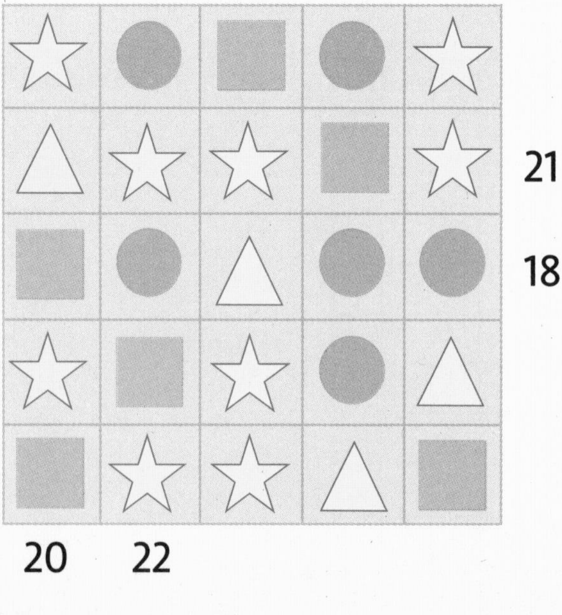

Arrow Direction

In each square, the arrow shows the direction you must move in. The numbers in some squares show that square's position in the correct sequence of moves. Move from top left to bottom right, visiting each square in the grid exactly once.

Finish the Sum

What number should replace the question mark?

Circlular Dilemma

What number should replace the question mark?

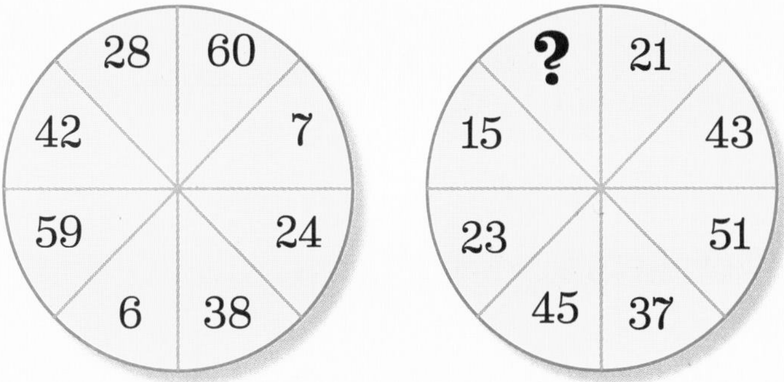

Answers at the back of this section

Pick a Pattern

Which of the designs A to E is the odd one out?

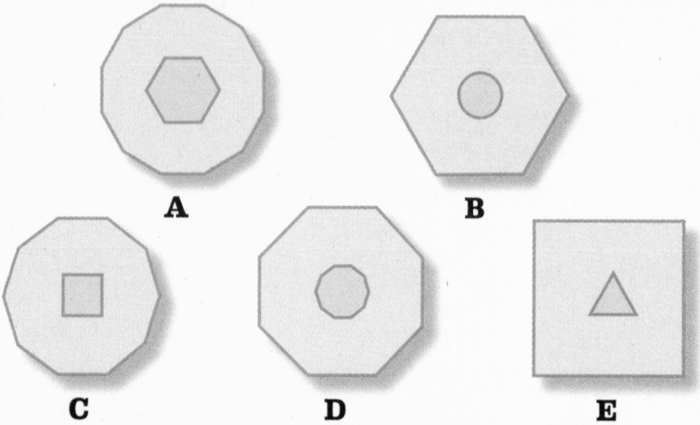

Missing Numbers

What numbers should replace the question marks?

4	1	3	2	0	6
9	5	8	5	4	4
6	5	4	?	?	?

Around the Clock

What time should the second clock in the sequence of four indicate?

Find the Sign

Fill in the missing plus, minus, multiplication, division, and/or factorial signs to make the equation below correct, performing all calculations strictly in the order they appear on the page.

All Square

What number should replace the question mark?

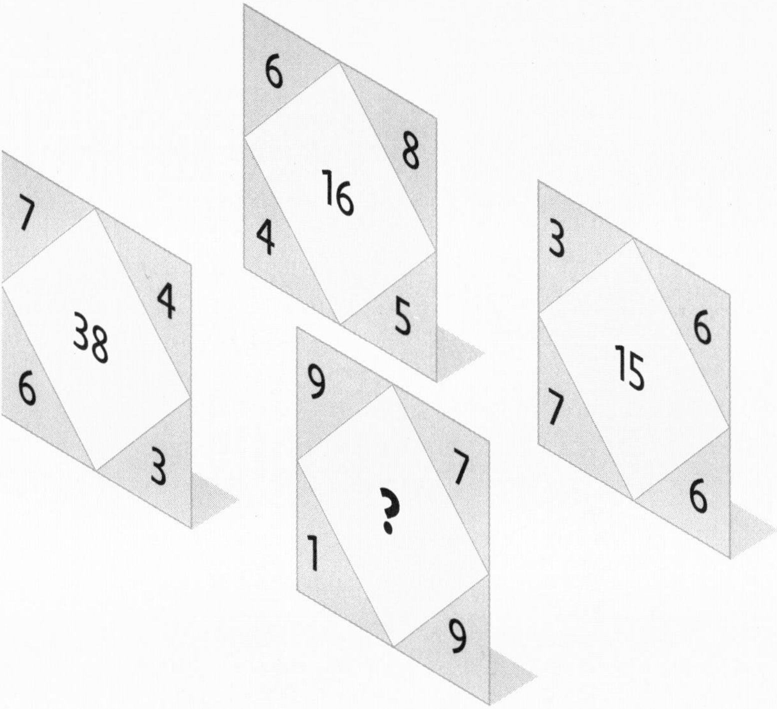

Answers at the back of this section

Sudoku Challenge

	3					2	4	
	2	4		3	5		6	
			4					
		6	2			9	3	
2			1		3			5
	3	5			9	6		
					6			
	6		9	7		3	1	
	9	2			8			

Complete the grid below so that every row, column, and 3x3 square each contains the digits 1–9 precisely once.

Battleship Hunt

Ten vessels are hidden in the grid below, four one cell ships, three two-cell ships, two three-cell ships, and one four-cell ship. Ships are positioned horizontally or vertically. No two ships are immediately adjacent to each other, including diagonally. The numbers next to each row and column show the total number of ship segments in that line. Identify the exact locations of all ten vessels. Some ship segments and/or spaces of empty ocean are shown to assist you.

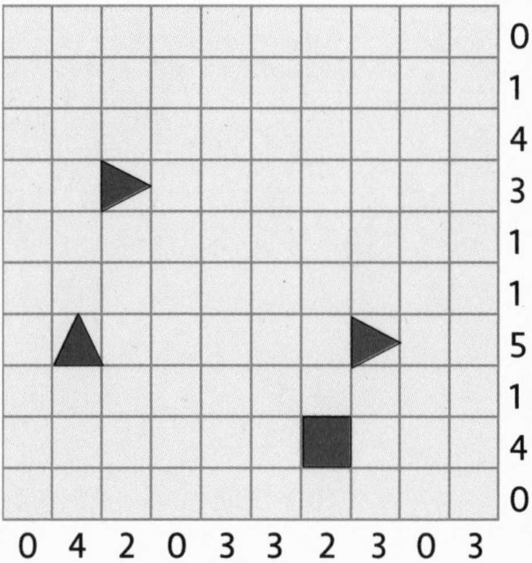

Shape Sum

In the grid below, how much is each symbol worth?

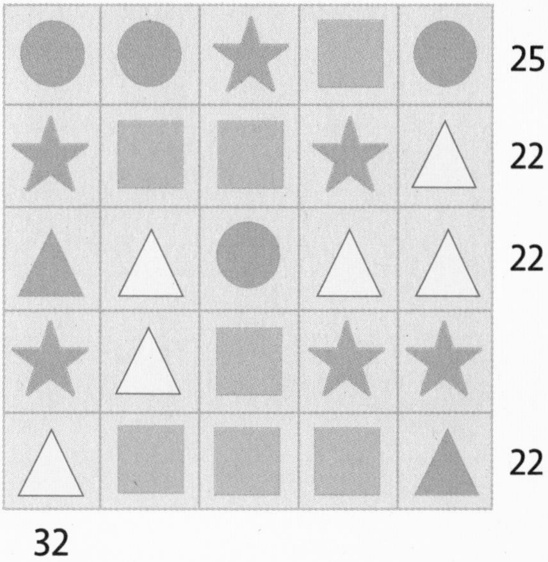

Square Solution

Which of the cubes A to E can be made using the layout shown?

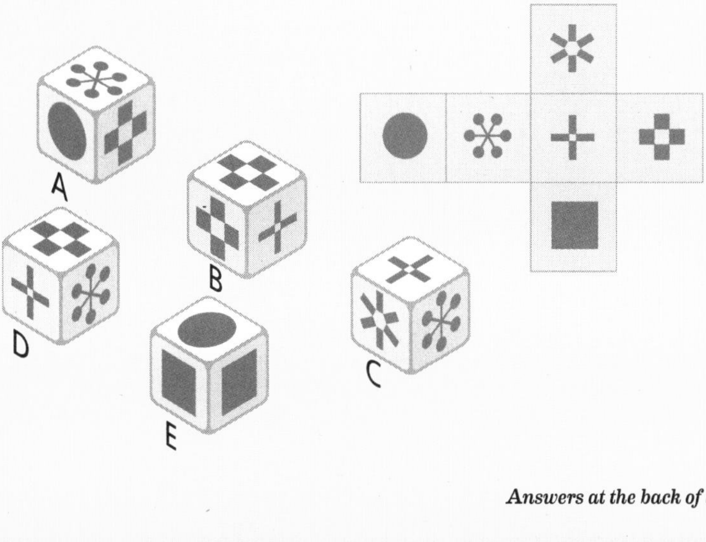

Answers at the back of this section

Around the Clock

What time should the final clock indicate?

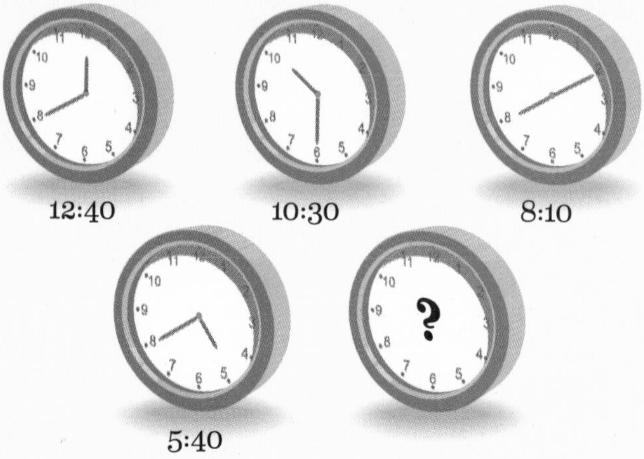

Tricky Squares

Use four straight lines to divide the field below into six sections each containing 16 squares, at least one of which must be of each colour.

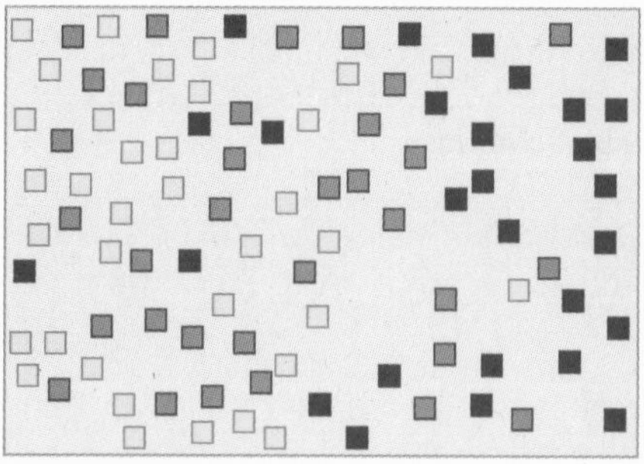

Tricky Triangles

What number should replace the question mark?

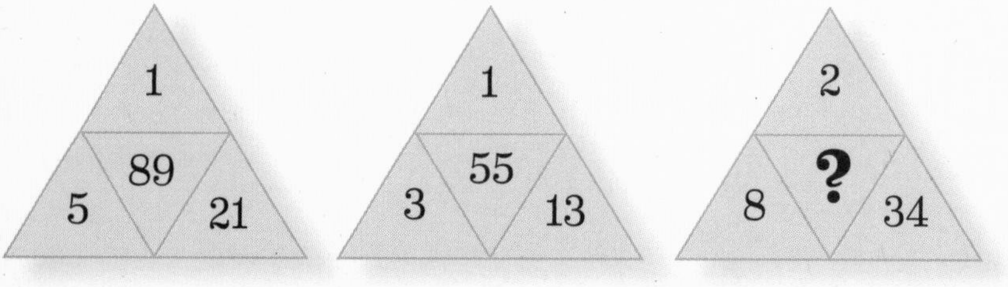

Tricky Tiles

Complete the grid below so that each unbroken horizontal and vertical stretch of light cells sums to the total indicated in the cell to the left or above the stretch respectively. Each cell may contain only the digits 1–9, and no digit may be repeated in any given stretch of cells.

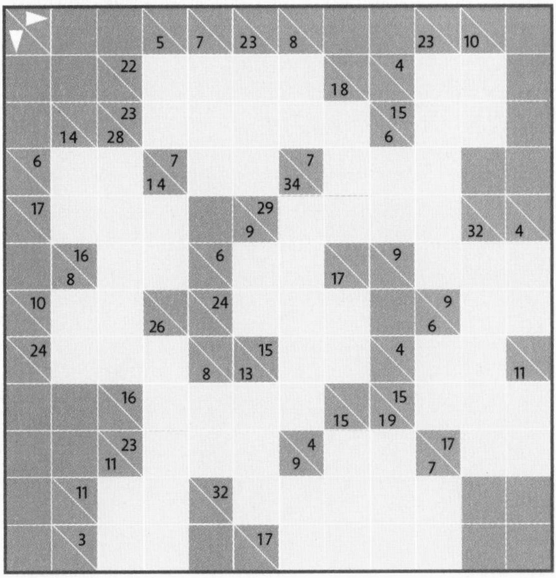

Domino Dilemma

The grid below shows the numbers on a full set of dominoes, from 0–0 to 9–9 inclusive, that have been pushed together horizontally and vertically to make a solid rectangle. Complete the grid to show where each domino lies.

5	3	3	5	9	2	0	7	4	1	4
6	4	6	9	5	8	2	1	4	6	4
7	1	8	7	2	2	7	3	5	6	9
8	6	8	3	2	0	0	1	5	9	4
8	8	2	0	8	9	6	2	5	3	2
3	5	7	4	6	0	6	2	3	9	7
3	0	9	1	9	3	1	3	6	6	1
5	0	4	1	0	6	8	0	7	3	8
2	7	7	0	1	0	4	7	4	8	2
5	1	7	5	9	1	4	5	9	9	8

Answers at the back of this section

Pyramid Plot

Two faces, on separate cubes, show identical symbols.

To which cubes do they belong?

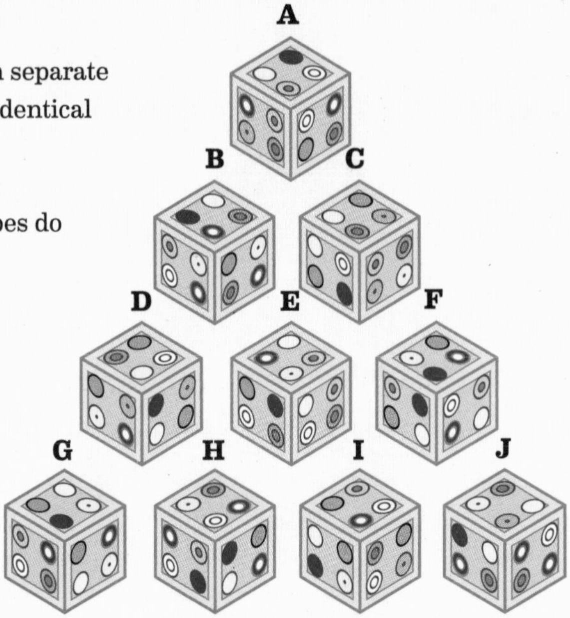

Missing Numbers

Complete the grid below so that each number shown forms part of a group of horizontally and/or vertically connected cells. The number of cells in the group must be the same as the number shown on the grid. So a '2' indicates a group that is a pair of two cells. No group shares a horizontal or vertical boundary with another group of the same size/number. Every group of cells has at least one number shown.

	4	2	3						2
			8		4	4			8
	2	8				7	7	8	
			8	5				7	
	2	9				7		9	
4	4							8	
6								7	
		5	5	3	7			2	4
4	4		5		2				
				2					5

Pick a Pattern

E.

Triangle Teaser

11+10-8 = 13.

Hidden Pattern

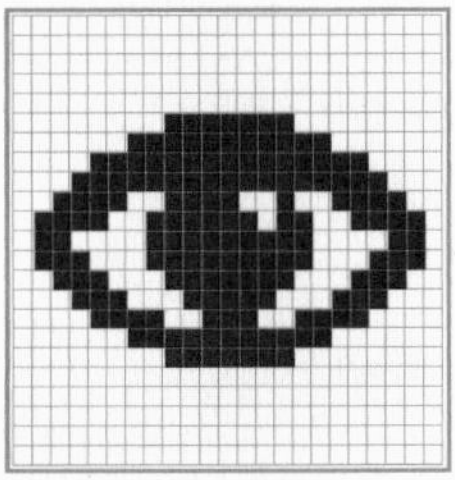

Sudoku Challenge

6	3	7	1	2	5	8	9	4
5	8	2	6	4	9	7	1	3
9	1	4	3	8	7	6	5	2
1	7	5	2	9	4	3	6	8
4	9	3	7	6	8	5	2	1
8	2	6	5	3	1	4	7	9
2	6	1	8	7	3	9	4	5
3	5	9	4	1	6	2	8	7
7	4	8	9	5	2	1	3	6

Tile Teaser

Off Balance

7.

Find the Sign

28+38-41/5+6*5 = 55.

Tricky Triangles

(one possible solution)

Cube Crisis

C.

Pick the Shapes

C. (All three shapes overlap).

Crossword Numbers

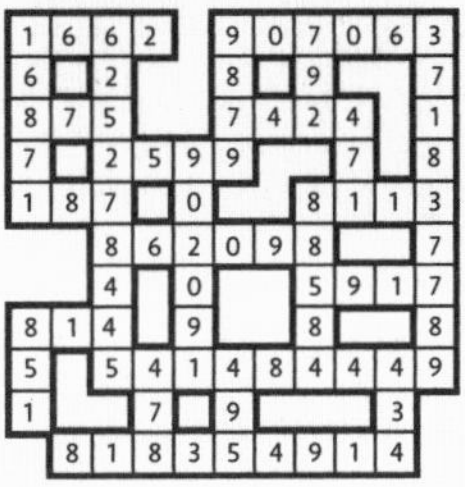

Battleship Hunt

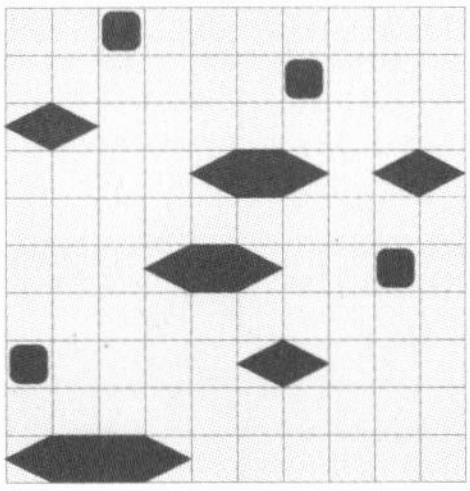

Shape Sums

▲ = 2, ■ = 4, ● = 4, ★ = 5.

Arrow Direction

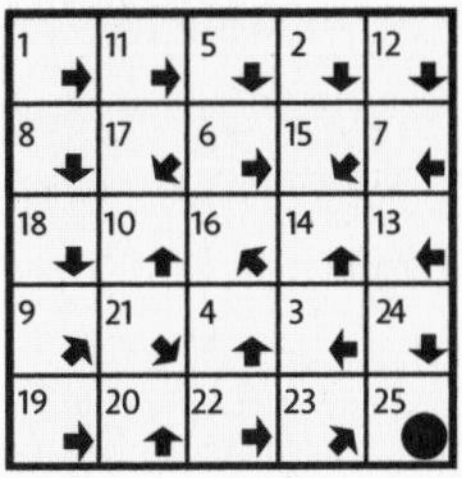

Finish the Sum

56. (For each position number n in the sequence, value is n^2 + n).

Circular Dilemma

29. (Each segment plus the opposite segment adds to total 66, so 29 + 37 = 66).

Pick a Pattern

D. (Shape inside has greater number of sides.)

Missing Numbers

(2*5) = 10. (0*4) = 0. (6*4) = 24.

Taking final units = **0 0 4**.

Around the Clock

4:20. (8/2 = 4, 40/2 = 20.)

Test Your IQ Answers

Find the Sign

20+1*23/7-16*20/4 = 265

All Square

(9*1)-7 = **2.**

Sudoku Challenge

8	5	3	6	9	1	2	4	7
9	2	4	7	3	5	1	6	8
6	1	7	4	2	8	5	9	3
4	8	6	2	5	7	9	3	1
2	7	9	1	6	3	4	8	5
1	3	5	8	4	9	6	7	2
3	4	1	5	8	6	7	2	9
5	6	8	9	7	2	3	1	4
7	9	2	3	1	4	8	5	6

Battleship Hunt

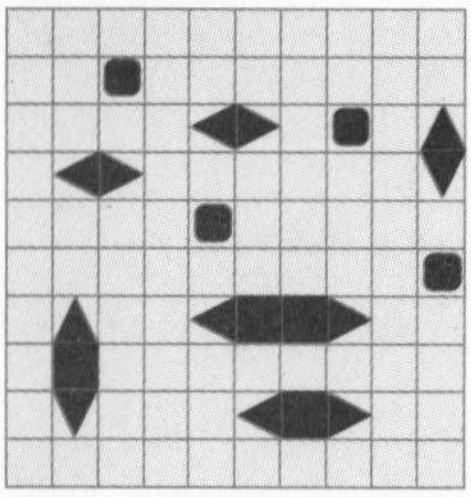

Shape Sum

▲ = 2, ■ = 3, ● = 5,

★ = 7, ▲ = 11

Square Solution

C.

Around the Clock

3:00. The clocks are turned back by an increasing 10 minutes each iteration, with the first reduction being 130 minutes.

Tricky Squares

(one possible solution)

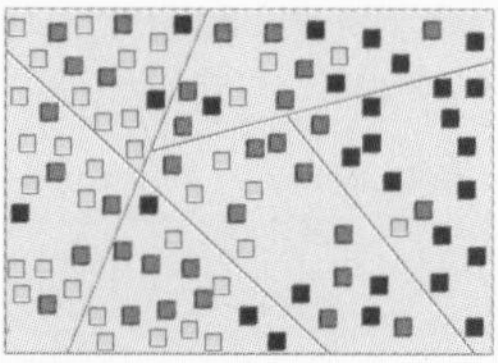

Tricky Triangles

144. (Numbers are Fibonacci sequence running centre, to left, to right along top, then bottom left corner, then bottom right corner, and finally centre)

Tricky Tiles

Domino Dilemma

5	3	3	5	9	2	0	7	4	1	4
6	4	6	9	5	8	2	1	4	6	4
7	1	8	7	2	2	7	3	5	6	9
8	6	8	3	2	0	0	1	5	9	4
8	8	2	0	8	9	6	2	5	3	2
3	5	7	4	6	0	6	2	3	9	7
3	0	9	1	9	3	1	3	6	6	1
5	0	4	1	0	6	8	0	7	3	8
2	7	7	0	1	0	4	7	4	8	2
5	1	7	5	9	1	4	5	9	9	8

Pyramid Plot

B (top) & **J** (left).

Missing Numbers

4	4	2	3	3	3	4	4	2	2
4	4	2	8	8	4	4	7	8	8
2	2	8	8	5	5	7	7	8	8
8	8	8	8	5	5	7	7	7	8
2	2	9	9	9	5	7	9	9	8
4	4	4	4	9	9	9	9	8	8
6	6	6	6	3	7	7	7	7	7
6	6	5	5	3	7	7	2	2	4
4	4	5	5	3	2	2	4	4	4
4	4	5	2	2	5	5	5	5	5

8. Where on the moon did Apollo 11 land?

9. Who was the first person to engage in a spacewalk?

10. In which spacecraft did Grissom, White and Chaffee die due to fire?

11. Who did the cosmonaut Andriyan Nikolayev marry?

12. Name one of the two astronauts who nearly lost their lives when Gemini 8 went out of control?

13. For what sort of mission was Apollo 18 used (it had nothing to do with Moon)?

14. When Apollo spacecraft split into two whilst in lunar orbit, each separate craft adopted call names. Give one of the names adopted by the two parts of Apollo 10 when it split up.

15. Who was the commander of the Challenger shuttle mission that suffered the fatal explosion?

Answers see page 316

Round the Dial

The circles of letters below contain the names of three works of literature (one French, one from the Middle East, one American). Can you unravel them?

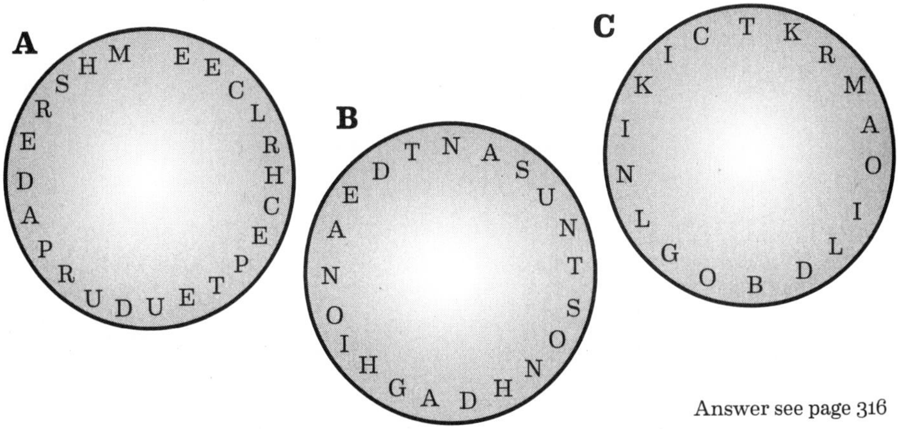

Answer see page 316

1. The 'Little Blue' is the smallest type and the 'Emperor' is the largest type of what living creature?

2. Who was the 'sea-green incorruptible'?

3. Which city is sometimes referred to as the 'Big Orange'?

4. The Golden Hamster stems originally from which country?

5. Which group did Ritchie Blackmore form after leaving Deep Purple (both times)?

6. Who stands on a column in Newcastle, erected to honour his part in the First Reform Bill?

7. At the end of *The Pink Panther*, who was convicted and imprisoned for being the Phantom, the person responsible for stealing the said jewel?

8. What is a *Porterhouse Blue*, in Tom Sharpe's novel of the same name?

9. Which city derives its name from the Celtic words for 'green valley'?

10. In which country would you find the 'White Sausage Boundary'?

11. What was the first name of the Black Prince?

12. Storeyville was the red-light district of which town?

13. According to its Latin name, where does a brown rat come from?

14. What role did Marlene Dietrich, pictured here, play in *The Blue Angel*?

Answers see page 317

Round the Dial

Time is moving strangely again on these clocks. What time should the fourth clock show?

Answer see page 317

Timed Puzzle

These clocks move in a certain pattern. Can you work out the time on the last clock?

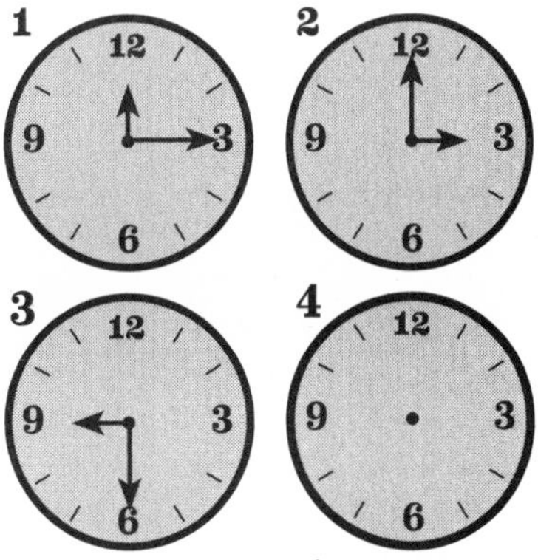

Answer see page 317

1. Which Irish scientist formulated the law that relates the pressure and volume of an ideal gas at constant temperature?

2. Faraday initially became an assistant to which other scientist at the Royal Institution?

3. Which element has a name derived from the Greek for 'producing acid' because it was wrongly believed that all acids contained it?

4. The Swiss physicist Johann Balmer studied the spectrum of which substance in the 1880s, producing the eponymous Balmer series?

5. 'Standing on the Shoulders of Giants' is an expression connected with Isaac Newton. Where would British people see this expression in a more everyday setting?

6. Which physicist, seen here, was a pioneer in using X-rays to establish atomic structure, before being killed in Gallipoli in 1915?

7. In which town or city did Einstein attend university?

8. Which astronomer and scientist was a scientific advisor to Tsar Peter I when the latter spent some time in England (as well as being an important drinking companion, if the stories are to be believed)?

9. Which steel process was discovered by Benjamin Huntsman in 1740, a process commemorated in the name of a theatre in Sheffield?

10. The Law of the Conservation of Energy is identical to which engineering law?

11. Name the two companies involved in developing the compact disk and bringing it on to the market?

12. In which university of the Venetian state did Galileo teach?

13. Maria Sklodowski, born in 1867, became well-known in which field?

Answers see page 317

Brain Twister

Which of the following comes next in the sequence?

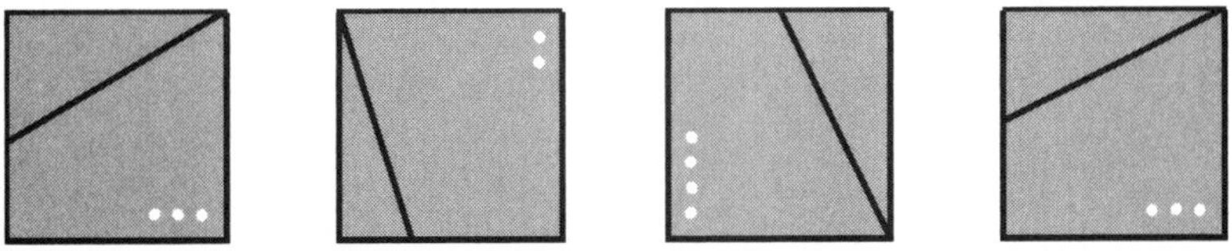

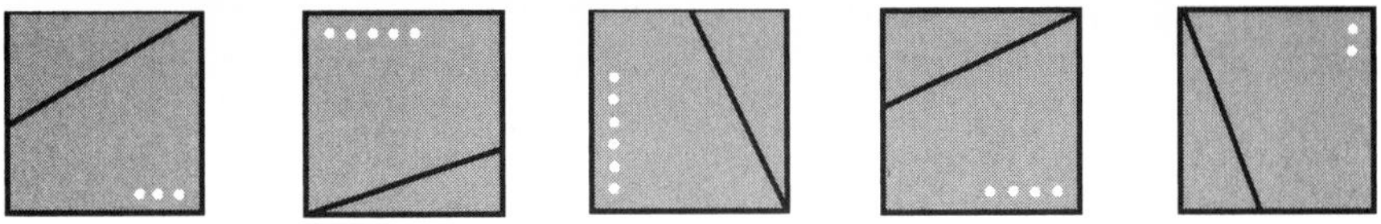

A **B** **C** **D** **E**

Answer see page 317

1. The German dudelsack is similar to which musical instrument in Britain?

2. Which musical instruments are traditionally made from wood which has been hollowed out by white ants?

3. A Basset Horn is a form of which type of instrument, specifically (more specific than 'woodwind')?

4. Which early musical instrument diminished in popularity with the rise of orchestras but has experienced a bit of a comeback in the 20th. century due to the efforts of Arnold Dolmetsch?

5. Black piano keys are traditionally made from which wood?

6. Which musical instrument of the lute family has a triangular-shaped body and is derived from the Dombra of Central Asia?

7. In a traditional British brass band, which is usually the most numerous instrument despite it having being displaced in classical orchestras by the trumpet?

8. Which musical instrument has a name derived from the French phrase for loud (or maybe high) wood?

9. The ukulele has its origins in which part of the world?

10. In an orchestra, which is the only stringed instrument which is not bowed?

11. The firm of Hohner mainly produces two types of musical instrument. Name one.

12. Which present-day instrument is descended from the sackbut?

13. What is the musical instrument pictured opposite and which family is it considered to be a member?

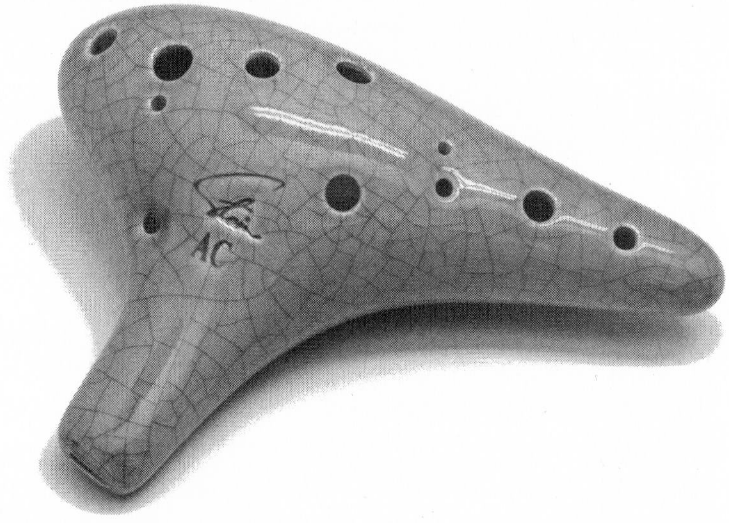

Answers see page 317

Make Up

Which cube can be made using:

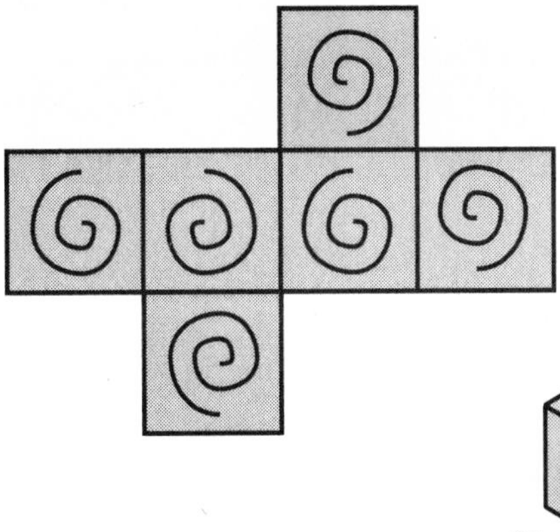

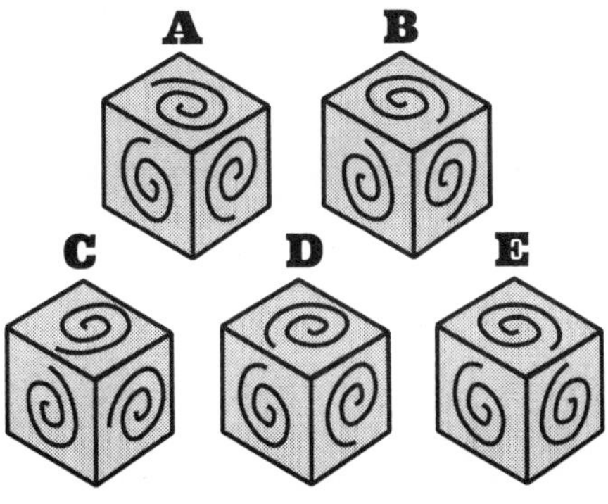

Answer see page 317

1. The cinchona tree, which was invaluable in counteracting malaria, is a native of which region or country?

2. Which was the first human disease to be identified as being caused by a virus?

3. Calmette and Guerin were responsible for combatting which disease?

4. In 1964 which British city experienced an outbreak of typhoid?

5. The 1981 Grand National was won by which horse, ridden by Bob Champion who had just recovered from cancer?

6. Which book consists of 100 tales related by escapees from an outbreak of plague in Florence?

7. The actor Michael J. Fox suffers from which serious disease?

8. What was declared extinct in 1977?

9. During an outbreak of plague in 1665–76, which village in Derbyshire allegedly cut itself off ?

10. Which animal is primarily responsible for spreading Weil's Disease?

11. What do you call dangerous bacteria or other material that causes disease or illness to its host?

12. Gin & tonic came into being as a by product of the fight against what?

13. Which disease had to be overcome before the canal shown opposite could be built?

Answers see page 317

Suspicious Circles

Which of these circles is the odd one out?

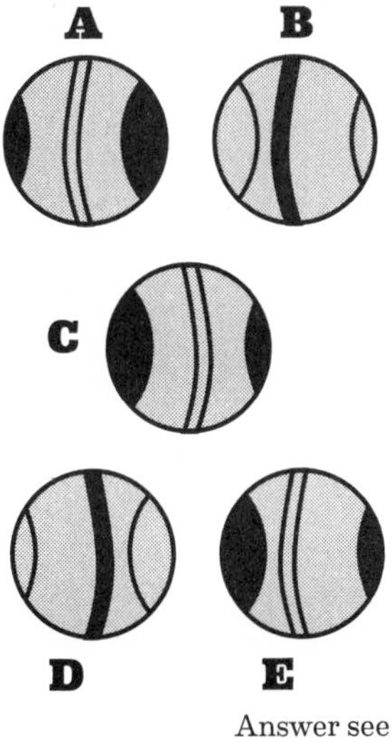

Answer see page 318

Number Placement

The numbers 4–16 have already been inserted into the grid, almost – but not quite – at random. Following just two simple rules, where would you place the numbers 1, 2 and 3 in the grid?

	14	10	7
9	6		4
16		13	11
12	8	5	15

Answer see page 318

1. Name one of the participants in the Chaco War?

2. In 1902, Britain allied with Germany to threaten which American country?

3. The Cerrado savannah region is located in which country?

4. What country does Paddington Bear originally come from?

5. The port of Antofagasta on the Pacific Coast belonged to which country immediately prior to its present owner?

6. When did the Tupamaros guerrilla group operate?

7. Where can you find the Atacama Desert, as seen here?

8. Rubber was once the monopoly of which country?

9. Where does the singer Shakira hails from?

10. Alberto Fujimora was president of where?

11. In which country was the Nazi leader Adolf Eichmann discovered in 1961?

12. Who hosted the first football World Cup?

13. Angostura (since re-named) is in which country?

Answers see page 318

Take a Tile

Look at the pattern of tiles. Which of the following tiles replaces the question mark?

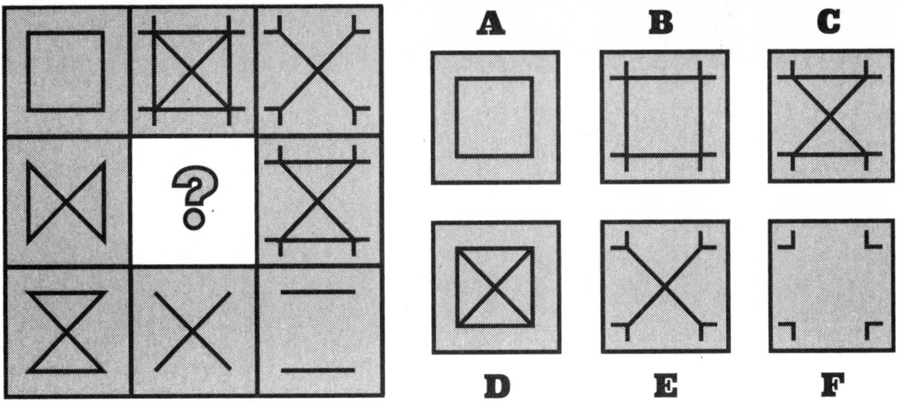

Answer see page 318

1. A so-called Egyptian Triangle has a perimeter 12 units long. What are the lengths of each of its sides in these same units?

2. What are referenced by Köchel numbers?

3. What number is equal to 4 factorial?

4. The faintest stars visible with the naked eye have a magnitude of what number?

5. If binoculars are described as 7 X 50, what does this mean?

6. How far do you have to go underwater before the pressure doubles to that at the surface (to nearest metre)?

7. What characteristic of photographic film is given by its ISO number?

8. How many milliliters are in one pint (you're allowed 5 either way)?

9. What number is the ratio of the circumference of a circle to its diameter?

10. A SWIFT number (sometimes called a BIC number) is used in which area of activity?

11. What is the commonest number of petals possessed by flowers?

12. In which program did Patrick McGoohan play a character called Number Six?

13. What is the length of the Trans-Siberian Railway, as shown opposite, to the nearest thousand kilometres?

Answers see page 318

Timed Puzzle

These clocks follow a weird kind of logic. What time should the fourth clock show? Choose from the four options provided.

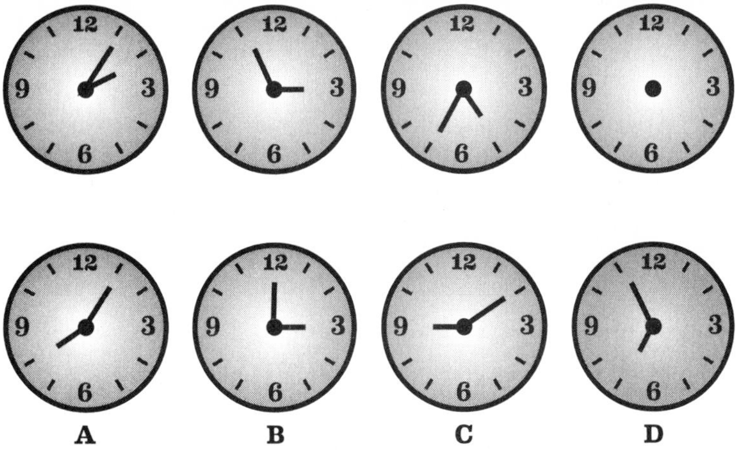

Answer see page 318

1. Which children's toy is based on a Filipino weapon?

2. Use of which object gave rise to the slang expression 'A Flash in the Pan'?

3. A twig of what was used to kill the Scandinavian god of light, Balder?

4. The weapons known in the British Army as Piats (Pro-jectile Infantry Anti-Tank), were known by what name in the American army?

5. What weapon was used to kill the albatross?

6. In which film does Alec Guinness play a character who is killed when a railway signal drops on his head?

7. Which Swedish person was brought in by the UN in 2003 to search for Weapons of Mass Destruction in Iraq?

8. In which atoll did France explode a nuclear device in 1995?

9. Who was the Bulgarian dissident murdered on Waterloo Bridge by a poisoned umbrella?

10. Give one of the two-word names given to the first two A-bombs?

11. In modern warfare, what is a Tomahawk?

12. What is an arquebus?

13. Britain's first operational nuclear weapon had what 'watery' or 'musical' name?

14. Greek Fire was a secret weapon employed by which empire, as demonstrated here?

Answers see page 319

Figure Columns

Look at the three columns of figures. Which column comes next in the sequence?

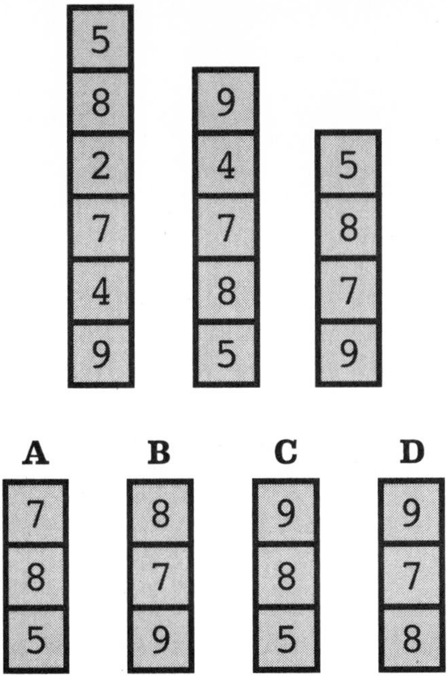

Answer see page 319

1. What was the name of both William the Conqueror's father and his eldest son?

2. Don Camillo was involved in a dispute with Mayor Peppone, when he refused to baptize Peppone's son, because of the name Peppone had given his son. What was the offending name?

3. In Macbeth, what is the name of Banquo's son?

4. Which son of King Priam was killed by Achilles?

5. The descendants of George Rex, the alleged eldest son of George III, live in which country?

6. Which Trojan hero was the son of Venus?

7. Who is this describing: as a member of the Committee of Public Safety he played a leading role in the organization of the French Armed Forces. His name is also known in Engineering and Science, albeit sometimes referring to his son?

8. Sam West, the theatre producer, is the son of which actress?

9. Which son of Sweyn Forkbeard was proclaimed King of England in 1017?

10. Who was the famous son of Hamilcar Barca?

11. Which pop star had a son called Rolan?

12. The novelist Erskine Childers who was executed by the British, had a son who became president of which country?

13. Who set sail in 1611 to try to find the Northwest Passage but was later – as the scene here depicts – set adrift with his 14-year-old son when the crew mutinied?

Answers see page 319

1. Who was the last non-seed to win Wimbledon?

2. Which was the last country in South America to abolish slavery?

3. Which was the last film that Clint Eastwood made for Sergio Leone?

4. After defeat at Stalingrad, which city in the Ukraine saw what the Germans could claim to be their last victory on Soviet soil?

5. Which was the last big cat to become extinct in Britain, around about the third century, although small colonies still exist in Continental Europe?

6. Who was the last Catholic Archbishop of Canterbury?

7. Who is pictured below, and what was he the last man to do?

8. What town was the last Dutch outpost in Belgium, holding out from 1601 to 1604 in a dispute in which 40,000 Spanish troops were killed?

9. Which gory-sounding individual is classed as the last Viking king of York, dying in AD 954?

10. Who was the last prisoner to be held by the state in the Tower of London?

11. Which European country adopted the Gregorian Calendar in 1923, possibly the last country to get rid of the Julian calendar?

12. What was the name of the last Shah of Iran?

13. The last example of which type of pigeon died in Cincinnati Zoo in 1914?

Answers see page 321

Number Crunching

Look at the diagrams. What number should replace the question mark?

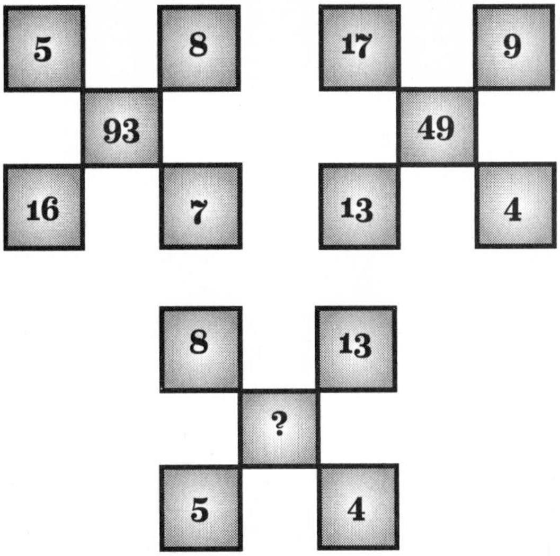

Answer see page 321

The Answers

Ancient Rome

1. Trajan
2. Pygmalion
3. Leptis Magna
4. Mercury, the god of commerce and protection of traders
5. Augsburg
6. Sweet Chestnut
7. Corinth
8. Crassus
9. Rio Tinto
10. The Colosseum & Vespasian
11. Claudius
12. Ovid
13. When August was named after the first Roman emperor its number of days was raised to 31 by taking one from February, so as not to be inferior to July (named after Julius Caesar). Previously all months alternated between 30 and 31, except the 29 for February. The months after August were re-arranged in the opposite way to previously
14. Patricians and Plebians could marry each other
15. The wind was blowing in the right direction
16. Nero
17. Geese
18. Cincinnati
19. Fabians
20. Caligula

The Solar System

1. Galileo
2. Methane
3. Achilles
4. Will Hay
5. Shoemaker-Levy 9
6. Shakespeare
7. The planet Mars
8. Cassini
9. Io
10. Great Red Spot
11. Mercury
12. Kepler
13. Olympus Mons

Stick Men

It is the only one consisting of an odd number of elements.

Artists

1. Margate
2. van Gogh, Gauguin
3. Monet
4. Michaelangelo
5. Damien Hirst
6. Upside down motifs
7. Velázquez
8. Titian
9. Pre-Raphaelites
10. Peter Lely
11. Degas
12. David Hockney
13. Botticelli
14. Canaletto
15. (Orthodox Byzantine) Icons
16. Millais
17. (Gustave) Courbet

18. Malaga
19. Rembrandt
20. Holbein

Islands

1. Robben Island
2. Vancouver Island
3. Hispaniola
4. Zeeland
5. Norfolk Island
6. Edmond Dantés
7. Sardinia
8. Isla de Perejil/Parsley Island
9. Bahamas
10. Marshall Islands
11. Chile
12. Nova Scotia
13. Formentera
14. Tristao da Cunha
15. Marseilles
16. Roanoke Island
17. Sicily
18. Albert Londres
19. Santorini
20. Capri

January

1. Kobe
2. *Mother Courage*
3. Paris
4. Morning Star
5. Canaan Banana
6. Use of the word 'Spam'
7. HAL
8. Casablanca
9. Glasgow
10. Paris
11. Rosa Luxemburg
12. Monarch Butterfly
13. (Western) Samoa

Odd One Out

B. It is a mirror image of the other shapes, which are all rotated variations of each other.

Puzzle Around

10. Multiply the two numbers on the outside of each segment, divide the product by the number on the outside of the segment and put the new number in the middle of the opposite segment.

Actors and Actresses

1. Charlie Allnutt
2. Anne Bancroft
3. 3
4. Buster Keaton
5. Orson Welles
6. Pele
7. Sugar Kane
8. Jerry Mouse
9. Guy of Gisborne
10. Laurence Olivier
11. Jill Masterton (played by Shirley Eaton)
12. Geraldine Chaplin
13. Horst Bucholz
14. Fred Kite
15. She was black and the premiere was in an all-white cinema
16. Claire Grogan

17. Laurel and Hardy
18. James Cagney
19. Ilsa Lund
20. Richard Roundtree

Inventions and Inventors

1. Coca-Cola
2. Rudolf Diesel
3. (John) Harrison
4. CERN
5. A Steam Engine
6. James Hargreaves
7. Isaac Newton
8. Personal Stereo
9. Monsanto
10. Trampoline
11. Häagen-Dazs
12. Photography
13. Tractors
14. Camembert
15. Maxim
16. Maxwell's Demon
17. Wristwatch
18. Siemens
19. Pergamon
20. Matsushita

European Cities

1. Swansea
2. Graz
3. Marseille
4. Brussels
5. Antwerp
6. Basel, Mulhouse, Freiburg
7. Vienna and Bratislava
8. Manchester
9. Sunderland
10. Lucca
11. Toledo
12. London
13. Mainz

Square Solution

3. The numbers rotate anti-clockwise from one square to the next and decrease by 2 each time.

Odd One Out 15

B. The digits of all the others add up to 6.

Thirds

1. Edmund Hilary
2. Napoleon
3. Passchendale
4. Comintern
5. Sightings of UFOs (one of his designations was used as the title of Close Encounters of the Third Kind, in which he made a cameo appearance)
6. Ural
7. Ghent
8. 'Now is our winter of our discontent'
9. Zither
10. To try and find the Northwest Passage
11. Peggy Guggenheim
12. *The Three Musketeers*
13. Izmir

Dartboard Dilemma

8 ways.

Squared Up

Leave only the 12 outside lines and the 4 inside lines.

Sculpture

1. Samothrace/Samothráki
2. Elgin Marbles
3. Centenary of Brazil's independence
4. Nelson
5. John Betjeman
6. General Sir Charles James Napier, Major General Sir Henry Havelock, King George IV
7. *Angel of the North*
8. Alfred The Great
9. Molly Malone
10. *Burghers of Calais*
11. Jacob Epstein
12. Apollo/Helios
13. Bernini

Words

1. A lake
2. Poker
3. Porcelain
4. PET
5. Diaspora
6. French
7. Rhyming slang - Scapa Flow
8. Magnetic Levitation
9. Ar(e)
10. Disaster
11. Ecu
12. Bar
13. Arabic
14. Marshall
15. Portuguese
16. Golgotha
17. It belongs to the first two names – the University was actually named by the founder in memory of his son
18. Transfer Resistor
19. Eye
20. Antirrhinum

Bands

1. The Band
2. Blur
3. Stevie Winwood
4. Manfred Mann
5. Supertramp
6. Montreux
7. Rotterdam
8. Herman's Hermits
9. CCS (or Collective Consciousness Society)
10. Ladysmith
11. Mungo Jerry
12. Kilimanjaro
13. Bonzo Dog Doo Dah Band

Box Clever

E.

Time Travel

6.00 am.

February

1. Sea Empress
2. Italy
3. Rugby (League)
4. Lubeck, Rostock

5. Fitzroy
6. Clean/Cleanse/Purification
7. Holland
8. Difference between Julian and Gregorian calendars
9. Torrey Canyon
10. Kasserine Pass
11. The Scream
12. Earl Grey
13. Truk

Pattern Poser

Anticlockwise spiral. The sequence is clockwise spiral, dot, square, anticlockwise spiral, square, dot. It starts from the top-left corner and moves in a clockwise spiral.

Odd One Out

20. The circle contains the squares of 13, 18 and 26 and as well as those numbers themselves.

South America

1. Belo Horizonte
2. Che Guevara
3. Rubber Seeds
4. Bernardo O'Higgins
5. Santos
6. Quechua
7. Galtieri
8. Amazons
9. Buenos Aires
10. Saint-Malo
11. Carlos
12. Aztec Stadium
13. Rio de Janeiro
14. Spectacled Bear, and it is the only bear native to South America

Round the Dial

10.50. The time moves backwards 1 hour, 5 minutes on each clock.

Missing Number

6. Add 1 to the number in the first column to give the second number. Column three has 3 subtracted from column two and column four is double the value of column three.

James Bond

1. Telly Savalas
2. *Dr. No*
3. SMERSH
4. *Thunderball*
5. Michael Lonsdale
6. *From Russia with Love*
7. Lotte Lenya
8. *Goldfinger*
9. Tanaka
10. Autogyro
11. *You Only Live Twice*
12. *From Russia with Love*
13. Lois Maxwell

Time Travel

1.00a.m.

Box Clever

B.

World Rivers

1. Camargue
2. Omo
3. Moselle
4. Canadian River
5. Parana
6. Arno
7. China, Korea
8. Hudson
9. Sea of Azov
10. Iron Gate
11. Turkey
12. Congo
13. Rance
14. Lena
15. Kwai
16. Russia, China
17. Darling
18. Originally assumed they led to China
19. Baghdad
20. Columbia

Classic Literature

1. *Black Beauty*
2. Canada
3. *Swiss Family Robinson*
4. *Bleak House*
5. *Nostromo*
6. *The Wind in the Willows*
7. Nantucket
8. *Fanny Hill*
9. *History of Mr Polly*
10. Laura Ingalls (Wilder)
11. *Ulysses*
12. *Wuthering Heights*
13. *The Castle*

Make Up

D.

Food

1. Cheese
2. Eggs Florentine
3. Bananas
4. (Kilo)Joules
5. A potato
6. Bread
7. The Big-Enders promoted eating of an egg from the Big-End, and vice-versa for Little-Enders.
8. Linseed
9. Branston Pickle
10. Glamorgan sausages
11. Atreus
12. Essen
13. Milk, Egg Yolk, Sugar

Puzzle Around

It should have the dot in the bottom left-hand corner. The sequence starts at the top right square and moves in an anti-clockwise spiral to the centre.

Piece It Together

A.

General Knowledge 1

1. 21cm by 29.7cm (21cm by 30cm is acceptable)
2. Gelert
3. French horns
4. *Catch-22*
5. Catherine de Medici
6. Great Star of Africa
7. Chile

8. France
9. Penguin Books
10. Underground Railway/ Rapid Transit
11. John Betjeman
12. Astronaut (i.e. due to be first British astronaut but career blighted by Shuttle explosion)
13. Berlioz
14. David Attenborough
15. Buildings, Antennas, Spans, Earth
16. Design of Tay Bridge (which collapsed)
17. Julie Andrews
18. Alexander Kielland
19. A duck
20. Joshua

US Presidents

1. Theodore Roosevelt
2. Spiro Agnew
3. James Buchanan
4. Monrovia
5. Eleanor
6. Nixon
7. Gadsden
8. Cuba
9. George McGovern
10. Wilson
11. Andrew Johnson
12. Harrison
13. Polk
14. Eugene Debs
15. George Wallace
16. MacArthur
17. Caroline
18. Bull Moose Party
19. James Madison
20. Aaron Burr

Poetry

1. Robbie Burns
2. Keats
3. Federico Garcia Lorca
4. Ezra Pound
5. Walter Scott
6. Petrarch (or Petrarca)
7. Hugh MacDiarmid
8. The darling buds of May
9. The French Revolutionary Calendar
10. Arthur Rimbaud
11. John Betjeman
12. Pablo Neruda
13. Peter the Great
14. Paul Revere
15. *Rime of the Ancient Mariner*
16. *Waltzing Matilda*
17. Jerusalem
18. Silvery
19. Tintern
20. Ozymandias

Science

1. Doppler Effect
2. Radiation given off when something travels faster than the local speed of light in a medium
3. Switzerland, France
4. Ears or end of nose
5. Lift obtained from a spinning body
6. An astronomer

7. Brownian Motion
8. Catenary
9. Angstrom
10. Bernoulli Effect
11. Tunneling
12. Planck's Constant
13. Aluminium

In The Balance

5 (4 large and 1 small).

Plays

1. *Arms and the Man*
2. *School for Scandal*
3. *Salome*
4. Confusing DH with TE Lawrence
5. *A Midsummer Nights Dream*
6. Willy Loman
7. Henrik Ibsen
8. *Cat on a Hot Tin Roof*
9. 'Me no Leica'
10. The Weavers
11. Sean O'Casey
12. *The Merry Wives of Windsor*
13. *Maria Stuart*

Scotland

1. Inveraray Castle
2. Produced in Scotland, at least 3 years old
3. Procurator Fiscal
4. Moray Firth
5. John Paul Jones
6. Scottish Lowland Dialect
7. Loch Leven
8. Perth
9. Lighthouses
10. Edinburgh Castle
11. Oban
12. Loch Lomond and Trossachs
13. Malcolm III (Canmore)
14. Ben MacDhui
15. Bonnie Prince Charlie
16. Darien (Isthmus of Panama)
17. *Kidnapped*
18. Glen More/Great Glen
19. Shinty
20. Falkirk

March

1. Brest-Litovsk
2. Remagen
3. My Lai
4. 20th. or 21st. March
5. Tokyo
6. Pembroke College, Oxford
7. Evening Star
8. Crush in a tube station, serving as a shelter
9. Liechtenstein
10. E-Type
11. Nanterre
12. Meriden
13. Rodney King

Squared Up

8. Subtract the bottom left corner from the top left corner. Now subtract the bottom right corner from the top right corner, then subtract this answer from the first difference and put the number in the middle.

Odd One Out

D, the diamond. It is a closed shape

French Revolutions

1. Germinal
2. Marianne
3. Avignon
4. Haiti
5. Thomas Carlyle
6. Wordsworth
7. David
8. Pantheon
9. Thermidor
10. Rousseau
11. Winds
12. Fronde
13. 1830

Sum Body

56. Head x left foot ÷ waist = right hand; head x right foot ÷ waist = left hand. 14 x 15 ÷ 5 = 42; 14 x 20 ÷ 5 = 56.

Squared Up

5. Three numbers in a horizontal line add up to the fourth number.

Trains and Railways

1. London, Glasgow
2. Train de Grand Vitesse
3. Wrought iron
4. Watt forbade them, his patent allowed him to do so
5. The Flying Scotsman
6. Snowdon
7. Dublin
8. Great Central
9. Widnes
10. Solar eclipse
11. South Africa
12. USA
13. Huskisson

Arrow Hunt

N. The sequence is NWSNEN.

Word Slice

Darwin, Newton and Pascal.

Film Adaptations

1. Ian Fleming
2. *Silence of the Lambs*
3. *The Outlaw Josey Wales*
4. *Brighton Rock*
5. Agatha Christie
6. Bates Motel
7. Max Von Sydow
8. *Midnight Cowboy*
9. *2001: A Space Odyssey or 2010*
10. *Gorky Park*
11. *Get Carter*
12. Joan Hickson
13. Donald Pleasance
14. Alfred Hitchcock
15. Uncle Remus/Brer Rabbit
16. True Grit
17. Che Guevara
18. Pat Reid
19. *Slumdog Millionaire*
20. *Mosquito Coast*

Mammals

1. Hedgehog, Mouse, Rabbit
2. Red Deer

3. Zebra
4. Wolf
5. Raccoon
6. Rhinoceros
7. Caspian, Java, Bali
8. Otter
9. A squirrel
10. Squealer
11. Grey squirrels
12. Seal, sealion, walrus
13. Platypus

Symbolic Value

3. Apples = 6, Bananas = –1, Cherries = 4.

Box Clever

B.

Further Islands

1. Tahiti
2. Sao Tome and Principe
3. Jamaica
4. Madagascar
5. Hawaii
6. Sicily
7. Majorca
8. Amelia Earhart
9. Richmond
10. Hong Kong
11. Corsica
12. Aleutians
13. Martinique
14. Laputa
15. Moluccas
16. Borneo, Sumatra
17. Franz Josef Land
18. Oahu
19. Curacao
20. Crete

The World Cup

1. Wales
2. North Korea
3. Uruguay
4. Dino Zoff
5. East Germany
6. United States
7. Ecuador
8. Valderrama
9. Munich
10. Eusebio
11. Marco Materazzi
12. (American) Samoa
13. Algeria
14. 1958, 1962, 1970
15. Jules Rimet

Pattern Poser

7. The sides are worth: Shaded 4, Solid line 5, Dots 6, Dash 8. The formula is left side plus base, minus right side.

Shape Shift

E. The others all have an equal number of straight lines and curves.

Songs

1. Lemmy
2. Chicago
3. 'La Bamba'
4. The Hurdy-Gurdy Man
5. 'I Walk the Line'

6. Joe DiMaggio
7. Ozzy Osbourne
8. Bossa Nova
9. Bob Dylan
10. 'Daisy Bell'
11. 'Londonderry Air'
12. Lulu
13. 'Proud Mary'

Arty Anagram

N: Monet, Rodin, Munch, Ernst.

Squared Up

40. Star = 7; Tick = 8; Cross = 14; Circle = 11.

Lakes

1. Geneva
2. Havasu
3. Edmund Fitzgerald
4. Zeppelin
5. Suez Canal
6. Coniston Water
7. Lake Tanganyika
8. Ghana
9. Ontario, Erie
10. Loch Ness, Lochy, Oich, Dochfour
11. Lake Nasser (Lake Nubia is also an acceptable answer)
12. Lake Baikal
13. Lake Lucerne
14. Zuider Zee
15. Interlagos
16. Garda
17. The Long Water
18. St. Petersburg
19. Lake Vyrnwy
20. Windermere

Circular Logic

13. Dove = 2; stars = 3; earth = 5; spiral = 4.

Russian Literature

1. Gorky
2. Tolstoy
3. *Solaris*
4. *The Seagull*
5. Pushkin
6. *Taras Bulba*
7. *The Master and Margarita*
8. *Lady Macbeth of the Mtsensk District*
9. Isaac Babel
10. Irina, Masha
11. A Witch or Ogress in Russian literature
12. Tolstoy
13. Hit by a train

April

1. Cuckoo
2. Ernst Toller
3. Georges Danton
4. A380
5. Chartists
6. Portugal
7. Great (or First) Reform Act
8. TSR2
9. Dennis Tito
10. San Francisco
11. The Girl from U.N.C.L.E.
12. Jenin

13. Grand National, Lincoln Handicap

Safe Path

1E on row 2, column 2.

Missing Number

4. The sum of diagonally opposite segments are the same.

Wars

1. Venice
2. Dukla
3. Tilsit
4. Crimean War
5. Grand Fenwick
6. Beaumarchais
7. War of Austrian Succession
8. End of World War I
9. Holland
10. DH Lawrence
11. Peloponnesian War
12. Sierra Leone
13. George Custer
14. Netherlands
15. George Orwell

Mountains

1. The Catskills
2. Matterhorn
3. Annapurna
4. Mount St. Helens
5. Mauna Kea
6. 8,850
7. Ireland
8. Snowdon Mountain Railway
9. Cwm
10. Drakensberg
11. Cumberland Gap
12. Carpathians
13. Haifa
14. Montevideo
15. Alaska
16. Isle of Skye
17. Jurassic
18. New Zealand
19. Mount Elbrus
20. Jungfrau

General Knowledge 2

1. Trombone
2. Nicaragua
3. Railways
4. Cosmonauts
5. Signal Passed At Danger
6. Ruddy Duck
7. Victoria Line
8. Tom Stoppard
9. Architect
10. Isle of Man
11. Whist
12. Mario Puzo
13. Morecambe Bay
14. David Cassidy
15. Henry Fonda
16. Barkis
17. Frogs' Legs
18. Edmond Halley
19. Johannesburg
20. Kirkcaldy and Cowdenbeath

Answers

Non-Fiction

1. Gorky
2. John Maynard Keynes
3. Machiavelli
4. JK Galbraith
5. Alfred Russel Wallace
6. *How To Make Friends and Influence People*
7. R.L. Stevenson
8. Edvard Munch
9. Lenin
10. Richard Dawkins
11. Lanfranc
12. Francis Wheen
13. Elizabeth Gaskell

Cycle Logical

4:22. Start time A minus Finish A equals Finish B. Start time B minus Finish B equals Finish C, etc.

Art

1. Steve McQueen
2. Tracey Emin
3. Pre-Raphaelite Brotherhood
4. Emulsion
5. Goya
6. Antwerp
7. *Mona Lisa*
8. Gauguin
8. Santi / Sanzio (da Urbino)
10. Vincent van Gogh
11. Slade
12. Milan
13. Luftwaffe

Number Pattern

2. The outer numbers, when multiplied, give the inner double-digit number.

A Question of Balance

24 squares.

Japan

1. Honshu
2. Suzuka
3. Quezon
4. Kamikaze
5. Rollercoaster
6. He was classed as Japanese, whereas in reality he was from Japanese-occupied Korea
7. Tokyo
8. Yamamoto
9. Russia and Japan
10. New Hampshire
11. Okinawa
12. B-29 Superfortress
13. Frank Lloyd Wright

Perfect Fit

2.

Figure It Out

11. It is a series of prime numbers.

Musicals

1. *Hair*
2. *Blood Brothers*
3. *Oklahoma!*
4. *Cabaret*
5. *Kipps*

6. The Four Seasons
7. Bert and/or Mr Dawes, Sr.
8. Salzburg
9. *Spamalot*
10. Kurt Weill
11. *Sweet Charity*
12. *Kiss Me Kate*
13. Gavroche

Missing Link

D. The number of edges of the shapes in each square increases by 1 in each row, starting from the left.

Death

1. Janet Leigh
2. Dostoyevsky
3. Greece
4. La Rochelle
5. Tasmanian Tiger
6. Constance Markiowecz
7. Syracruse (Sicily is also an acceptable answer)
8. Jesse James
9. *Ophelia*
10. By approaching too close to Vesuvius
11. Sonny Bono
12. Spanish settlements were attacked (while Raleigh was instructed not to upset the Spanish)
13. Jeanne D'Arc
14. Haydn
15. Chicago
16. Little Nell
17. *Sunset Boulevard*
18. St. John the Evangelist
19. The Beatles
20. *Macbeth*

May

1. Mount St. Helens
2. Ticonderoga
3. Möhnesee
4. Torino
5. *Spirit of St. Louis*
6. Goya
7. Hadrian's Wall
8. Dublin
9. Lavoisier
10. (Colonel) Thomas Blood
11. Cherwell
12. Liverpool
13. Crash of the Hindenburg

Pattern Poser

14. Sides are worth: Shaded 2, Dots 3, Dashed 5, Line 6. Add sides together and put sum in centre of triangle.

William Shakespeare

1. John of Gaunt
2. Cyprus
3. *Troilus and Cressida*
4. Theseus
5. Caliban
6. *Macbeth, Otello, Falstaff*
7. *The Comedy of Errors*
8. Portia
9. Harfleur
10. Falstaff
11. *Julius Caesar*
12. Owain Glyndwr

13. Macduff

14. *A Midsummer Night's Dream*

15. Earl of Southampton

16. Spain and England were using different calendars at the time

17. *Hamlet*

18. Antonio

19. *Romeo and Juliet*

20. Horatio

US States

1. Columbia

2. Missouri

3. New Mexico, Arizona, Colorado, Utah

4. Kansas, Nebraska

5. Maryland, Pennsylvania

6. Gray Davis

7. Key West

8. Kentucky

9. Pennsylvania (pen is a welsh word)

10. Rhode Island

11. *Indiana*

12. Providence

13. Florida

14. Georgia

15. Hawaii

16. 1848

17. Wyoming

18. Vermont

19. Indiana

20. Illinois

Movie Themes and Soundtracks

1. Matt Monro

2. *Gone with the Wind*

3. Richard Strauss

4. Vangelis

5. Buffy St. Marie

6. *Cat Ballou*

7. Henry Mancini

8. Clint Eastwood

9. Lulu

10. McCarthyism

11. The Corrs

12. Ron Goodwin

13. Verdi

Sum Puzzle

The formula is (right x left) - top x shaded fraction of circle = bottom. The missing shape is half a circle.

Nicknames

1. Empire State

2. Barbarossa

3. Eric Clapton

4. Papillon

5. The Yardbirds

6. *To Serve Them All My Days*

7. Franz Josef

8. 617

9. The Birdman of Alcatraz

10. Molotov

11. Charles Blondin

12. Charlotte Brontë

13. Michael Douglas

14. Margaret Kelly

Puzzle Around

5. Add both numbers in one

segment, add the digits of that sum and place new number in the next segment, going clockwise.

Odd One Out

625. The cubes of 7, 9 and 13 are listed as well as those numbers.

Astronomy

1. The fact that it had satellites that it was carrying along with it (it had been argued that a moving Earth would leave the Moon behind)
2. Christiaan Huygens
3. *The Tempest* (Miranda, Ariel)
4. Mapping Venus
5. 1066
6. Mauna Kea
7. Southern Cross
8. Took bearings (6 months apart) on a star and detected parallax
9. SOHO
10. Transient Lunar Phenomena
11. Jupiter
12. Scorpius/Scorpio
13. Swan (Cygnus)
14. Venus (Ve) and Halley's Comet (Ga – there being no 'H' in Russian characters)
15. Pulsar
16. Copernicus
17. Somerville
18. Edmond Halley
19. Algol
20. W (or M)

The Olympic Games

1. 1924
2. 1936 (Berlin)
3. Emil Zatopek
4. For traveling part of the way by automobile
5. 1,500 metres
6. 1984
7. Tommy Smith
8. Buster Crabbe
9. Marathon
10. Jim Thorpe
11. Ulrich Salchow
12. Lasse Viren
13. Calgary
14. 100m, 200m, Long Jump, 4 × 100m Relay

Missing Number

56. Take 2/3 of the number in the top left square and multiply it by twice the number in the top right square. Put the new number in the bottom square.

Who Wrote It?

1. Jilly Cooper
2. Friedrich Engels
3. Julius Caesar
4. Frederick Marryat
5. Prosper Merimée
6. Thackeray
7. Thucydides
8. Gaston la Roux
9. Wilfred Owen

10. Pushkin
11. Charles Wesley
12. Agatha Christie
13. Ezra Pound

Puzzle Around

16. The sum of inner and diagonally opposite outer segments totals 29.

Symbol Value

21. Star=5, circle=4, square=8.

Classical Music

1. Leipzig Gewandhaus
2. Pin
3. Prokofiev
4. Shostakovitch
5. Brahms
6. Mahler
7. Chopin
8. Constanze (Weber)
9. Daniel Barenboim
10. Beethoven
11. Rimsky-Korsakov
12. Tchaikovsky
13. Surprise Symphony

Square Solution

19. Shades are worth: Waves 3, Grey 4, Black 5, Straight lines 7.

Cog Query

It will fall.

In the Dictionary

1. Annealing
2. Choctaw
3. Viscosity
4. Beauty
5. Harrier
6. Hawaiian
7. Pacific
8. Holocene
9. Bar
10. Shoes/clogs
11. Passim
12. Perestroika
13. Vandals
14. Chine
15. Forest
16. Pergamon
17. Alexandrine
18. Beech
19. Dunnock
20. Welsh

June and July

1. Midway
2. New York
3. Parachute did not open
4. King David Hotel
5. Henry Hudson
6. Caen
7. Dante
8. Shoemaker-Levy
9. Brendan Barber
10. Vicksburg
11. Roswell
12. Catalonia
13. Dickens
14. K2
15. Bretton Woods Conference
16. J

17. Tempel 1
18. Genoa
19. Magenta
20. Falkirk

World War II

1. James Stewart
2. PG Wodehouse
3. SMERSH
4. River Plate
5. Lithuania
6. Spruce Goose
7. Robert (Gordon) Menzies
8. Mitchell
8. Monte Cassino
10. Babi Yar
11. Navajo
12. (Mother of) Pearl Coast/ Cote de Nacre
13. Italians invaded Egypt from Libya

Cycle Logical

15. Take the number of minutes in the hours, add the minutes and divide by 10. Ignore the remainder.

The Ancient World

1. Akhenaton
2. Alexander the Great
3. Valley of the Queens
4. Demotic
5. Ptolemy
6. Pompey
7. Marathon
8. Demosthenes
9. Thermopylae
10. Mycenae
11. Herodotus
12. Thebes
13. Ziggurats
14. Darius
15. Cairo
16. Cut it with his sword
17. Alexandria (Heliopolis is also acceptable)
18. Howard Carter
19. Pompey
20. Athena

General Knowledge 3

1. To build an underground railway
2. Saul
3. Abbey Theatre
4. Seal
5. Albert Camus
6. Rope making
7. E (Napoleone)
8. Apples
9. Scandinavian Airline System
10. John Major
11. Andromache
12. Ralf Schumacher
13. Scott McKenzie
14. UFO sightings
15. Serge Danot
16. Acongagua
17. Ratatouille
18. Fossils
19. Butch Cassidy and the Sundance Kid
20. Warned of the dangers of

the Trojan Horse

Square Solution

27. Add all the numbers for each square. For light shade add 5, for dark shade subtract 5. Then swap the numbers in adjacent light and dark squares.

The Beatles

1. Rory Storm and the Hurricanes
2. Parlophone
3. *The White Album*
4. Granny Smith
5. Star Club
6. Ryde
7. The Ruttles
8. Get Back
9. Strawberry Fields
10. Yoko Ono
11. Lucy
12. Pete Best
13. *All You Need Is Love*
14. *Mull of Kintyre*
15. Wilfred Brambell

Missing Number

29. Add together the corner squares of each row or column in a clockwise direction. Put the sum in the middle of the next row or column.

Take Time

Back (10.30), back (2.00), forward (7.15), back (6.45).

Flags and Anthems

1. Ensign
2. Haydn
3. 1896
4. Netherlands
5. Belgium
6. Colours of Italian Flag
7. Ira Hayes
8. *Waltzing Matilda*
9. India
10. Alaska
11. Ireland
12. *O Tannenbaum*
13. Beethoven's Ninth Symphony
14. Mozambique
15. Baltimore

Card Challenge

Spade = 2, Club = 4, Diamond = 6, Heart = 8.

Pattern Poser

12. The shades are worth: Dots 5, Dashed 3, Shaded 6, Line 4.

Daughters

1. Marie Antoinette
2. Ingrid Bergman
3. Antigone
4. Loretta Lynn
5. Eleanor
6. Charles I (Henrietta Maria)
7. Iphigenia
8. Wagner
9. Jamie Lee Curtis

10. Buxtehude
11. Catherine of Aragon
12. Cleo Laine
13. Sylvia, Christabel, Adela

Missing Number

72. Halve the number on the top left, multiply the number on the top right by 3. Multiply the two resulting numbers by each other and put the product in the bottom square.

African Countries

1. Somaliland
2. Sudan
3. Angola
4. Ghana
5. South Africa
6. Nigeria
7. Botswana
8. Sudan
9. Lesotho
10. Tanzania
11. Namibia
12. Mozambique
13. Ghana

All Square

B.

August and September

1. India gained independence
2. Space-walking
3. Kursk
4. Jaffa
5. Switzerland
6. 11th September
7. Black September
8. Berliner
9. Because it didn't exist (Calendar Reform)
10. Leila Khaled
11. Leeds and Liverpool
12. Worcester
13. 'Lili Marleen'
14. Battle of Lake Erie
15. Vienna

Puzzle Around

10. The three numbers in each sector are added together and the totals in the bottom four segments are double those of their diagonally opposite ones.

Prime Ministers of the World

1. Barry
2. Alexander Kerenski
3. Portugal
4. Bettino Craxi
5. Cecil Rhodes
6. Luxembourg
7. Edith Cresson
8. (Jan) Smuts
9. Leon Blum
10. Yatzhik Shamir
11. Gough Whitlam
12. (Mohammed) Mossadegh
13. Bulgaria

Sum Circles

72. Multiply all the numbers in the top sections to arrive at the number in the opposite bottom section. Multiply by 3 in the first circle, by 6 in the second one, and by 9 in the third circle.

Animals

1. Jackass Penguin
2. Fish
3. Limpet
4. A dog
5. Lark
6. Calf
7. Shoveller Duck
8. Rhinoceros
9. Bat
10. Sea lions have visible ears
11. Beetles
12. Form
13. Parrot

Rectangle Assembly

E.

Film Directors

1. *Alexander Nevsky*
2. Ken Loach
3. Leni Riefenstahl
4. *A Fistful of Dollars*
5. Erich Von Stroheim
6. Joan Littlewood
7. Jacques Cousteau
8. Russian, French
9. Stanley Kubrick
10. Robert Stevenson
11. Renoir
12. Red, White, Blue
13. *The Cabinet of Dr Caligari*

Odd One Out

91. All the others are prime numbers

European rivers

1. Somme
2. Weser
3. Alabama
4. Poland/Belarus
5. Elba
6. Medina
7. Rhein
8. Richard (sometimes known as Richard I of England, although he was French)
9. Marne
10. Asti
11. Neandertal
12. Spey
13. Eau de Cologne
14. Humber
15. Shrewsbury
16. Volga
17. Bann
18. Adige
19. Douglas
20. Severn

Alcohol

1. Peaches
2. Beer
3. Ethanol
4. Sarsaparilla
5. Piña Colada

6. Whisky
7. Vermouth
8. 13
9. Chardonnay
10. Ullage
11. *The Iliad*
12. 119.24
13. Blue Moon
14. Gin
15. Ricard
16. Tokay
17. Rum
18. Drambuie
19. Liebfraumilch
20. Singapore Sling

The Lives of Writers

1. Goodbye, Mr Chips
2. Daniel Defoe
3. Cardinal (John) Newman
4. No temptation to go out elsewhere
5. Marcel Proust
6. Germaine Greer
7. DH Lawrence
8. Thirsk
9. Byron
10. Emile Zola
11. John Milton
12. *Down and Out in Paris and London*
13. Belgian Congo

Odd One Out

C. The others are all rotated variations.

Team Sports

1. World Cup (Jules Rimet Trophy)
2. Jamaica entering a bobsleigh team
3. Octopush
4. 3 times 20 minutes
5. Ice Hockey
6. Brooklyn Dodgers
7. Rugby League
8. Water polo
9. Football
10. Hexagons and Pentagons
11. Honduras, El Salvador
12. West Germany Winning the World Cup
13. Rugby League
14. Football is American football, and Fussball is soccer
15. Ice hockey

Weigh-in

No. 2. Subtract the first digit of the weight from the second to arrive at the answer.

British Islands

1. Chesil Beach
2. May 1945
3. *Thunderbirds*
4. Holy Island
5. Calf of Mann
6. Long John Silver
7. Brownsea Island
8. *Notes from a Small Island*

9. Alderney
10. Grace Darling
11. Guernsey
12. Newfoundland
13. Mull

Odd One Out

D. In the other sets the single spot is in the flipped reflection of the point of intersection of the two lines.

Translation

1. Sir Richard Burton
2. Bat
3. William Tyndale
4. Committee for State Security
5. Egyptian hieroglyphics
6. Glasnost
7. Amsterdam
8. English and Welsh
9. Marcel Proust
10. Alcohol (Arabic translation)
11. The Haka
12. Nuremberg Trials
13. Red Windmill

Triangulation

7. Add the three numbers at the corners, multiply by 2, and place that number in the middle.

Clock Wise

1 o'clock. The hour hand moves 1 hour back and the minute hand 20 minutes forward each time.

The Pope

1. The Great Schism
2. Constantine
3. St. Bartholomew's Massacre
8 Joseph Ratzinger
4. Heinrich (Henry) IV
5. Transferred recognition to Avignon
6. Julius II
7. Rodrigo
9. After Pope Sixtus
10. Castel Gandolfo
11. Avignon
12. Vatican
13. Pius XII

Pattern Poser

a. The edges of all the symbols in one square added together, increase by 2 with each square (i.e. 12, 14, 16, 18, 20).

October

1. Aachen
2. Kerenski
3. Zinoviev Letter
4. San Giuliano
5. Imre Nagy
6. Discovery of America
7. Eureka Uprising
8. Anna Politkovskaya
9. Leipzig
10. Yom Kippur (or Ramadan)
11. Paris
12. India

13. US

Squared Up

- x + - ÷ +: 9 - 3 x 4 + 19 - 8 ÷ 5 + 4 = 11.

America

1. Chaparral
2. El Paso
3. Amtrak
4. Their spelling of the gold measure is 'karat'
5. Enron
6. San Diego
7. 1913
8. It split America between Spain and Portugal
9. Jim Beam
10. Benedict Arnold
11. Matthew
12. Tadpole
13. Wells Fargo

Time Travel

9.15 pm.

General Knowledge 4

1. Snake
2. Football referee
3. The Invisible Man
4. Powys
5. Subscriber Identity Module
6. P.L. Travers
7. Wheat
8. Finistere
9. Look after horses
10. New Bedford
11. Peter Ustinov
12. Her voice
13. Australiopethicus
14. France
15. Galileo
16. Muckle Flugga
17. Mauled by lion
18. Folsom
19. Neuschwanstein
20. Skein

Money

1. Calcutta Cup
2. Napoleons
3. So they can be used in slot machines, etc.
4. Florin
5. Mont St Michael
6. Euro
7. Silver inside, gold outside
8. Dime
9. To discourage coin-clipping
10. Anna
11. Mark Twain
12. Pound (or Livre)
13. Germany
14. Peso

Shape Shift

A. The thinnest shape to cover an area always has the greatest perimeter.

Opera

1. McHeath
2. Countertenor
3. Richard Strauss
4. *Aida*
5. Mahler

6. *Kreutzer Sonata*
7. Lillian Hellman
8. *Lulu*
9. *Madame Butterfly*
10. Englebert Humperdinck
11. *Pearl Fishers*
12. Moses and Aaron
13. Hermann Melville

Clock Wise

10. The sum of hands on each clock is 15.

Sea Life

1. Crown of Thorns
2. Form
3. Haddock
4. Pups
5. Tuna
6. Nile Perch
7. Right Whales
8. Animal migrations due to man-made features, (e.g. Red Sea fish moving into Mediterranean)
9. A whale or a sturgeon
10. Basking Shark
11. Fish
12. Trout
13. Siamese Fighting Fish
14. Smolt

Square Assembly

Line A: 9 1 4 6 3; B: 1 2 5 3 1; C: 4 5 8 0 2; D: 6 3 0 9 6; E: 3 1 2 6 7.

Nobel Prize Winners

1. Marie Curie
2. Gunter Grass
3. Chile
4. Desmond Tutu
5. Yeats, Shaw, Beckett, Heaney
6. Wilhelm Roentgen
7. Fritz Haber
8. Sartre, Camus
9. Shimon Peres
10. Betty Williams, Mairead Corrigan
11. Albert Einstein
12. Andrei Sakharov
13. Saul Bellow
14. Pyotr Kapitsa
15. Howard Florey/Ernst Chain

Odd One Out

31. It is the only odd number!

Wales

1. Toilets
2. Captain Henry Morgan
3. Cromlechs
4. Rebecca
5. Paul Robeson
6. Conway
7. Aberystwyth
8. Everest
9. Gruffydd ap Llywelyn
10. Battle of Chester
11. Hedd Wyn/Ellis Humphrey Evans
12. Caernarfon
13. St Asaph

Pattern Poser

11. The shades are worth: Dots 5, Dashed 3, Shaded 2, Line 6. The formula is to add all of the sides together.

Stacked

21. Arrow = 12, Star = 9, Heart = 3, Percent = 5, @ = 7.

Musical Theatre

1. *Beggar's Opera*
2. *Carousel*
3. *Kismet*
4. Cosette
5. *Kiss me, Kate*
6. *Mary Poppins*
7. *Nordost* (North East)
8. *Man of La Mancha* (Don Quixote)
9. Sally Bowles
10. Israel
11. *Pickwick*
12. *The Sound of Music*
13. D'Oyly Carte

Paintings

1. Picasso
2. St. Lazare
3. Raphael
4. Pre-Raphaelites
5. *Mona Lisa*
6. Rain, Steam, Speed
7. Rembrandt
8. Medusa
9. *The Night Watch*
10. Manet
11. *School of Athens*
12. Dali
13. *Whistler's Mother*
14. Boccaccio
15. *The Starry Night*
16. Hannibal crossing the Alps
17. Willy Lott's Cottage
18. L.S. Lowry
19. Padua
20. Le Havre

November and December

1. Slate
2. Austerlitz
3. Smolny Institute
4. Alexander Dubceck
5. Brumaire
6. Wounded Knee
7. White Ship
8. Kirov
9. Montevideo
10. Coventry
11. Sarkozy
12. December 26th
13. General Theory of Relativity
14. Luxury Cars
15. Lindisfarne

Missing Number

8. Starting at the top left corner add the first three numbers. Place the sum below, beside or above the second number. Moving around the square in a clockwise spiral, repeat with the next three numbers, placing the sum below, beside or above, as appropriate.

Odd One Out

410. In all the others the first two digits added equal the third.

Modern Classics

1. *Murder on the Orient Express*
2. *The Mouse that Roared*
3. *1984*
4. Toby
5. *Slaughterhouse Five*
6. Wilbur
7. South Africa
8. *Brideshead Revisited*
9. *Name of the Rose*
10. Jean-Paul Sartre
11. Miranda
12. L-shaped room
13. Akela

Stargazing

1. Its angle above the horizon equals the latitude that it is viewed from
2. Galileo
3. Andromeda
4. 88
5. Sagittarius
6. Because you would need eyes like a lynx to see it
7. Sirius
8. Vega
9. Ursa Minor – Little Bear
10. Antares
11. After Table Mountain in South Africa
12. Right Ascension
13. Magellanic Clouds

Make Up

A.

Even More Food

1. 'Meat' - farewell to meat before Lent
2. Semolina
3. Shepherd's Pie is specifically made from mutton/lamb, Cottage Pie from other types of meat
4. Donkey
5. Stilton Cheese
6. Britain
7. Buckwheat
8. Rhubarb
9. Canada
10. Potatoes
11. Blue cheese
12. Buffalo
13. Lion

Timed Puzzle

4.20. The time moves forward by 1 hour and 5 minutes, 2 hours and 10 minutes, 4 hours and 20 minutes and 8 hours and 40 minutes.

Mathematics

1. Archimedes
2. Seven
3. Fermat's Last Theorem
4. Bell-shaped
5. A rhombus (kite is also acceptable)
6. Sector
7. Infinity
8. Hamilton
9. Fibonacci
10. Choosing the central item when all the data is arranged in order by magnitude
11. Trigonometric Functions (Sine/Cosine/Tangent)
12. Square Root of 2 (1.41)
13. Latin Square

Odd One Out

B. The number of sides of the internal figures should increase by one each time. B is the odd one out because its internal figures should have 2 sides.

Musicians

1. Kirsty MacColl
2. Cello
3. Frank Zappa
4. Modena
5. Geoff Love
6. Clara
7. Crystal Gayle
8. Sandie Shaw
9. Vince Hill
10. Guitar
11. Nana Mouskouri
12. Herb Alpert
13. Montserrat Caballae

Squared Up

23. Square = 9; X = 5; Z = 6; Heart = 7.

Triangulation

C. The number in the middle is the sum of the squares of the numbers at the points of the triangles. C does not fit this pattern.

Days

1. Henry Fonda
2. Penance, Confession
3. Alan Sillitoe
4. Reynolds News
5. Everton, Sheffield Wednesday
6. First Sunday after the first full moon following the Spring equinox
7. The Last Supper
8. Melbourne Cup
9. *Saturday Night Fever*
10. Widgery
11. Mardi
12. Black Monday
13. Simnel Cake

Total Mystery

3. The numbers in each circle add up to 30.

Number Pattern

19. The numbers denote the alphanumeric positions of the first letter of the words one, two three, four and five (o = 15, t = 20 etc.) Six begins with s (19).

British Authors

1. Evelyn Waugh
2. Ruth Rendell
3. Agatha Christie
4. Ulster (Belfast specifically)
5. John Bunyan
6. Kingsley Amis
7. Doris Lessing
8. Virginia Woolf
9. South Riding
10. D.H. Lawrence
11. Charles Dickens
12. Mary Wollstonecraft
13. King's Cross

Boxed In

4. The answer depends upon the number of the four-sided figures within which the number lies.

Other Rivers

1. Gironde
2. Vaclav Havel
3. Basel
4. Plate/Plata
5. US Airways
6. Lusitania
7. Rhone
8. Vltava or Moldau
9. Thames
10. Tigris, Euphrates
11. Phil Spector
12. Red River
13. *101 Dalmatians*
14. Nevsky Prospect
15. Biafra
16. Shenandoah
17. Niagara
18. *Aeneid*
19. Blackadder
20. Charon

American Cinema

1. *Snow White and the Seven Dwarves*
2. Bob Dylan
3. Marilyn Monroe
4. Searchers
5. *Duck Soup*
6. Philadelphia
7. *Thunderbolt and Lightfoot*
8. Michael Moore
9. Keystone Studios
10. *Duel*
11. *Arsenic and Old Lace*
12. Olivia de Havilland, Errol Flynn
13. Nakatomi Plaza

Triangulation

10. Add 2 to each value, place sum in corresponding position in next triangle, then subtract 3, and add 2 again. Alternatively, in each triangle, add together the top and bottom left figures, then subtract the bottom right figure.

Missing Number

1. On each row, subtract the two right numbers from the two left ones. The answer is put in the middle.

Russia

1. Dynamo
2. *The Seagull*
3. Kopeks
4. Vauxhall
5. Day of the saint after whom they were named
6. Potemkin
7. Alexander (or Alexandra)
8. Neva
9. Boris Spassky
10. Novosibirsk
11. Moscow Time
12. Boris Godunov
13. Volgograd
14. Beetroots
15. Molotov
16. Tea
17. Catherine
18. Solaris
19. Taiga
20. Peter and Paul Fortress

General Knowledge 5

1. Argentina, Brazil, Chile
2. Cactus
3. For the role of King of Siam
4. Green Line
5. Jim Bacchus
6. The introduction of the Gregorian Calendar
7. Industrial Workers of the World
8. Siberian
9. Victor
10. New Order
11. *Felix Holt*
12. Dante's Inferno
13. *The Untouchables*
14. Showerings
15. *Hound of the Baskervilles*
16. Elver
17. Wolves (or wolf pack etc.)
18. He had been changed into an insect
19. The Jam
20. Calais

Take Time

Forward (4.45), back (1.15), forward (7.45), back (5.30).

Birds

1. Penguin
2. Feathers
3. Great Auk
4. Legs
5. Manx Shearwater
6. Swallow (Hirondelle)
7. Austria
8. Kiwi
9. Vultures
10. Georgia
11. Nightingale
12. Grouse (also Ptarmigan, Capercaillie)
13. Kingfisher

14. House Sparrow
15. Roc
16. Wheatear
17. Common Gull
18. Penguin
19. Puffin Island
20. New Zealand

Too Much Food

1. It will have no buoyancy when fresh, and gradually gain more buoyancy the older it becomes
2. The Shambles
3. Upton Sinclair
4. Norway
5. Egg
6. Acorns (or beech nuts etc.)
7. Croque-monsieur
8. Grass
9. Spam
10. Potatoes (and are types used for chips)
11. Roquefort
12. A melon
13. Lobster / Scampi / Dublin Bay Prawn (or similar)

Make Up

B.

World Cities

1. Adelaide
2. Dunedin (Edinburgh)
3. Detroit
4. Samaria
5. Paris-Istanbul
6. Bhopal
7. Brigham Young
8. Bam
9. Dallas, Fort Worth
10. Constantinople
11. Jaffa
12. Sao Paulo
13. Atlantic City
14. Vienna
15. Dawson City
16. Mannheim
17. Geneva Bible
18. New Orleans
19. Welsh
20. San Antonio

Military Vehicles

1. Scharnhorst
2. Normandie
3. Halifax
4. Canberra
5. Potemkin
6. The Flying Fortress
7. Typhoon
8. Valiant, Vulcan, Victor
9. Mustang
10. Hurricane
11. Polaris
12. Meteor or Vampire
13. Cheonan

Squared Up

116. The shades are worth: Straight lines 8, Black 6, Grey 3, Waves 2. The halves of each square are multiplied.

Literature

1. *Ben Hur*
2. Lilliput
3. Mallorca/Majorca
4. *Three Men in a Boat*
5. Boccaccio
6. Washington Irving
7. *To Serve Them All My Days*
8. *Our Man in Havana*
9. Kilimanjaro
10. Harriet Vane
11. Peter the Great
12. *Bridge on the River Kwai*
13. La Mancha

Triangle Logic
44. Add the three outer numbers together, and put double that number in the centre.

Classic Rock

1. Jefferson Starship
2. Ginger Baker
3. Argent
4. The Isle of Wight Festival
5. The Kinks
6. The Byrds
7. John Paul Jones
8. *Led Zeppelin*
9. The Grateful Dead
10. Uriah Heap
11. Tyrannosaurus Rex
12. Fleetwood Mac
13. Free

Make Up
D.

European Words

1. Swift
2. Trabant
3. Russian
4. Benjamin
5. Swedish/Norwegian/Danish
6. Earl
7. Raisin
8. Anthracite
9. Zorro
10. Langue d'oc
11. Rhaiadr (town-Rhayader)
12. Lev
13. Mortgage
14. Concorde
15. Alcatraz
16. Rod, stick (etc.)
17. Railway station
18. Norwegian
19. Petanque
20. Granada

Myths and Legends

1. Mesopotamian
2. Tuonela (also known as Manala)
3. Heracles/Hercules
4. Aesop's fables
5. Lethe
6. Lemmings
7. Beowulf
8. Gessler
9. Locksley
10. 'End of World' or 'Rebirth of the World'
11. Lorelei

12. *The Mabinogion*

13. Lars Porsenna

Make Up

D. The small square moves clockwise and the circle gains an extra line each time. The T moves anticlockwise and rotates through 180º.

British Cinema

1. D'Ascoyne (in *Kind Hearts and Coronets*)

2. Portobello Road (Blenheim Crescent is also acceptable, which was another location)

3. 'Hot Stuff' by Donna Summer

4. Frank Muir and Denis Norton

5. Edward Woodward

6. Keighley and Worth Valley

7. Richard Burton

8. *Chariots of Fire*

9. *The Italian Job*

10. George Harrison

11. *Where Eagles Dare*

12. Eric Cantona

13. Millicent Martin

Squared Up

27 ÷ 9 x 6 + 12 ÷ 3 – 5 = 5.

Bodies of Water

1. Cyclones

2. Niagara Falls

3. Gulf of Aden

4. Bayou

5. Diego Garcia

6. Reichenbach

7. Vietnam

8. Canada

9. Magellan

10. Kielder (water)

11. Australia

12. Loch Lomond

13. Straits of Malacca

Puzzle Around

7. Multiply the numbers in the outer section, divide the product by 2 and put it in the middle of the segment two ahead.

Shapes

11. Multiply the number of sides of each number by 3, and then subtract the number printed

Even Further Islands

1. Maelstrom

2. Java

3. Anguilla

4. Monte Cristo

5. Corfu

6. Madeira

7. Haiti

8. Canary Islands

9. Jamaica

10. Mauritius

11. Sicily

12. Coney Island

13. Prince Edward Island

Germany

1. Trier
2. Volkswagens
3. Belgium
4. Newly re-unified Deutschland had two different currencies
5. Kalinningrad
6. Scapa Flow
7. Pinot Noir
8. Auric Goldfinger
9. Dynamo Dresden
10. Augsburg/Nurnberg (Nuremburg)
11. Magdeburg
12. A canary
13. Robert Stephenson & Co.

Far From Home?

10. This is the alphanumeric value of the town's first letter (A=1 etc.), multiplied by 10.

Grid Challenge

The faces follow a pattern from the bottom right-hand square going up then down the columns: full face, left open, right open, full face, right open, left open, full face, left open, right open, full face, right open, left open. The face replacing the question mark would have a smile and two eyes.

Individual Sports

1. Lawn tennis
2. Swim the English Channel
3. Tour de France
4. Butterfly, back, breast, crawl
5. Max Schmeling, Joe Louis
6. Spain, Italy
7. King of the Mountains
8. Wightman Cup
9. Kati (Katerina) Witt
10. Swimming, cycling, running
11. Nancy Kerrigan
12. Tom Simpson
13. Swimming
14. Angular momentum
15. Monica Seles

Odd Ones Out

A. 695, the other numbers have the same first and third digits.
B. 10, the numbers double each time so this should be 16.

More US States

1. New Jersey
2. Bill Clinton
3. Delaware, Maryland, Kentucky, Missouri
4. South Carolina
5. Mississippi
6. Kansas
7. Texas
8. George Wallace
9. Vermont
10. Missouri
11. Kansas
12. New Jersey
13. South Dakota

Square Solution

90. Shades are worth: Straight 25, Black 17, Grey 36, Wavey 12.

Line Up

4 and 1. Add the top line to the bottom line to give the middle line.

Tea Break

1. Earl Grey
2. Liquorice
3. Cappuccino
4. Ice cream
5. *Moby Dick*
6. Madeleine
7. Tamils
8. Salman Rushdie
9. Coconuts
10. Santos
11. Chocolate
12. Orange and (Bitter) Lemon
13. Coffee

Make Up

C.

Memorable Lines

1. *Under Milk Wood*
2. Roald Dahl
3. Figaro
4. 'Woodstock'
5. Spike Milligan
6. *Anna Karenina*
7. *West Side Story*
8. *Aeneid*
9. *The Bible* (Ecclesiastes)
10. *'O sole mio*
11. *All You Need Is Love*
12. Christopher Marlowe
13. 'MacArthur Park'

Triangulation

3. The formula is top corner x left corner ÷ right corner = middle number.

Watch this Space

21.14.51. The hour decreases by an extra hour each iteration. The minute doubles the previous increase. The second decreases by an extra second each iteration.

Discoveries

1. Helium
2. Ernst Mach
3. Tyrannosaurus Rex
4. Rosetta Stone
5. Mohenjo Daro
6. Nitroglycerine
7. After a Mr. Salmon (who discovered the bacteria)
8. Humphrey Davy
9. Clockwork radio
10. Quantum Mechanics
11. Joseph Swan
12. Copernicus
13. Van der Waal's Forces

Odd Ones Out

A: 26. Multiples of 6 should make it 24;

B: 689. The other numbers' digits increase by 1.

Roads and Automobiles

1. Samoa
2. Cadillac
3. Fiat
4. Havana
5. Karen Silkwood
6. MG
7. Fosse Way
8. Volvo
9. 57 Chevrolet
10. Volkswagen
11. Kraftwerk
12. Audi
13. Gravelly Hill Junction

Square Solution

68. To get the central number, multiply the numbers on the diagonally opposite corners of each square and add the products.

Puzzle Around

Grey = 9 and black = 8.

Battles

1. Sedgemoor
2. Russia
3. Yorktown
4. War of Spanish Succession
5. Actium
6. Russia
7. Mannassas
8. Waterloo
9. Brian (Boru)
10. Poitiers
11. Tostig
12. Athens and Sparta
13. Blucher
14. Brandywine
15. Dunsinane
16. Ulm
17. Constantine
18. Isonzo (Soca) [the last battle is also known as Caporetto]
19. (Second) Punic War
20. Thomas (Stonewall) Jackson

General Knowledge 6

1. Gipsy Moth
2. Priest
3. Severn
4. Haiti
5. Hamburg
6. Peter Cook
7. Peach
8. Comes back to life after drying out completely
9. Chickenpox
10. Tarantula
11. Special Administrative Region
12. Diana
13. Semibreve
14. Because it was named by a Polish citizen
15. Snake
16. Llewelyn The Great
17. Jemima Puddle-Duck
18. Marvin
19. Chess

20. Gudmundsdóttir

Africa

1. Nkrumah
2. Gold Coast
3. Yoruba, Ibo, Hausa
4. South Africa
5. Katanga
6. Pretoria
7. Lourenço Marques
8. Danikil Depression
9. Western Sahara
10. Anglo-American
11. Sudan
12. South Africa
13. Uhuru

Triangle Teaser

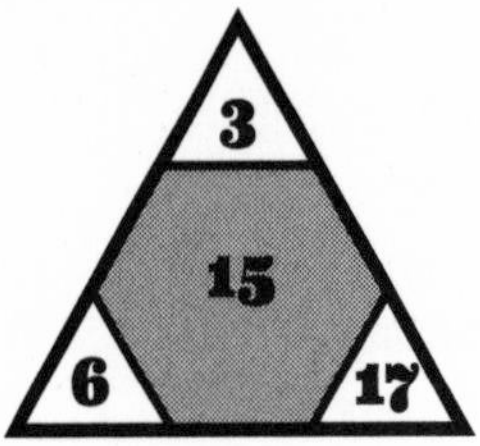

Divide the central number by 5 to give the top number. Add the digits of the central number to give the bottom left number. Reverse the digits of the central number and divide by 3 to give the bottom right number.

Reptiles and Amphibians

1. Alligator
2. Toad
3. Chameleon
4. Komodo Dragon
5. Cobra
6. Mexico
7. Mick
8. Robin
9. (Saltwater) Crocodile
10. Gila Monster
11. Crocodile
12. The Lizard
13. Brontosaurus

Stars

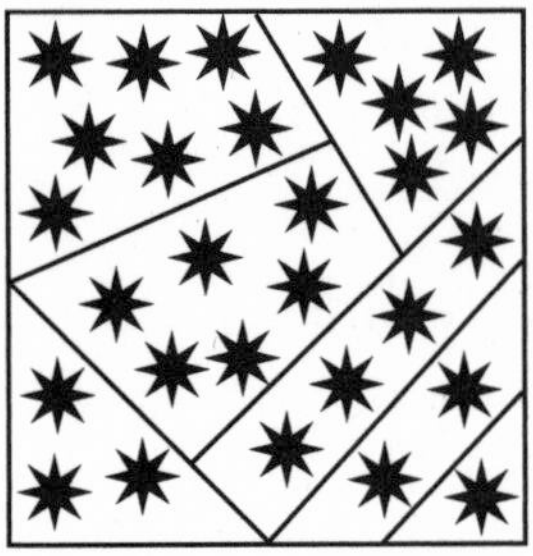

Acronyms

1. All Points Bulletin
2. American Standard Code for Information Interchange
3. Non-Inflationary Constant Expansion
4. Additional Voluntary Contributions
5. Kosovo
6. Online Public Access Catalog
7. Charged-Coupled Device
8. Universal Serial Bus
9. Automated Teller Machine
10. Video Home Systems

11. Byway Open to All Traffic
12. Power of hydrogen
13. Federation International de Football Associations

Odd Ones Out
C. In all other cases, the biggest shape is also the smallest.

World leaders

1. Hindenburg
2. Poincaré
3. Benito Juarez
4. Ireland
5. Brazil
6. Ukraine
7. Isabel
8. Louis Napoleon (Napoleon III is acceptable)
9. Ireland
10. Charles Taylor
11. Najibullah
12. Archbishop Makarios
13. President of France

Missing Number
Outer 3, inner 9. The numbers in the outer sectors are added together and the sums of the top half are double those of the diagonally opposite bottom halves. The top half numbers in the inner part of the sectors are three times those of the diagonally opposite bottom half ones.

Symbol Value
2A and 3C.

Journalism

1. The Guardian
2. Surviving the Titanic sinking
3. Daily Herald
4. International Times
5. Gorbachev
6. The (Daily) Beast
7. Robert Maxwell
8. Morning Star
9. Sign up for the Chicago Cubs baseball club
10. Jayson Blair
11. William Randolph Hearst
12. 1821, the Manchester Guardian
13. Karl Marx

Brain Twister
C.

Authors

1. Nevil Shute
2. Remarque
3. Heinrich Mann
4. Maxim Gorky
5. Bram Stoker
6. Gaston Leroux
7. Jean-Paul Sartre
8. James Joyce
9. A.F. Schumacher
10. Alexandre Dumas
11. Simenon
12. Hungarian

13. John James Audubon

Theatre

1. Russia/USSR
2. Ireland
3. *A Doll's House*
4. Robespierre
5. *Under Milk Wood*
6. Quantum Mechanics
7. Lady Bracknell
8. Androcles (and the Lion)
9. Alan Ayckbourn
10. Bruno
11. *The Comedy of Errors*
12. Don Diego
13. Beaumarchais

Matchpoints

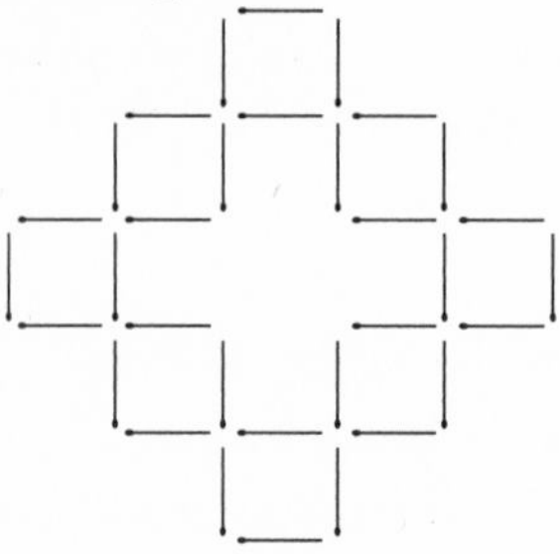

Bridges

1. Telford
2. It was the original locomotive that fell off the bridge in 1879
3. Kittiwake
4. Golden Gate Bridge
5. Nijmegen
6. Ponte Vecchio
7. Denmark, Sweden
8. Verrazano Narrows
9. Dublin
10. Bristol
11. Golden Horn
12. It collapsed
13. Tam O'Shanter

Odd One Out

D. The formula is: left + (middle x right) = top + (middle x bottom), but in D, the answers are 26 and 25 respectively.

Astronauts

1. Michael Collins
2. Fred Haise, John Swigert
3. Alan Shepard
4. Vanguard
5. Soyuz 11
6. Christmas
7. Saturn V
8. Sea of Tranquility
9. Alexei Leonov
10. Apollo 1
11. Valentina Tereshkova
12. David Scott, Neil Armstrong
13. Link up with craft from the USSR (Soyuz 19)
14. Charlie Brown, Snoopy
15. Dick Scobee

Round the Dial

A *La Recherche Du Temps Perdu,*
B *A Thousand And One Nights,*
C *To Kill A Mockingbird.*

Colours

1. Penguin
2. Robespierre
3. Tel Aviv/Jaffa
4. Syria
5. Rainbow
6. Earl Grey
7. Clouseau
8. A stroke caused by overeating
9. Glasgow
10. Germany
11. Edward
12. New Orleans
13. Norway
14. Lola

Round the Dial

1.00. In each case, the time is moving back 2 hours 10 minutes.

Timed Puzzle

6:45. The minute hand moves back to 15, 30 and 45 minutes. The hour hand moves forward to 3, 6 and 9 hours.

Scientists

1. Boyle
2. Humphry Davy
3. Oxygen
4. Hydrogen
5. On the side of a £2 coin
6. Henry Moseley
7. Zürich
8. Edmond Halley
9. Crucible
10. The First Law of Thermodynamics
11. Phillips/Sony
12. Padua
13. Physics/Chemistry/Radioactivity (Marie Curie)

Brain Twister

B. The sequence here is less one dot, plus two dots, and the box rotates in a clockwise direction for each dot.

Musical Instruments

1. Bagpipes
2. Didgeridoos
3. Clarinet
4. Recorder
5. Ebony
6. Balalaika
7. Cornet
8. Oboe
9. Hawaii (Portugal is also acceptable as the Hawaiian instrument appears to have been based on a Portuguese one)
10. Harp
11. Accordion, harmonica
12. Trombone
13. Ocarina, member of the flute family

Make Up

A.

Disease

1. Peru (Andes)

2. Yellow Fever
3. Tuberculosis
4. Aberdeen
5. Aldaniti
6. *Decameron*
7. Parkinson's
8. Smallpox
9. Eyam
10. Rats
11. Pathogens
12. Malaria
13. Yellow Fever (the Panama Canal was pictured)

Suspicious Circles

E. A is a mirror image of C; B is a mirror image of D.

Number Placement

2	14	10	7
9	6	1	4
16	3	13	11
12	8	5	15

1. No two consecutive numbers appear in any horizontal, vertical or diagonal line;
2. No two consecutive numbers appear in adjacent squares.

South American Countries

1. Paraguay, Bolivia
2. Venezuela
3. Brazil
4. (Deepest, darkest) Peru
5. Bolivia
6. Uruguay
7. Chile
8. Brazil
9. Colombia
10. Peru
11. Argentina
12. Uruguay
13. Venezuela

Take a Tile

B. Looking both across and down, any lines common to the first two tiles disappear in the third tile.

Numbers

1. 3, 4, 5
2. Works by Mozart
3. 24
4. 6
5. Magnification of 7, (Objective) Lens of 50mm
6. 10
7. Sensitivity to light/Film speed
8. 568
9. Pi (or 3.142 approx.)
10. Banking
11. 5
12. The Prisoner
13. 9,000

Timed Puzzle

A. The minute hand moves back thirty minutes and the hour hand moves forward three hours.

Weapons

1. Yo-yo
2. Gun
3. Mistletoe
4. Bazookas
5. Crossbow
6. *The Ladykillers*
7. Hans Blix
8. Muroroa
9. Georgi Markov
10. Little Boy/Fat Man
11. Cruise Missile
12. Gun
13. Blue Danube
14. Byzantine

Figure Columns

D. The smallest number is dropped each time and the remaining numbers appear in reverse order.

Sons

1. Robert
2. Lenin
3. Fleance
4. Hector
5. South Africa
6. Aeneas
7. (Lazare) Carnot
8. Prunella Scales
9. Canute
10. Hannibal
11. Marc Bolan
12. Ireland
13. Henry Hudson

Lasts

1. Goran Ivanišević
2. Brazil
3. *The Good, Bad and the Ugly*
4. Kharkov
5. Lynx
6. Reginald Pole
7. Eugene Cernan, walk on the moon
8. Ostend
9. Eric Bloodaxe
10. Rudolf Hess
11. Greece
12. Reza (Pahlavi is also acceptable). Name in full is Mohammed Reza Pahlavi
13. Passenger Pigeon

Number Crunching

33. Multiply diagonally opposite squares and subtract the smaller product from the larger:
(13 x 5) - (8 x 4) = 33.

Picture credits

The publishers would like to thank the following sources for their kind permission to reproduce the pictures in this book.

Page 13: Viacheslav Lopatin/Shutterstock; 15: NASA; 16: Public Domain; 19: Tupungato/Shutterstock; 21: Chainfoto24/ Shutterstock; 23: MGM/Wikimedia Commons; 25: Patrik Bitner/Wikimedia Commons; 27: Public Domain; 28: Public Domain; 31: Alvesgaspar/Wikimedia Commons; 33: Chatree.l/Shutterstock; 34: Travel Addicts/Shutterstock; 37: Darryl Leniuk/age fotostock/Alamy; 39: Christian Musat/ Shutterstock; 41: Wikimedia Commons; 43: U.S. Department of the Interior; 44: Charles Curtis/Shutterstock; 47: CKP1001/ Shutterstock; 48: Public Domain; 51: Public Domain; 53: Natalya Okorokova/Shutterstock; 55: SAPhotog/Shutterstock; 57: Public Domain; 59: Wikimedia Commons; 60: David Ingham/Wikimedia Commons; 63: Wikimedia Commons; 64: K. Jähne/Wikimedia Commons

Moons of the Solar System: A, B, C & E: NASA; D: Private Collection. **Black-and-White Animals**: A: Ehrman Photographic/Shutterstock; B: Nagel Photography/ Shutterstock; C: MKworldphoto/Shutterstock; D: Claude Huot/Shutterstock; E: Erni/Shutterstock. **Edvard Munch**: A-E: Public Domain. **Anniversaries**: A: Billion Photos/ Shutterstock; B: kavring/Shutterstock; C: josefauer/ Shutterstock; D: Photographee.eu/Shutterstock; E: Dimj/ Shutterstock. **Dessert**: A: AS Food studio/Shutterstock; B: EQRoy/Shutterstock; C: espies/Shutterstock; D: Gossip/ Shutterstock; E: j.chizhe/Shutterstock. **Sport**: A: Natursports/ Shutterstock; B: A_Lesik/Shutterstock; C: Mitch Gunn/ Shutterstock; D: Lucy Clark/Shutterstock; E: Scott Lomenzo/ Shutterstock. **The Cross and the Ensign**: A-E: Public Domain. **Famous Faces**: A: Wikimedia Commons; B & C: Public Domain; D: University of Texas at Austin; E: Joost Evers/Anefo/Public Domain

67: ullstein bild/Getty Images; 68: F. W. Bond/Wikimedia Commons; 71: Bagrin Egor/Shutterstock; 73: ullstein bild/ Getty Images; 74: Bettmann/Getty Images; 77: Kevin Eaves/Shutterstock; 79: SNAP/REX/Shutterstock; 81: Lesley Rigg/Shutterstock; 83: Wikimedia Commons; 85: Galyna Andrushko/Shutterstock; 87: Javen/Shutterstock; 89: Universal History Archive/Getty Images; 90: Public Domain; 93: Hulton Archive/Getty Images; 94: canadastock/ Shutterstock

Seeds: A: Fablok/Shutterstock; B: Thamizhpparithi Maari/ Wikimedia Commons; C: Glenn Price/Shutterstock; D: Victor Cardoner/Shutterstock; E: abc1234/Shutterstock. **Cocktails**: A: Public Domain; B: Ralf Roletschek/Wikimedia Commons; C: Blueclaude/Wikimedia Commons; D: Dasha Petrenko/Shutterstock; E: Steve Cukrov/Shutterstock. **The Northern Renaissance**: A: Private Collection; B-E: Public Domain. **Velocipedes**: A & E: Public Domain; B: Tetedelacourse/Wikimedia Commons; C: Nationaal Archief/Wikimedia Commons; D: National Archives and Records Administration. **Neolithic Burial Sites**: A: Gianf84/ Wikimedia Commons; B: Public Domain; C: Nick Hawkes/ Shutterstock; D: Wikimedia Commons; E: Joachim Jahnke/ Wikimedia Commons. **Presidential Pets**: A: Public Domain; B: The National Archives, U.S.; C & D: Library of Congress; E: National Archives and Records Administration. **Inventions**: A: MaraZe/Shutterstock; B: gosphotodesign/Shutterstock; C: Brian A Jackson/Shutterstock; D: Chattapat/Shutterstock; E: Dmitry Tkachanko Photo. **Unusual Animals**: A: State of Queensland/Wikimedia Commons; B: Richard Crossley/ Wikimedia Commons; C: U.S. Fish and Wildlife Service/ Wikimedia Commons; D: Cyril Henry H. Jerrard/Wikimedia Commons; E: Fotos593/Shutterstock

97: Public Domain; 98: Wikimedia Commons; 101: Library of Congress; 103: Everett Collection/Shutterstock; 105: Public Domain; 107: Public Domain; 108: esfera/Shutterstock; 111: Library of Congress; 113: E. O. Hoppe/Mansell/The LIFE Picture Collection/Getty Images; 114: Everett Historical/ Shutterstock; 117: Josfor/Shutterstock; 119: Patrick Poendl/ Shutterstock; 120: San Diego Air & Space Museum/ Wikimedia Commons; 123: Andreas Mariotti; 125: Javizal Darriaga/Wikimedia Commons; 126: Michael S. Koren/ Wikimedia Commons; 128: defenseimagery.mil/Wikimedia Commons; 131: Museum of London/Heritage Images/ Getty Images; 132: Vadim Petrakov/Shutterstock; 135: Public Domain; 137: Public Domain; 138: Tom Reichner/ Shutterstock; 140: Public Domain; 143: Pamela Reynolds/ Shutterstock; 145: vbmark/Shutterstock; 146: Granger Historical Picture Archive/Alamy; 149: Pe3k/Shutterstock; 151: David Falconer/Shutterstock; 152: Gerald Penny/AP/ REX/Shutterstock; 154: Public Domain; 157: Public Domain; 158: Matthew Field/Wikimedia Commons; 161: Lone Wolf Photography/Shutterstock; 162: Steve Gray/Freeimage. com; 165: Public Domain; 166: Bildagentur Zoonar GmbH/ Shutterstock; 169: Public Domain; 170: Milosz Maslanka/ Shutterstock; 173: Public Domain; 175: Public Domain; 176: Public Domain; 179: Public Domain; 181: Library of Congress; 182: Lisovskaya Natalia/Shutterstock; 185: Héctor Rodríguez/Wikimedia Commons; 186: Public Domain; 189: SMarina/Shutterstock; 191: c.muangkeaw/Shutterstock; 193: Public Domain; 195: Wikimedia Commons; 197: dimbar76/Shutterstock; 199: Nicolas Primola/Shutterstock; 201: Morphart Creation/Shutterstock; 202: phatisakolpap/ Shutterstock; 205: Mattstone911/Wikimedia Commons; 206: U.S. Air Force; 209: Tatyana Vyc/Shutterstock; 210: National Park Service Museum Collections; 213: Kyselova Inna/ Shutterstock; 214: Henrietta Elizabeth Marshall/Wikimedia Commons; 216: Helena/Wikimedia Commons; 218: Jeanrenaud Photography/Shutterstock; 221: Public Domain; 223: Jürgen Heegmann/Wikimedia Commons; 224: Alain Lauga/Shutterstock

Astronauts: A, C & D: NASA; B: Public Domain; E: Svilen1970/Wikimedia Commons. **Whistler and Ruskin**: A, B, D & E: Public Domain; C: Wikimedia Commons. **Notable Bridges**: A: Jenny Lilly/Shutterstock; B: s4svisuals/ Shutterstock; C: dibrova/Shutterstock; D: FiledIMAGE/ Shutterstock; E: Pete Spiro/Shutterstock. **Flags of the World**: A: Giro720/Wikimedia Commons; B: Jeff Dahl/Wikimedia Commons; C: seav/Wikimedia Commons; D: SKopp/ Wikimedia Commons. **Roman Emperors**: A: PLRANG ART/ Shutterstock; B: Till Niermann/Wikimedia Commons; C: Wikimedia Commons; D: Cnyborg/Wikimedia Commons; E: Marie-Lan Nguyen/Wikimedia Commons. **Artists and Religion**: A: Charlotte Salomon Foundation; B: Wikimedia Commons; C: Public Domain; D: Universal History Archive/ UIG/Getty Images. **Romantic Poets**: A, C & D: Public Domain; B: Everett Historical/Shutterstock; E: Wikimedia Commons. **Space Rovers**: A: Public Domain; B-E: NASA

227: Russell Weller/Freeimages.com; 228: Public Domain; 230: Downtowngal/Wikimedia Commons; 232: Olecrab/ Wikimedia Commons; 235: Neil Mitchell/Shutterstock; 237: Public Domain; 239: Featureflash Photo Agency/ Shutterstock; 241: NASA; 242: Department of Defense; 244: ImYanis/Shutterstock; 247: Public Domain; 249: Public Domain; 251: John James Audubon; 253: Wikimedia Commons; 254: kimson/Shutterstock; 256: NASA; 259: Ufa/Kobal/REX/Shutterstock; 260: Public Domain; 263: Wikimedia Commons; 265: Galina Savina/Shutterstock; 266: Luca Galuzzi (www.galuzzi.it); 269: Aleksandr Riutin/ Shutterstock; 271: Public Domain; 273: Public Domain; 274: NASA

Every effort has been made to acknowledge correctly and contact the source and/or copyright holder of each picture and Carlton Books Limited apologises for any unintentional errors or omissions, which will be corrected in future editions of this book.